ROSE WYLIE

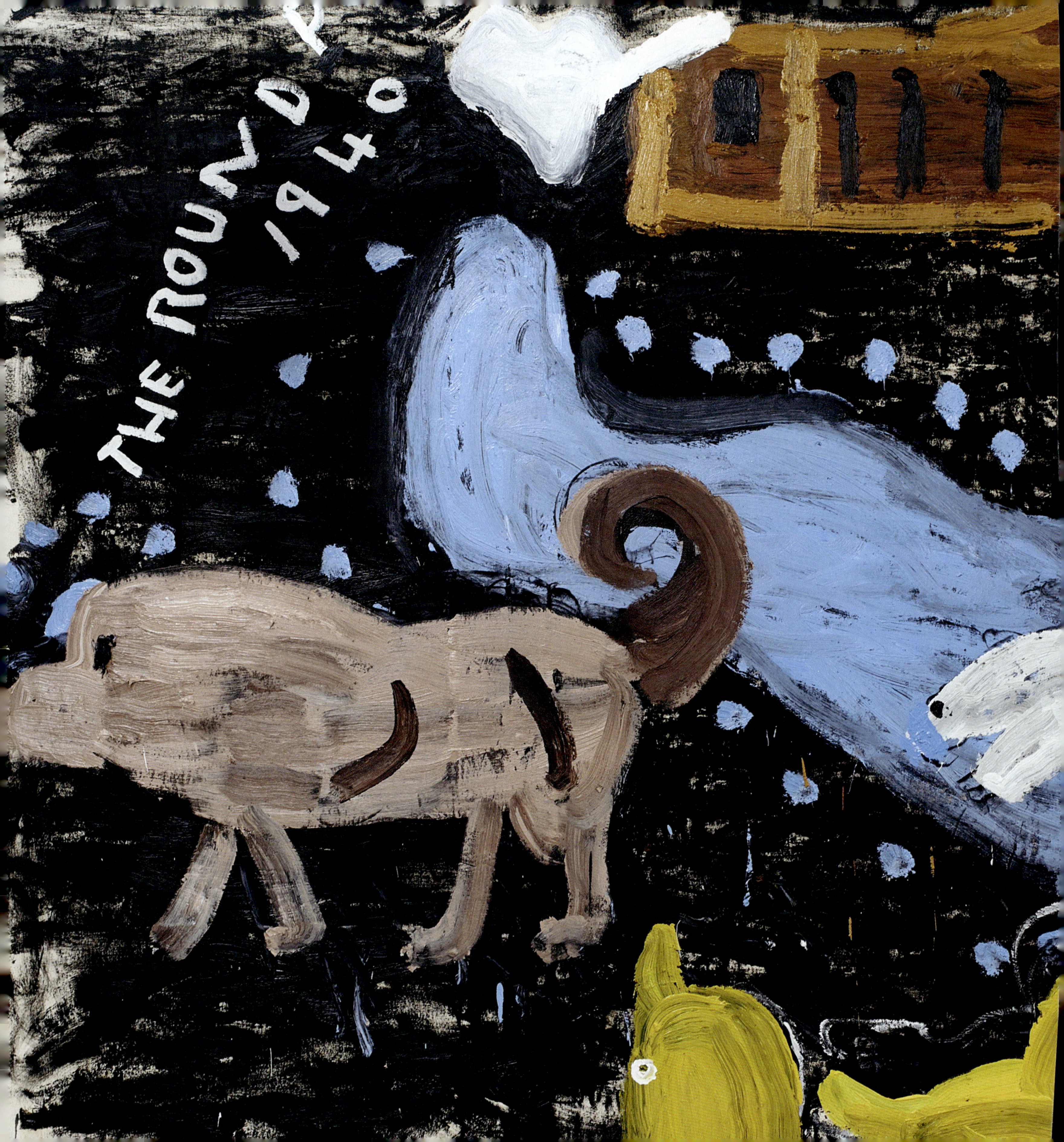

THE ROUND
1940

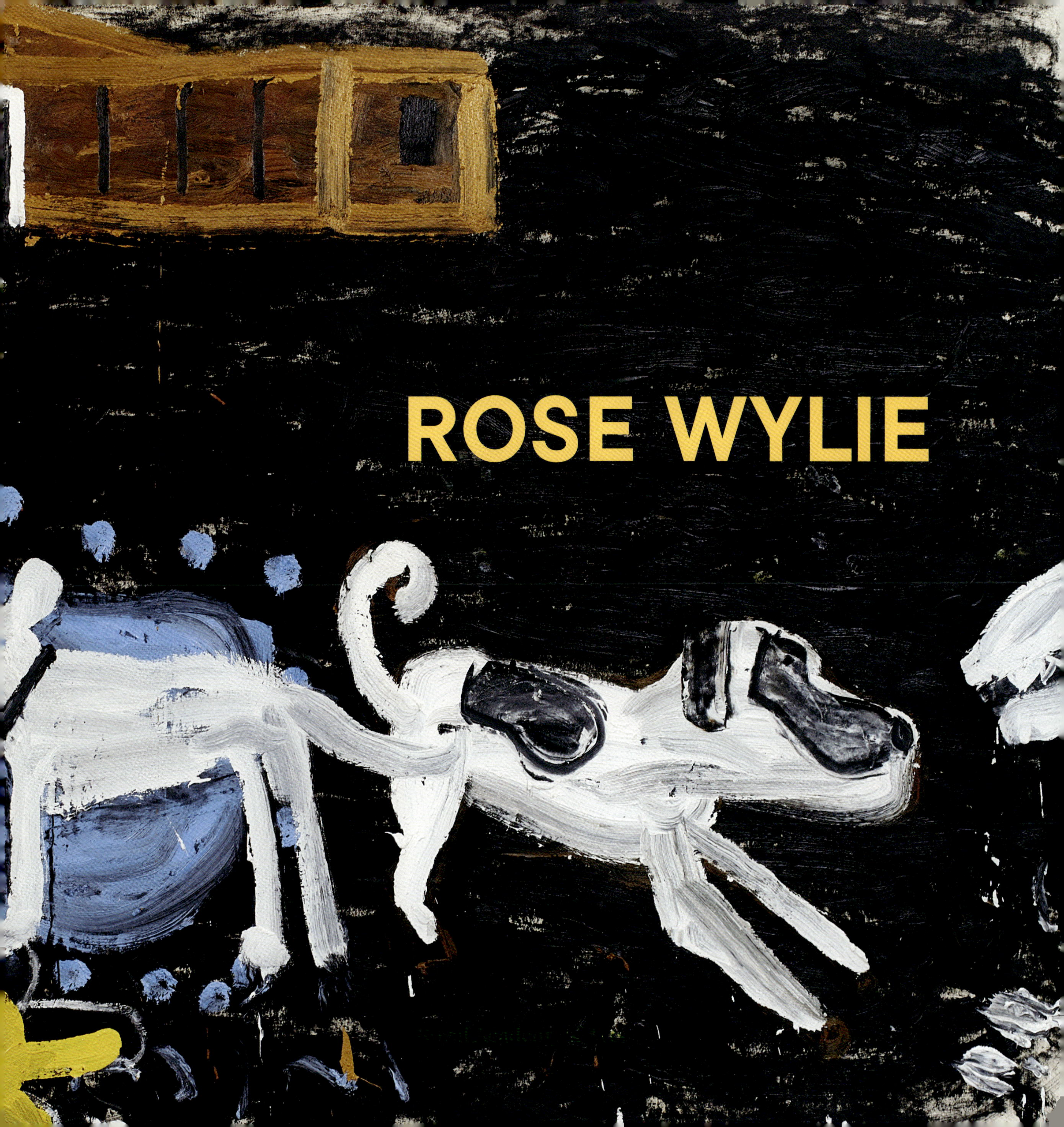

ROSE WYLIE

First published on the occasion of the exhibition
'Rose Wylie: The Picture Comes First'

Royal Academy of Arts, London
28 February – 19 April 2026

Supported by

David Zwirner

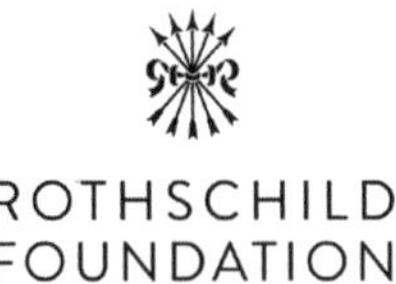

With additional support from

Christian Levett and Musée FAMM

Jake and Hélène Marie Shafran
and The Magic Trust

This exhibition has been made possible by the provision of Government Indemnity. The Royal Academy of Arts would like to thank HM Government for providing Government Indemnity and the Department for Culture, Media and Sport and Arts Council England for arranging the indemnity.

Department
for Culture,
Media & Sport

DIRECTOR OF EXHIBITIONS
Andrea Tarsia

EXHIBITION CURATORS
Katharine Stout
Tarini Malik
with Colm Guo-lin Peare

EXHIBITION ORGANISATION
Guy Carr
with Rourke Bonar

PHOTOGRAPHIC AND
COPYRIGHT CO-ORDINATION
Giulia Ariete

EXHIBITION CATALOGUE
Royal Academy Publications
Florence Dassonville, Production and Distribution Co-ordinator
Carola Krueger, Production and Distribution Manager
Peter Sawbridge, Head of Publishing and Editorial Director

Copy-editing and proofreading: Susannah Lawson
Design: Kathrin Jacobsen
Colour origination and printing: Gomer Press, Wales

Royal Academy of Arts, Burlington House
Piccadilly, London W1J 0BD
www.royalacademy.org.uk

EU Authorised Representative
EAS Europe, Mustamäe tee 50, 10621 Tallinn, Estonia: gpsr.requests@easproject.com

British Library Cataloguing-in-Publication Data. A catalogue record for this book is available from the British Library

ISBN 978-1-915815-22-4
ISBN 978-1-915815-31-6 (special edition)

Distributed outside the US and Canada by ACC Art Books Ltd, Riverside House, Dock Lane, Melton, Woodbridge, IP12 1PE

Distributed in the US and Canada by ACC Art Books, 6 West 18th Street, Suite 4B, New York, NY 10011

EDITORIAL NOTE
All works illustrated are by Rose Wylie unless otherwise stated.

Dimensions of all works of art are given in centimetres, height before width.

ILLUSTRATIONS
On the cover: detail of cat. 61
Pages 2–3: detail of cat. 2
Page 6: detail of cat. 83
Page 9: detail of cat. 30
Pages 38–39: detail of cat. 1
Pages 46–47: detail of cat. 6
Pages 70–71: detail of cat. 24
Pages 94–95: detail of cat. 57
Pages 106–07: detail of cat. 67
Pages 126–27: detail of cat. 79
Pages 140–41: detail of cat. 82

Contents

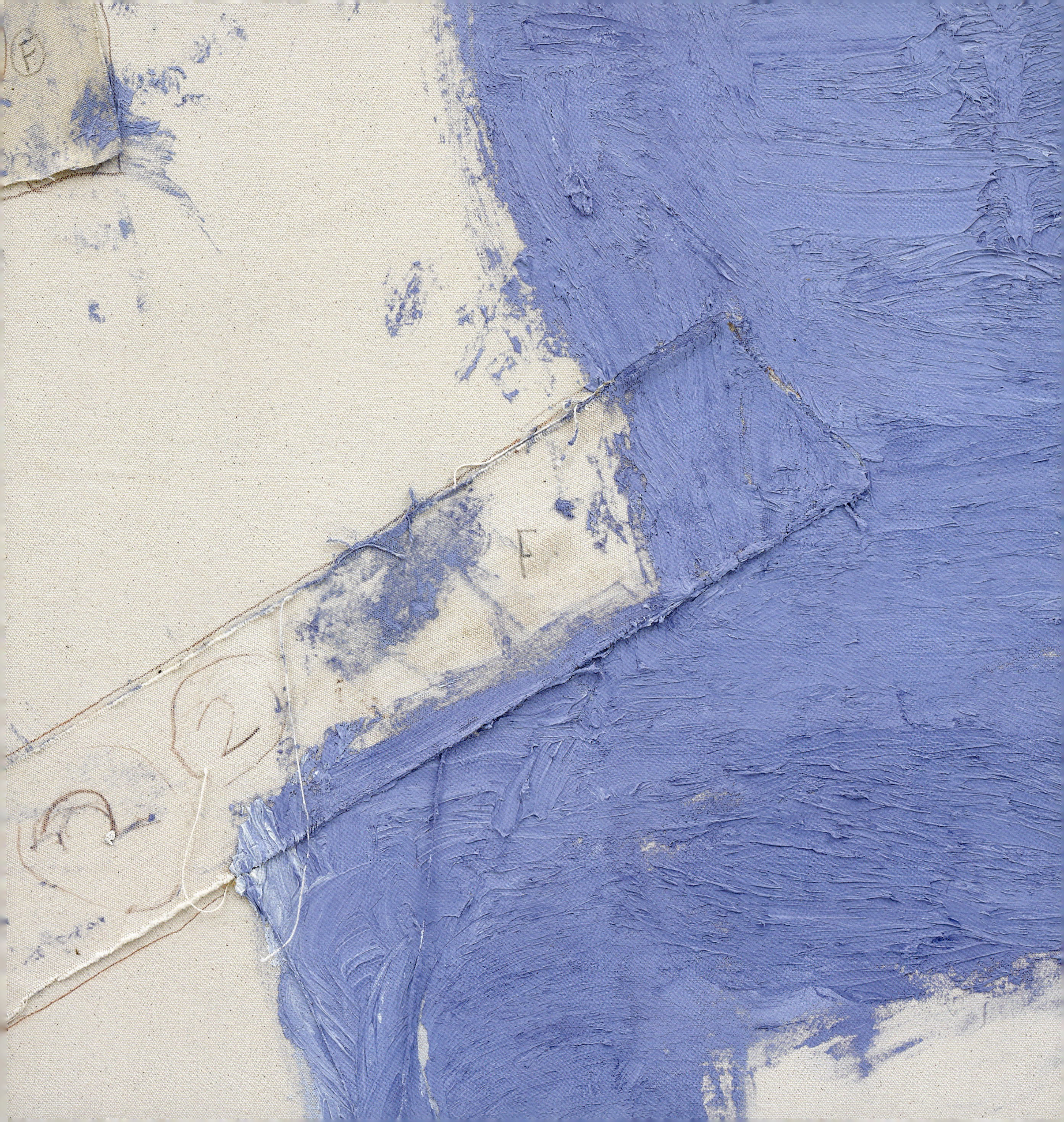

President’s Foreword

One of Britain’s most innovative artists, Rose Wylie OBE RA is celebrated for her bold, figurative practice that draws its subject-matter from art history, ancient civilisations, literature, cinema, celebrity culture and current affairs. A painter of contemporary life, she chronicles the times she has lived through in her works, from the Blitz to quotidian events such as an exhibition opening or an evening with friends. Wylie was born in 1934, and her memories offer a rich source of inspiration, allowing her to extract ideas from different times and places and re-present them here and now. Struck by an artwork by a favourite painter, an arresting shot in a film, or an incident from her own life, she might first record it in a drawing, before carefully distilling her subject’s essential qualities in paint and creating a unique, arresting picture.

This exhibition, the biggest survey of her practice to date, shows Wylie’s most iconic pieces alongside new and previously unseen artworks. There is a rare focus on her drawings, and we have also gathered diverse thematic groupings of Wylie’s large paintings from nearly four decades. Elected a Royal Academician in 2014, Rose Wylie is the first female British artist to have a solo exhibition in the RA’s Main Galleries.

None of this would have been possible without the considered and attentive participation of the artist, who has dedicated her time and energy to realise this extraordinary show. We are grateful also to her family, whose support has been indispensable. We thank the exhibition’s curator Katharine Stout, co-founder of the Drawing Room, London, and an independent curator, for her passionate and thoughtful work.

We are immensely grateful to Rodolphe von Hofmannsthal, Eve Baer Reilly and Yasmin Namdjou at David Zwirner and Jari Lager at JARILAGER Gallery for advice and organisational support. Our thanks go to Tarini Malik, Curator, and Colm Guo-lin Peare, Assistant Curator, for delivering the exhibition, supported by Guy Carr, Exhibition Manager, and Rourke Bonar, Assistant Exhibition Manager, with Idoya Beitia, Head of Exhibitions. Jason Wolfe and Luke Hall, assisted by Izi Thexton, of Wolfe Hall have designed the exhibition, alongside Tom Johnson of Sanford Lighting Design. Our thanks go to Giulia Ariete, Rights and Reproduction Manager, for sourcing and licensing images.

This publication offers a lasting record of the exhibition, and we are extremely grateful to Katharine Stout, Jennifer Higgie, art writer and novelist, and Frances Morris, former Director of Tate Modern and independent curator, for their insightful texts. Our thanks go also to Peter Sawbridge, Head of Publishing and Editorial Director, and his colleagues, and to Kathrin Jacobsen for her beautiful book design.

We are sincerely grateful to all those who have generously lent to the exhibition. We acknowledge with gratitude our supporters David Zwirner and the Rothschild Foundation. We also extend our thanks to Christian Levett and Musée FAMM, alongside Jake and Hélène Marie Shafran and The Magic Trust.

We also thank Cornelia Parker CBE RA, who championed Wylie’s election to the Royal Academy over a decade ago, for her article on Rose for *RA Magazine*, and Clarrie Wallis and Melissa Blanchflower from Turner Contemporary, Margate, for their encouragement and advice.

Rebecca Salter PRA
President, Royal Academy of Arts

Acknowledgements

The Royal Academy is exceptionally grateful to the following individuals without whose help the making of this exhibition and its accompanying catalogue would not have been possible:

Nadia Alting von Geusau, Maria Balshaw, Kathryn Blacker, Poppy Clover, Charlotte and Philip Colbert, Paula Cooper, Kate Davies, Emma Dexter, Fabienne Eggelhöfer, Brett and Julia Frankle, Brian Garish, Christos Giamakis, David Kennedy, Cristina Kolomines, Jeremy and Kathryn Levison, John McGill, Emily Oldfield, Edwin Oostmeijer, Amy Ormrod, Vladimir Ovcharenko, Luke and Louisa Oxlade, Alona Pardo, Sandra Penketh, Sven Petersen and Holly Frean, Laura Pye, Eleanor Reid, David Roberts, Cait Scott, Indrė Šerpytytė, Philippe Van Cauteren, Jana Van De Mierop, Gordon Veneklasen, Michael Werner and Nina Zimmer.

Additional thanks go to the staff at the Royal Academy for their unwavering support and their contribution to the successful realisation of this project.

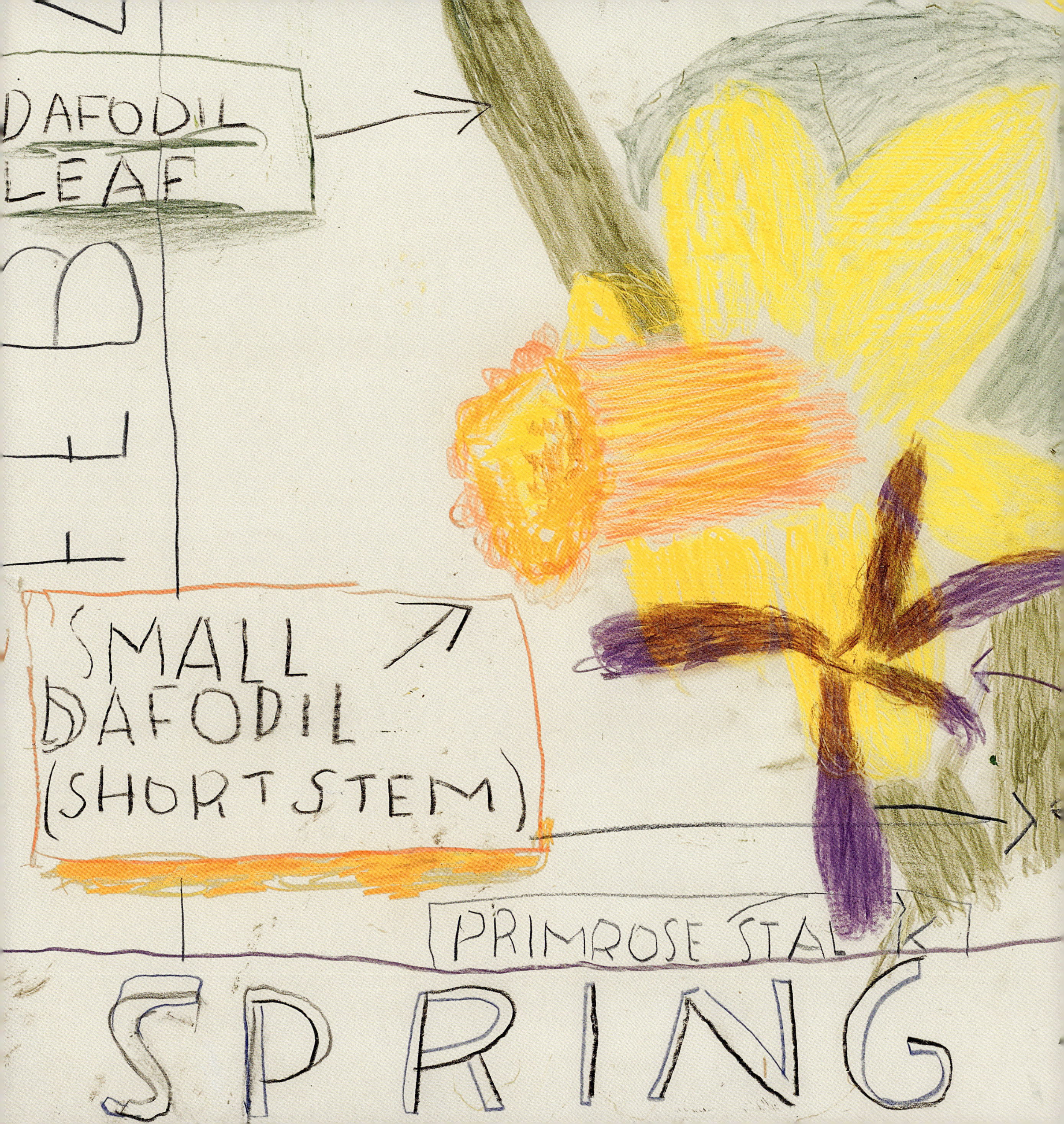

DAFODIL
LEAF
FEB
SMALL
DAFODIL
(SHORT STEM)
PRIMROSE STALK
SPRING

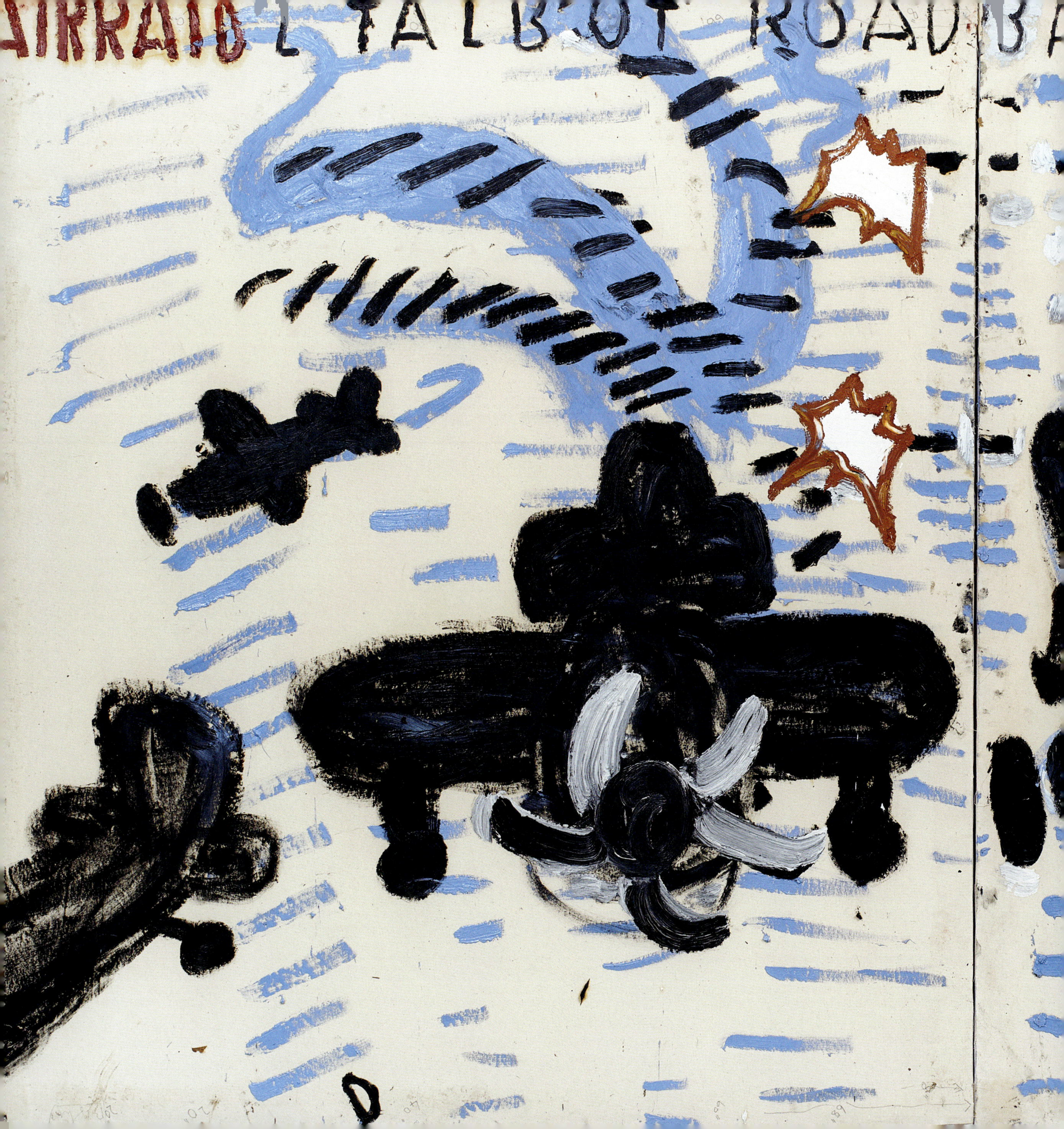
AIRRAID
TALBOT ROAD

The Picture Comes First

KATHARINE STOUT

Early memories

In a world saturated with a fleeting array of images, Rose Wylie's paintings have a singular ability to make you stop and enjoy the act of looking slowly and deeply. As we focus our gaze, a contrasting colour juxtaposition or use of bold outline draws attention to a particular detail; a motif out of scale with the other elements creates visual intrigue; painted words introduce a lateral reference. Wylie's figurative pictures reveal the evidence of their own making with impasto areas of paint scraped back or accidental blobs and exposed areas of canvas left *in situ*, reminding us that the work is not in the servitude of representation, but exists as a formal picture plane that is an end in itself. Wylie's works possess the 'essential quality of being present', an attribute of 'The Painter of Modern Life' assigned by Charles Baudelaire in his essay of 1860, reimagined for the twenty-first century.[1]

The artist's memories offer a rich databank for her paintings, allowing Wylie to extract ideas from different time zones, often years later, and re-present them within a new context and in the here and now. These might recollect an artwork by a favourite painter from art history or an ancient civilisation; an arresting shot seen in a film; or an incident from her own life. She usually records these first in a drawing. The process of turning specific memories into paintings makes concrete something intangible and very personal. Often, they are retrieved through repetition in both drawings and paintings and are therefore secure in Wylie's long-term memory, to be retained and accessed at will, as opposed to our more transitory working memories. In selecting these memories, Wylie comments, 'I think it's sifting. I sift. I go through it and think I remember certain things. It is the things I remember that I'm interested in. The memory may not be accurate but if I have a fond memory of something, the work I make gives me a chance to relate the work to the memory.'[2]

Wylie's earliest childhood memories are of German bombers targeting different parts of London during the Second World War, including areas close to where she was living in Bayswater. The painting *Park Dogs & Air Raid* (2017; fig. 1 and cat. 2) reveals not only this specific memory, but also a childlike perspective and something of the excitement of this time. Children notice the small things and often have a skewed sense of scale and viewpoint, designating the size and order of things according to

FIG. 1 Detail of *Park Dogs & Air Raid*, 2017 (cat. 2). Oil on canvas, 393 × 331 cm (overall). Private collection

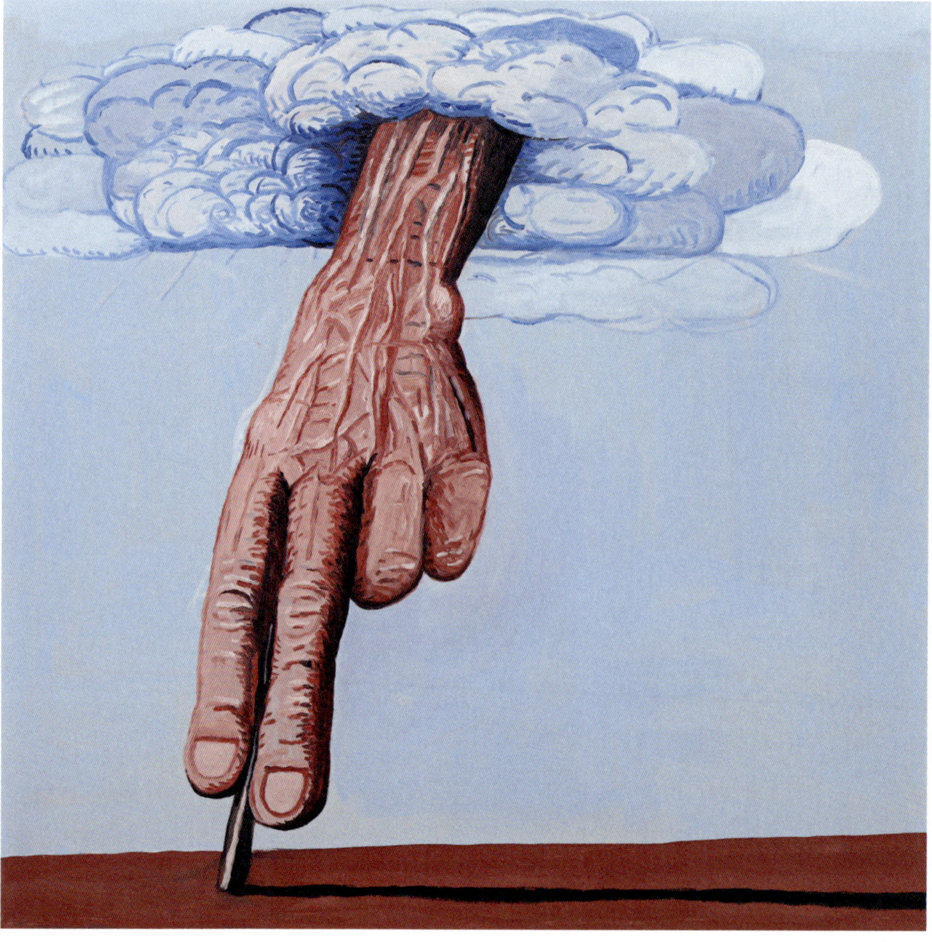

FIG. 2 Philip Guston, *The Line*, 1978. Oil on canvas, 180.3 × 186.1 cm. Promised gift of Musa Guston Mayer to The Metropolitan Museum of Art, New York, PG.Guston. P78.020.74

their importance. The planes overhead and the dogs in the foreground loom large over the present-day Serpentine Gallery building in Kensington Gardens, whose invitation to Wylie for an exhibition in 2017 prompted this work. Wylie describes her impression of this time, 'I think the war probably had something to do with it, because it was a kind of exciting moment, from the point of view of bombs coming down, and air raids and stuff. From a child's point of view, that was quite special, quite unusual... I wasn't really frightened, because it was going on all the time, that was what it was.'[3]

Transformation, synthesis and specific

Wylie feels an affinity with the late work of Philip Guston (1913–1980) from the late 1960s, which sees a shift away from his founding role in the New York School of abstraction during the 1950s and signals a return to his earlier figurative interests. At the time, Guston's seemingly abrupt stylistic change received a mixed response, with some critics labelling it 'crude',[4] just as Wylie's painting has mistakenly been called 'naïve' by some conservative reviewers. Guston arrived at this new interest in figuration through an intensive period of drawing between 1967 and 1968, observing, 'I'm always excited by the thin line which divides the image from the nonimage [see fig. 2]. What's exciting about an image is that at any given moment it would take so little to wipe it out completely, to have chaos, to have nothing there.'[5]

Both Guston and Wylie share an aversion to representational art as 'waxworks',[6] for which Wylie cites Samuel Taylor Coleridge,[7] who counsels against art as nothing more than an imitation of nature: 'Why are such simulations of nature, as wax-work figures of men and women, so disagreeable?'[8] Wylie, like Guston before her and as Coleridge before both of them, believes that a transformation needs to take place in the process of painting, which Coleridge sets out in his 1818 treatise, *On Poesy or Art*: 'It is sufficient that philosophically we understand that in all imitation two elements must coexist, and not only coexist, but must be perceived as coexisting. These two constituent elements are likeness and unlikeness, or sameness and difference, and in all genuine creations of art there must be a union of these disparates.'[9] It is this process of transformation and disjuncture that makes Wylie's paintings so intriguing: we may recognise the source imagery and the subject but that is not of foremost importance; it is Wylie's newly created depiction that holds the meaning. As Wylie explained to Clarrie Wallis, 'The image is arrived at through many drawings, evolving from a process of observation, personality and response; keeping something of the original subject, but hoping for a transformation into a poetic and particular form or whole, free from conventional representation.'[10] Notably, this non-academic approach is at odds with Wylie's traditional art-school training at Folkestone and Dover School of Art in the 1950s, with its emphasis on technical ability and memorising the correct anatomy for drawing human and animal figures, a requirement that Wylie refers to in her painting *Irreverant Anatomy Drawing* (2017; cat. 12), which shows a horse with labelled parts. Wylie comments, 'I like stuff that goes across time, through trans-temporality, or whatever you want to call it. And I very much like cultures which were excluded from my art education when I was a student. They literally didn't exist in that education. It was all determined exclusion.'[11]

Wylie feels sympathy with a number of artists from across history. 'I see my paintings continuing an art-historical conversation in every sense, from all of art history but particularly from the ancients; they are always so good.'[12] Her interests in art history are broad and run in parallel with a fascination for the visual culture of a wide range of civilisations, from Egyptian wall paintings to Roman mosaics and frescoes to medieval tapestries, each considered for their formal properties as much as for their historical resonance. In this respect she is an admirer of the work of the influential art historian Alois Riegl (1858–1905), who carried out close, formal analysis through empirical observation of such disparate ancient artefacts as Roman sarcophagi and Persian rugs,[13] in a way that deviated from the widely held consensus that the trajectory of Western art history saw a linear progression culminating in the achievements of the High Renaissance artists. Riegl's definition of skill was also of interest to Wylie, who remembers that in his concept of *Kunstwollen*[14] he outlines the idea that 'skill in painting is not skill in accurately reproducing what you see, but in getting what you want, which of course you only know when you see it'.[15] Wylie is seemingly drawn to cultural artefacts from different periods and to artists whose work sits slightly to one side of the traditional art-historical narrative, in particular to those early Renaissance painters who do not follow classical rules of perspective or scale.

FIG. 3 Vittore Carpaccio, *The Meditation on the Passion*, c. 1510. Post-restoration. Oil and tempera on wood, 70.5 x 86.7 cm. The Metropolitan Museum of Art, New York, John Stewart Kennedy Fund, 1911, inv. 11.118

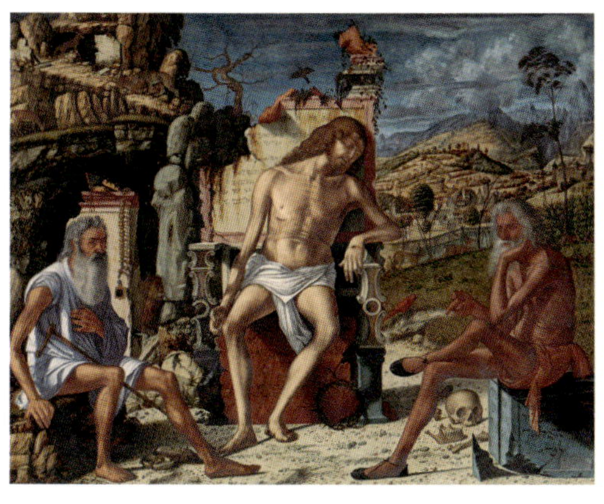

The foreground figure in Wylie's painting *London New York* (2000; cat. 9) is painted after the depiction of the Old Testament prophet Job in Vittore Carpaccio's *The Meditation on the Passion* (*c*. 1510; fig. 3), now in the Metropolitan Museum of Art,

New York. In Carpaccio's painting the foreground figures appear to have been placed against a theatrical backdrop, rather than a lifelike landscape. Wylie dispenses with a background altogether, incongruously positioning her rendition of Job next to an armoured figure from the Royal Armouries.

The paintings of modern artists who speak to Wylie's sensibility, such as Fernand Léger (1881–1955), Giorgio de Chirico (1888–1978) or Henri Matisse (1869–1954; fig. 4), similarly operate on a shallow, if not a flat, spatial plane, with their subjects delineated by clear, bold outlines rather than perspectival depth. While she was at art school, these artists offered Wylie adventurous alternatives to those more revered by her (all-male) tutors, who looked up to such exemplars of post-war British neo-romanticism as Graham Sutherland (1903–1980) and John Piper (1903–1992).

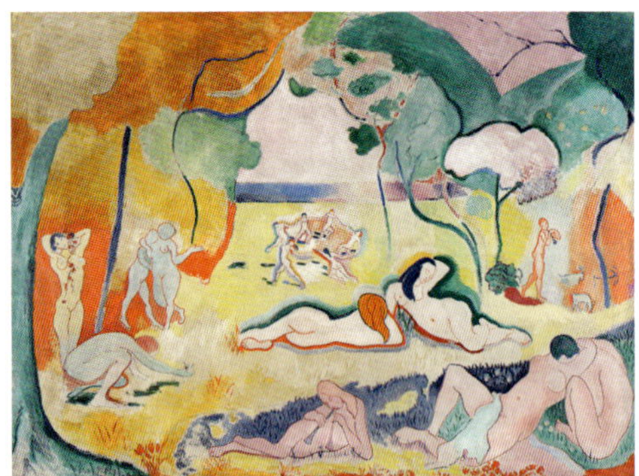

FIG. 4 Henri Matisse, *Le Bonheur de vivre*, also called *The Joy of Life*, 1905–06. Oil on canvas, 176.5 × 240.7 cm. Barnes Foundation, Philadelphia, inv. BF719

Room Project

Soon after leaving Folkestone and Dover School of Art, Wylie married the artist Roy Oxlade, whom she met while they were both at Goldsmith's College training to be teachers. Her energies then became focused on raising their three children with some occasional teaching work. Wylie speaks of this time not as lost years but as an opportunity to develop a set of skills and experiences that come with spending time with children – empathy, creativity, flexibility:

> Well, the break came about because of marriage and children. People will say, 'Did you find that... Are you angry about that?' And the answer is no, because the children are good, okay, great, knockout! But maybe you come back to it again with a bit more excitement, perhaps, than if you'd kept going all that time. But then your age is out of step. So people expect you to be twenty-four when you start painting, when you get known. In fact, that's completely gone. You can't retrieve that. But you've got a lot of experience in between.[16]

During this period, Wylie also read extensively – 'Dostoevsky and Chekhov, Mallarmé, Proust, Flaubert, Stendhal, Balzac'[17] – and visited exhibitions with her husband. When the children left home, she redeployed her time and space, converting a room in their Kent house as her studio – where she still works today – and enrolling to study at the Royal College of Art from 1979. Wylie's graduation from the Royal College in 1981 coincided with the influential exhibition 'A New Spirit in Painting', held at the Royal Academy of Arts, which introduced Britain to a new, international generation of expressive figurative painters, among them Frank Auerbach, Georg Baselitz, Philip Guston, Pablo Picasso and Julian Schnabel. Those selected ranged very widely in style and age and included no women artists – unremarkable at the time. The show validated a resurgence in figurative painting after a period that had been dominated by American abstraction, though it also revealed a wide stylistic variation across these new developments. Within this context, Wylie forged her own intuitive manner of painting.

The major series that comprised Wylie's first significant introduction to the London art scene depicts a magical, childlike world of make-believe, in which paper cut-out dolls have come to life and large totemic cats populate the landscape. *Room*

Project (2003–04), comprising 'Twink' paintings in yellow, green, blue and red, was painted for Trinity Theatre in Tunbridge Wells and gave Wylie the opportunity to work on a large scale, creating four large companion works totalling seventeen metres that offer a playful world in themselves (see cats 17, 22–23). Designed to be seen from afar as well as close up, giving life to different characters, these paintings offer a contemporary take on medieval tapestry, which was designed to animate large halls, providing colour and life. The artist herself also appears (cat. 15), wearing a favourite checked skirt as seen from different angles. When Wylie entered the paintings into the East International at Norwich Gallery, they were selected by the artists Neo Rauch and Gerd Harry Lybke, and Wylie was subsequently offered a London exhibition, giving impetus to her highly successful professional career.

Hand: Drawing as Central

Drawing lies at the core of Wylie's practice as a consistently accessible way to observe, record things or people and think through ideas. As many artists have found, the attraction of drawing is also its pragmatism, the fact that the pencil can be a constant companion and a way to give instant gratification to the impulse to create. Wylie explains: 'With drawing, you can do it anywhere. You can do it before going to bed or off the computer. It's more economic, it's simpler to carry around; it's small. It isn't "mess" like a painting. Painting is a physical mess, it gets everywhere. Also, drawing is very immediate, and I've always got pencils.'[18] Wylie draws what she sees around her, noticing the change in seasonal flowers or animal life in her garden, as well as sketching from the screen when watching a film or looking at the internet, sometimes in the moment, sometimes to capture a memory. People are a frequent preoccupation. She might return to the same subject, capturing different responses and versions that seek to go beyond conventional representation and transforming them into something more essential. Often this means focusing on a particular feature or characteristic that she finds interesting and exciting. Wylie's depository of thousands of drawings and works on paper acts as a vast visual diary from which she can extract ideas and subjects to transform into paintings.

Drawings can be large, autonomous artworks, rendered in ink or watercolour as well as pencil, as seen in *Hazelnut Leaf* (2017; cat. 27) or *Yellow Mexican Box* (2019; cat. 25), offering Wylie a greater fluidity and speed than when she paints on canvas. As seen in *Out in Garden Now, Feb 5th, 2022* (2022; cat. 30), they can also be precisely detailed drawings that are worked and reworked until Wylie achieves the qualities that she is looking to fix in her image. It is through drawings that Wylie will test out a composition or a combination of subjects for a painting. She reflects:

> Usually I paint something I've seen, but I may fiddle with the scale, context and rules of gravity. I draw from observation, memory and with 'conceptual projection' – how a stereotype would look from the unstereotypical view, or if made from a written list of observed particulars, then that list illustrated. The paintings often start from my drawings, but anything can change, depending on the way I feel about how it is, or if I know what that should be. The drawings can come from

> the excitement of anything I've seen, or from film (the swapping of one art form from another), newspapers and memory of personal events.[19]

Wylie often includes words within her paintings, as an integral part of the work rather than a detached commentary on it. She says, 'I like painting letters – they have all the options of other stuff you paint, but in a way are easier – they can be used to unify a painting, like Léger's use of black outlines… and used to oppose presuppositions. I paint in names and titles, as doing this settles them in the total framework of the painting and in my visual experience.'[20] Drawing and writing are indexically linked: as children our scribbles serve both as attempts to visualise something and to name it. Lev Vygotsky (1896–1934), a Russian psychologist best known for his work on the cognitive development of children, saw drawing as the preliminary stage of written language. 'A drawing is "a unique graphic speech, a graphic story", and drawing is often accompanied by speech. But later there must come the realisation that writing is a way of drawing speech, not objects. This then is "second-order symbolism", a drawing of the word for the thing, rather than the thing itself.'[21] Wylie adds another layer of symbolism by painting a word or words that might reinforce the imagery or cast another meaning onto the picture. In *HAND, Drawing as Central* (2022; cat. 24), she paints a hand and names it HAND (while also entitling the first panel THE PAINTING). In the middle section she describes what is happening when making THE DRAWING, itself the subject of the painting, 'SHADOW FROM THE SUN. A HAND TO HOLD THE PAPER DOWN, while rubbing out.' The third part is named THE OIL ON PAPER, in which a second version of the painted hand and its label appear, making the painting a conceptual word play to emphasise that images and words are always simulacra.

Film Notes

The muse-like role of Wylie's drawings is illustrated in how her paintings after the 1994 film *Natural Born Killers, Long Shot (Film Notes)* came about (2018; cat. 58). 'I went back on a set of drawings and found four *Natural Born Killers* drawings. I did the drawings close to the time of the film, and then forgot about them. And then I was looking for images and I found the drawings and I just picked them. But they came from a hugely good memory of the film.'[22] A voracious film-watcher, Wylie is often struck by a particular shot that stands in for the film in her memory. She explains her enthusiasm for the medium and for certain film-makers such as Quentin Tarantino, and how this feeling is translated into a painting such as *Kill Bill (Film Notes)* (2007; cat. 59), which allows us to view two versions of the same dramatic scene simultaneously:

> It's the sudden image of the film that's just wonderful and memorable… I used to try to put the excitement of the image from the film into the drawing. I did that a lot. Also, it helped me remember the film. It was respectful of the film-maker, which I like because it's another art form. The translation from one art form to a new and invented version of it is an interesting idea. Transposition – we've all done it. But if you do it from a different art form (film), I recently heard it's called ekphrasis…

> I try to make an equivalent image with a measure of the same excitement that I felt when I saw the original.[23]

Across her practice, Wylie's works resist categorisation and in some of her 'Film Notes' paintings she juxtaposes different sources that are unrelated to each other. For example, in *Bagdad Café (Film Notes)* (2015; cat. 54), the café's owner Brenda, a central character from Percy Adlon's 1987 film of the same name, is depicted in the left panel, whereas the right panel depicts moments from Wylie's life, such as red lips licking a coffee spoon, and flowers from her garden, set against a calendar page. Wylie always uses canvases of the same size (so that they will fit down the stairs from her studio), working on each separately before selecting and combining different pieces to form new diptychs. *Brunhilde (Film Notes)* (2024; cat. 52), a recent painting, depicts a particularly brutal scene, which relates to another Tarantino film, *Django Unchained* (2012); Wylie retains the German mythological name of the central character, who is called Broomhilda in the film. That the two are related is made explicit by the text 'LEGEND not FILM' inscribed above it (Broomhilda's death does not occur in the film). This is placed next to a rendition of an African wall painting of a tree entitled HOMAGE AFRICAN (above the image) and WALL PAINTING (below), an indirect reference to the film's central character's African American ancestry. These two images are brought together by a Pompeian frieze-like border across the top and dark reddish-brown colouring.

The mediated image

Occasionally images printed in newspapers, magazines or posted on the internet, particularly of figures, catch Wylie's eye and are translated into drawings, then sometimes a painting. Her relentless thirst for visual culture is well served by our digital information age, which makes it possible to gain easy access to a wealth of knowledge. The attraction might be a detail, or a pose, or a flash of colour rather than the identity of a person, although she is not opposed to the popular culture of the celebrity world. Wylie is first and foremost investigating an image, not the subject.

> If people saw my work as 'easily read', then that is not something I would immediately object to – it depends on what you define as 'easily read', and, importantly, whether that is all it is. After readability, I look for particularity, plus something more you can't quite put your finger on. In my painting it's not the subject matter that needs to be known about – that doesn't matter. It is more the objects/things/persons that need to be recognised, felt and understood: trees as trees, a skirt as a skirt, and the quality of how it's done.[24]

Wylie's caution against the drive to read meaning into her subject matter aligns her with one of her contemporaries, albeit the two were unknown to each other. In her 1964 article 'Against Interpretation', the influential American writer and critic Susan Sontag (1933–2004) makes a convincing case against the trend – one that still proliferates today – of reading more significance into the content of a work of art

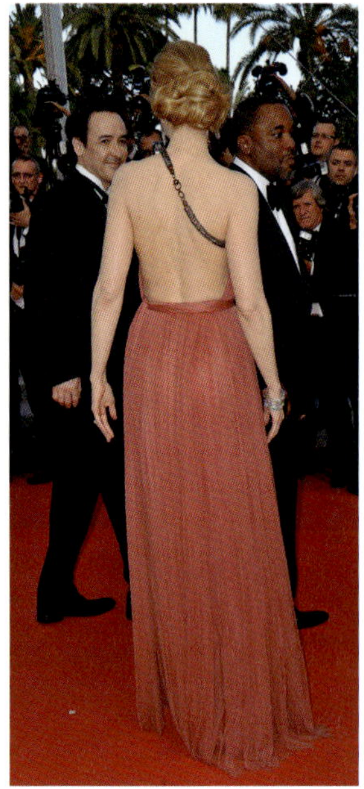

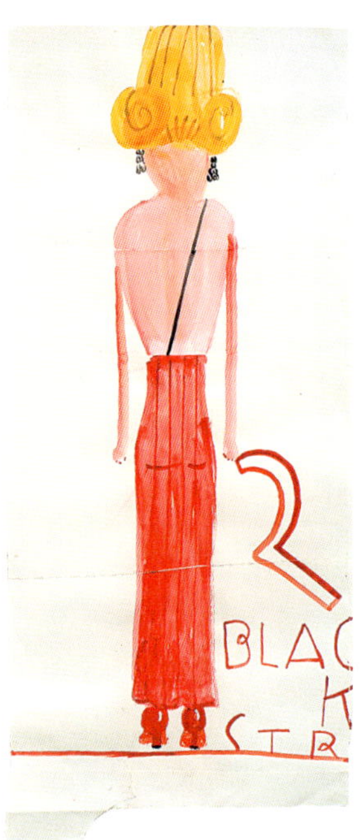

FIG. 5 Nicole Kidman wearing a backless dress for the première of Lee Daniels's *The Paperboy* at the Cannes Film Festival, 2012

FIG. 6 *NK and the Black Strap I*, 2013. Watercolour and collage on paper, 140 × 60 cm. Courtesy private collection and JARILAGER Gallery

than the experience of its appearance, not least since interpretations are often hijacked by the political or social world view of the critic in question. Sontag explains: 'In most modern instances, interpretation amounts to the philistine refusal to leave the work of art alone. Real art has the capacity to make us nervous. By reducing the work of art to its content and then interpreting that, one tames the work of art. Interpretation makes art manageable, conformable.'[25] Wylie's paintings do not shy away from visual discord and the awkwardness of the everyday, and it is this that makes them so beguiling. Incidentally, Sontag also shares Wylie's love of cinema, and unknowingly offers an account of Wylie's fascination with it: 'there is always something other than content in the cinema to grab hold of, for those who want to analyse. For the cinema, unlike the novel, possesses a vocabulary of forms – the explicit, complex and discussable technology of camera movements, cutting and composition of the frame that goes into the making of a film.'[26]

That's not to say that as viewers of Wylie's work we can't form our own cerebral responses. When I see *Girl in Lights* (2015; cat. 73), a nude with her back to the viewer, I can't help but think of it as a retort to all the nude women who have been painted by men throughout art history in front-facing poses, presenting themselves as readily available to the (assumed) male gaze. When Wylie paints women, they are exuberant rather than submissive. In *Pink Skater (Will I Win, Will I Win)* (2015; cat. 71), for example, the figure leaps from one side of the canvas to the other, while the painting's title and the skater's timid expression underline the anxiety of performance. Occasionally Wylie offers more overt commentary, as in *Snowwhite (3) with Duster* (2018; cat. 66), a sardonic depiction of Disney's original Technicolor version of the Grimm Brothers' fairy tale, in which Snow White's lack of agency in determining her own destiny means that her fate is to be an accidental housewife, reliant on a kiss from an unknown prince to rescue her from her death-like sleep. Wylie advocates that Snow White should herself strive for her release and independence. She was taken to see Disney's *Snow White* at the cinema in 1937, the year it came out, and remembers it as quite a terrifying experience. The film's graphic style, with its dramatic contrasts and viewpoints, can be seen to have had an impact on Wylie's own style of painting.

Sometimes a striking image, often related to film or media, compels Wylie to rework it into several compositions: this is a way of trying out different versions of the same scene without obliterating the previous painting, changing details and or backgrounds each time, and introducing notions of 'repeat'. Inspired by a website photograph of Nicole Kidman wearing a backless dress on the red carpet at the Cannes Film Festival for the première of *The Paperboy* in 2012, Wylie portrayed the particular features she found compelling in this image (fig. 5) – the actress's bare back, the black strap, her blonde hair piled up on her head and the swinging earrings – first in a number of works on paper (fig. 6), then in multiple canvases.

Views of 'NK' from the back are rendered in different positions in *NK (Syracuse Line-up)* (2014; cat. 63), whereas in *Black Strap (Eyelashes)* (2014; cat. 62), the same shot of the actress appears against a backdrop taken from another painting, *Rainham Oast* (2014; cat. 60), of a local community centre not far from where Wylie lives. Another version, *Black Strap (Red Fly)* (2012; cat. 61), sees the addition of oversize flies to the composition – one black, one red. The repetition of these bold images makes a visual statement that stays with us, the opposite of the relentless cacophony of digital images that cross our retinas daily, quickly to be forgotten. Wylie acknowledges society's fascination with celebrity in these paintings in a humorous and non-judgemental way: 'Icons are interesting. Clichés are interesting. It's not so much about glamour or beauty, or celebrity. It's about letting the viewer in on the process, permitting him or her to see how it started and where it ended.'[27]

Football performs a similar function in providing alluring subject matter – it is not that Wylie is a dedicated football fan, but she does recognise its widespread appeal. *Yellow Strip* (2006; cat. 67), nearly seven metres wide, offered the opportunity to depict figures in movement from different perspectives at the same time. The painting operates in the same way as medieval embroideries such as the Bayeux Tapestry (fig. 7), in which key figures appear more than once in the same scene in a continuous narrative, each enacting a different action important to the story being told. In Wylie's painting, a single figure is depicted in each of the five panels, separately performing a different ball technique, all set against Wylie's signature symbol for grass – three short vertical lines of green paint. *Arsenal & Spurs* (2006; cat. 68) alludes to the tribalism of a football match, a rivalry enjoyed by Wylie's family as they watched football together on television.

Gender is not an explicit concern for Wylie, although she acknowledges there is remedial work to be done in rebalancing which artists get to be selected and shown in museums and galleries, and the pricing that follows. The historical gendered control of whose story gets told prompted a recent painting, *Lilith and Gucci Boy* (2024; cat. 65), which was inspired by Wim Wenders's documentary on Anselm Kiefer (2023), in which Kiefer mentioned Lilith, the first wife of Adam. This came as a revelation to Wylie, whose education to date (as is the norm) had omitted any mention of Lilith. She set about researching this female figure in Jewish mythology. Created at the same time and from the same clay as Adam, therefore made his equal, Lilith left the Garden of Eden after she refused to become subservient to Adam. Other versions see her cast as a she-demon, and she has occupied an obscure role in both history and theology. Wylie realised that she had in fact encountered Lilith already, having made a drawing of the 'Burney Relief' in the British Museum (fig. 8),

FIG. 7 Unknown artist, 'Many fall in battle and King Harold is killed', detail of the Bayeux Tapestry, *c.* 1070. Wool embroidery on linen, 0.5 × 70 m (overall). Musée de la Tapisserie, Bayeux

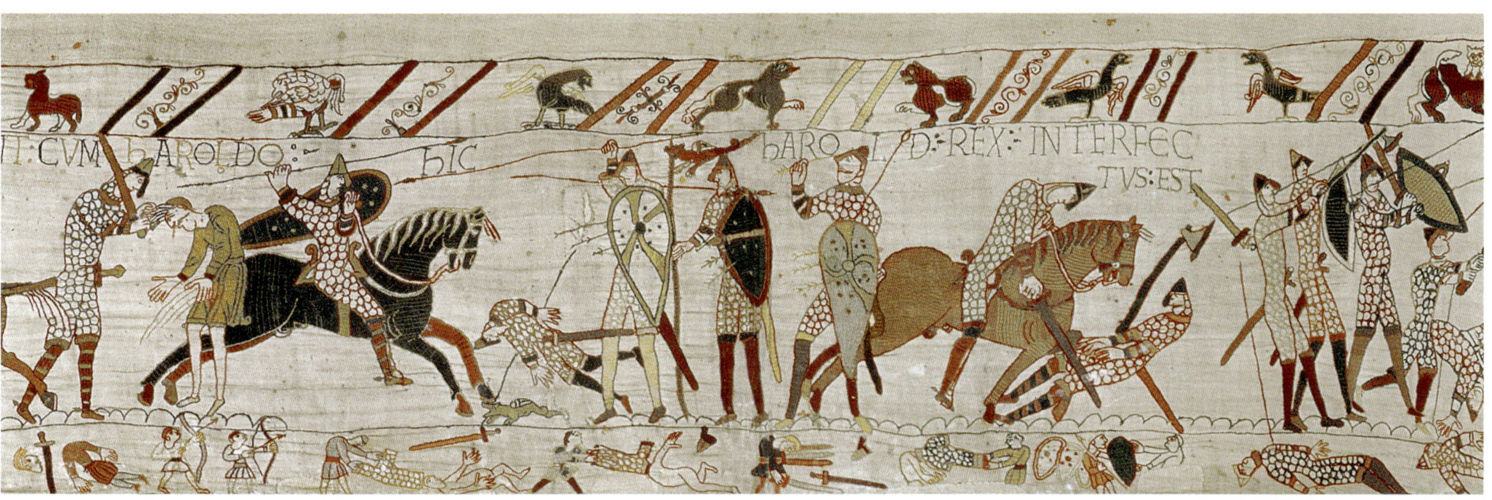

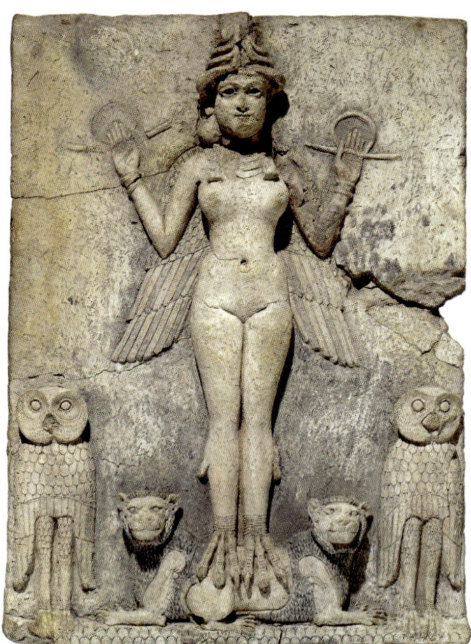

FIG. 8 The ‘Burney Relief’, an Old-Babylonian terracotta plaque depicting the ‘Queen of the Night’, believed by some to show Lilith, nineteenth–eighteenth centuries BC. Fired clay, height 49.5 cm. British Museum, London, inv. 2003,0718.1

an Old-Babylonian terracotta plaque of the ‘Queen of the Night’ that is believed by some to depict Lilith with owl wings and taloned feet, denoting her association with this night bird. Turning this drawing into a painting, in which she designates Lilith ‘the first feminist’, Wylie places her next to an image taken from a fashion event, showing the artist’s love of both pop culture and historical references.

Diary as history painting

Wylie’s paintings can all be seen as a form of diary, collectively an ongoing historical record of what the artist has done and seen. As Clarrie Wallis describes, ‘Anything and everything captures her attention, and she responds to the peculiarity of each experience in the hope that she can find a way to describe the character of things as vividly and accurately as possible.’[28] This includes everyday moments and encounters, seemingly incidental but in many ways the most real to the artist. *Breakfast* (2020; cat. 77) is atypical in that it was painted directly from the memory of a favourite meal rather than captured first as a drawing. The dark umber background creates a very flat spatial plane for an overhead view of the plate, with the addition of the word BREAKFAST helping to bring into focus the spoon, poised ready to scoop up the red and purple berries. The work can also be read obliquely as a climate-change painting, promoting the consumption of seasonal produce. Painted over 30 years earlier, *The Well-Cooked Omelette* (1989; cat. 78) depicts another dish and the satisfaction of a job well done.

The motivation for *PV Windows and Floorboards* (2014; cat. 74) arose from the gallerist Jake Miller’s description of the architecture of his London gallery, The Approach, with its Victorian floorboards and windows. When attending a private view, Wylie found that these exactly lived up to his description. This painting won Wylie the prestigious John Moores Painting Prize, a surprise and welcome accolade after years of entering.

Wylie’s enjoyment of being with people – neighbours, fellow artists, old friends and new acquaintances – also becomes material for her art. *Dinner Outside* (2024; cat. 79) evokes a summer evening, the two canvases presented quite literally as DIARY ENTRY with the date, August 10 2024, inscribed on the first. The painting offers two views of the same occasion, with the orientation of each inscribed on the canvases, together with compass markings. Wylie thinks of the painting as a map, a record by a seventeenth-century ship’s hired artist of the encounter with a new country, with its particular houses, dress and customs. Only this is now. The starting points for *3 Seating Plans and Seated Table* (2025; cat. 80) were jotted diagrams in Wylie’s diary, aides-memoire to remember who sat where after various art-world dinners. Important courtship rituals between artists, gallerists, collectors and curators, these dinners are rarely the subject of artworks, remaining private and exclusive. In Wylie’s painting, the canvas is covered with black initials, so that we can only guess who attended. As ever, it is not the story of who sat next to whom that interests Wylie, but the formal, diagrammatic image that offers us a bird’s-eye view of these social occasions, punctuated by disembodied heads, each imbued with a character of its own.

The process makes the image

In the moment of painting multiple canvases that together make four monumental compositions in black, blue, ginger and red (2015–16; cats 81–84), Wylie abandoned her paintbrushes and used her hands. Unlike most of her works, which are carefully planned and tested through many drawings, these images of various animals, among them an elephant, a bird and a worm, found their form through the process of painting. David Salle's comment about Wylie's work is particularly apt for this group: 'The handmade quality, the feeling of an image arrived at through careful in-the-moment looking, is always present.'[29] The animals, identified in words along the bottoms of the paintings, are reduced to their essential character, following Matisse's observation: 'Everything that is not useful in the picture is, it follows, harmful. A work of art must be harmonious in its entirety: any superfluous detail would replace some other essential detail in the mind of the spectator.'[30]

The raw energy of these paintings is derived from the physicality of the way Wylie has applied the paint. Smudges and accidental blobs are left to become part of the image; in other sections new strips of canvases are applied to amend the picture. For Wylie, 'The mistakes are, in fact, helpful. But I think as soon as you start making mistakes on purpose then you're in trouble. I'm intrigued by affectation, mannerism. So far I haven't done it. If there's a flick or correction, it's because I haven't liked what's underneath.'[31] Although the paintings are large, the areas of untreated canvas give the images space to breathe. The subjects are just a means to the end of creating a picture; again, Matisse captures the essence of Wylie's approach: 'I cannot copy nature in a servile way; I am forced to interpret nature and submit it to the spirit of the picture.'[32]

Ultimately, perhaps Gertrude Stein gives the best description of what it means to look at a Rose Wylie painting. In her own inimitable style, Stein reminds us that the visual encounter and the pleasure we draw from it are all that matter:

> And now, why does the representation of things that being painted do not look at all like the things look to me from which they are painted why does such a representation give me pleasure and hold my attention. Ah yes, well this I do not know and I do not know whether I ever will know, this. However it is true and I repeat that to give me this interest the painting must be an oil painting and any oil painting whether it is intended to look like something and looks like it or whether it is intended to look like something and does not look like it it really makes no difference, the fact remains that for me it has achieved an existence in and for itself, it exists on as being an oil painting on a flat surface and it has its own life and like it or not there it is and I can look at it and it does hold my attention.[33]

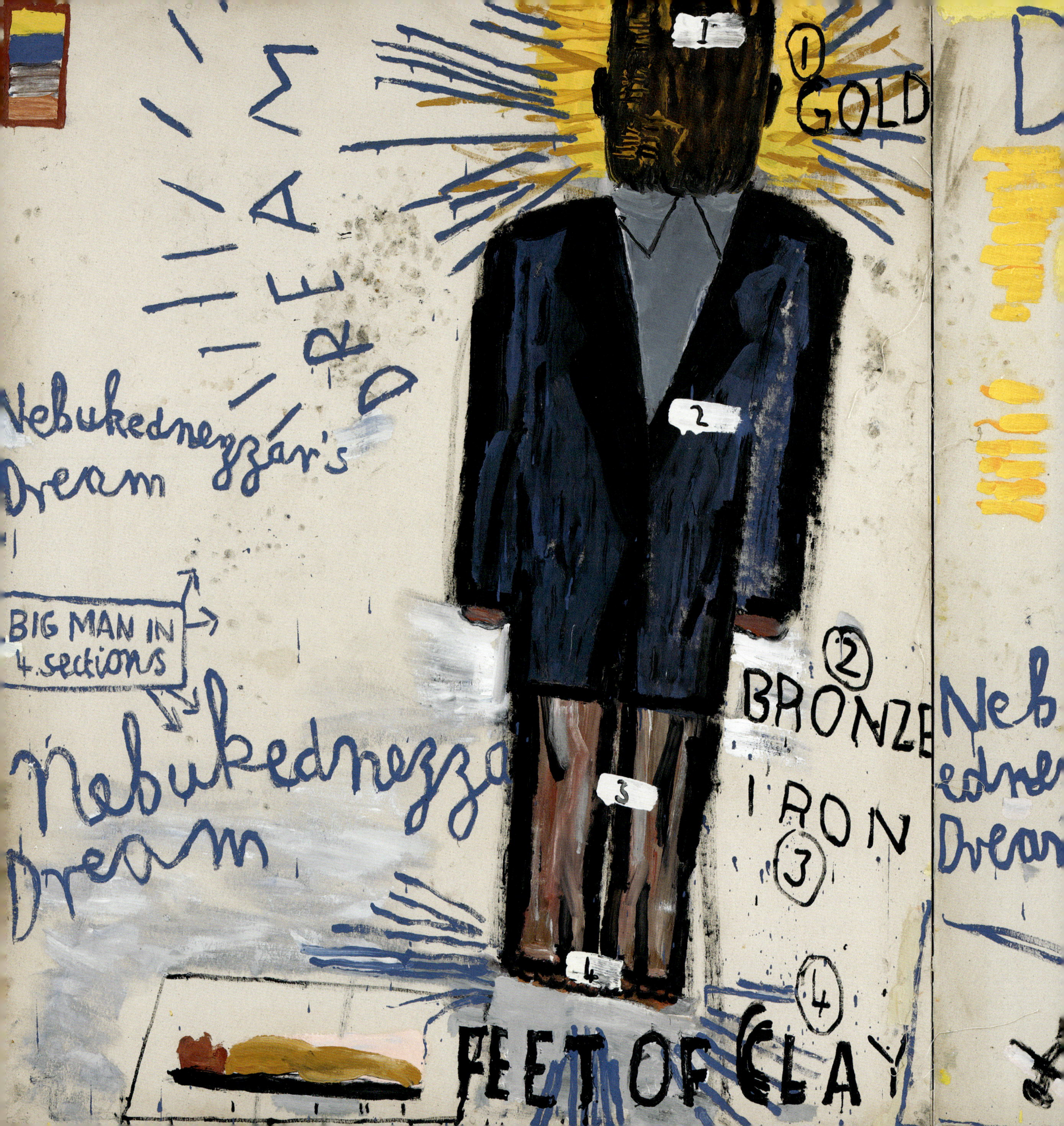
DREAM
Nebukednezzar's
Dream
BIG MAN IN
4 sections
Nebukednezza
Dream
1
① GOLD
2
② BRONZE
3
IRON ③
4
④
FEET OF CLAY

Various Instances: Rose Wylie's Relationship with Time

JENNIFER HIGGIE

About suffering they were never wrong,
The Old Masters: how well they understood
Its human position; how it takes place
While someone else is eating or opening a window
or just walking dully along...

W. H. AUDEN, 'MUSÉE DES BEAUX ARTS'[1]

Time, in Rose Wylie's paintings, is as malleable as paint. Uninterested in neat chronologies, she conjures scenes from her childhood as vividly as if they had occurred yesterday and converses with centuries-old painters who are as alive to her as someone she met last week. In myriad paintings and drawings, Wylie resurrects kings and queens who, metaphorically speaking, shake the dust from their tombs and proceed to rub shoulders with footballers and movie stars, all of whom appear at once immortal and all too human. Helen of Troy has taken centre stage, as has the biblical Adam's first wife, Lilith, who was banished from the Garden of Eden for speaking her mind. Wylie pictures her in *Lilith and Gucci Boy* (2024; cat. 65) as a naked, golden goddess, her hands raised, flanked by a wide-eyed owl and a fashionable young man in a smart suit. The painting has an earlier echo in *Nebuchadnezzar's Dream* (2023; fig. 9): the longest-reigning king of the Babylonian dynasty is reimagined twice as a very small figure, on a bed at the bottom of each canvas. He dreams of a monumental modern man in a sharp suit – an image informed by the chapter in the Bible that describes Daniel in the lions' den, dreaming of a giant statue made of four different materials: gold, bronze and iron, its feet composed of clay.

In Wylie's world, the dead and the living commingle like guests at a cosmic cocktail party; time often unfolds within the painting as the story progresses. For example, in the right-hand panel of the diptych *Mary and Philip and Little Rose (Hall)* (2025; fig. 10), Wylie's 21-year-old granddaughter, Little Rose, appears twice in the artist's pale-yellow hallway, both sitting and standing, long and slender in a blue dress, a brown coat and red shoes. In the left-hand panel, Mary Tudor, 'Bloody Mary', the first queen to rule England (from 1553 to 1558), her face a patchwork diamond,

FIG. 9 Detail of *Nebuchadnezzar's Dream*, 2023. Oil on canvas, 184.5 × 307 cm (overall). Courtesy of the artist and David Zwirner

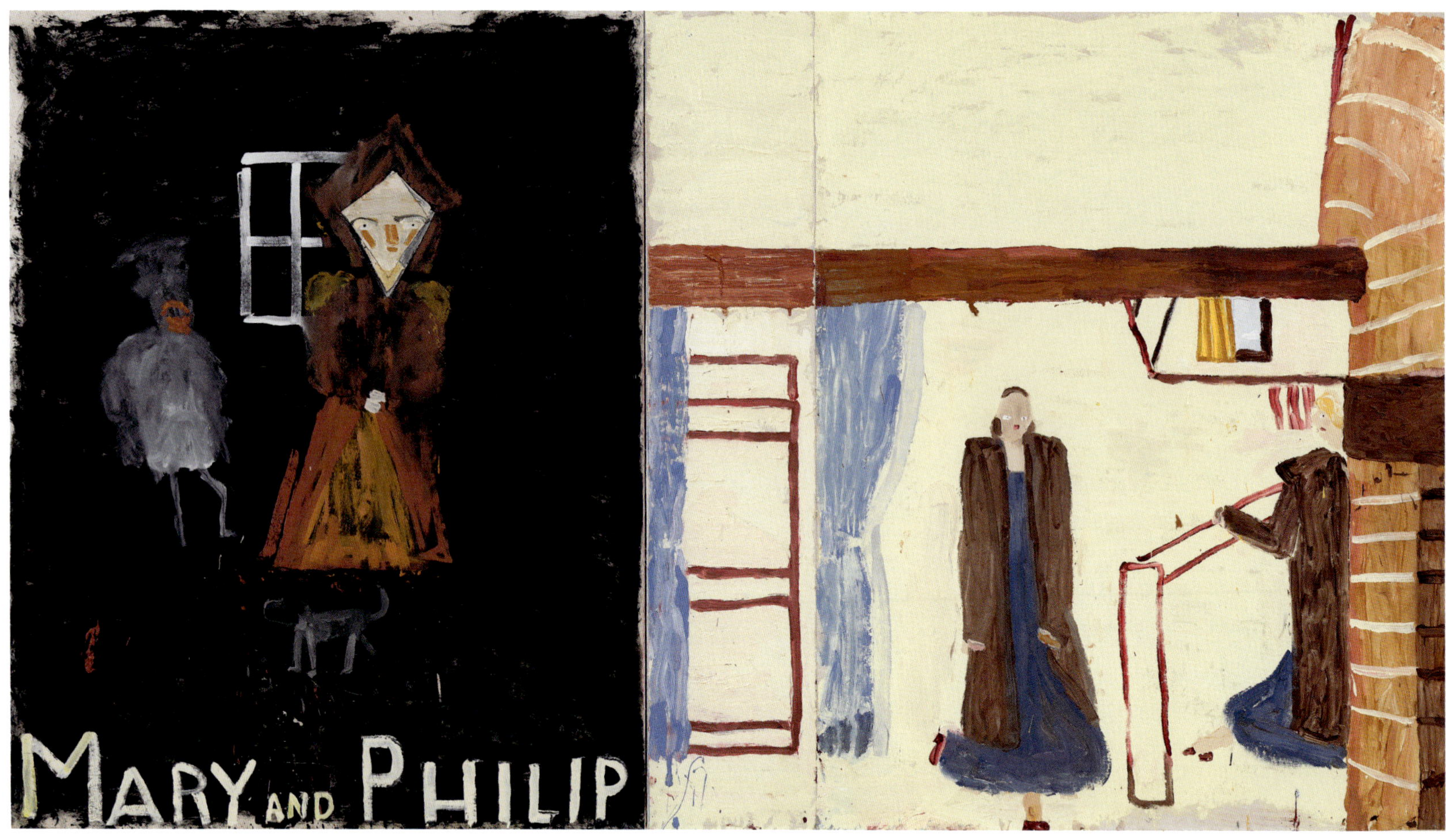

FIG. 10 *Mary and Philip and Little Rose (Hall)*, 2025. Oil on canvas, 183.5 × 329 cm (overall). Courtesy the artist and David Zwirner

hovers in a gloomy space illuminated by a stark white window frame. To her right, her small, ghostly husband, Philip II of Spain, his legs as thin as twigs, fades besides his wife; at her feet, a small, pale dog wags his tail. The work, which Wylie describes as 'a painting made from a painting and a painting made from my own context',[2] grew from a television programme. The artist had watched an episode of the 2025 BBC production *Lucy Worsley Investigates*, in which the historian discusses the life and reputation of England's first queen regnant. Wylie then did an online investigation and came across *Mary I of England and Philip II of Spain* (1558; Woburn Abbey, Bedfordshire), a portrait by Hans Eworth (or Ewoutsz). She was fascinated by the artist's indifference to proportion, in particular his rendering of Philip's spindly legs in their white shoes and stockings. If the inspiration for the left panel was, in Wylie's words, 'Philip's little legs', the right-hand panel grew from her desire to change the colour palette: to contrast the yellow with bright red and blue.

As we look at the world, we edit it. Ideas and objects and feelings and facts are jumbled together in the thousands of thoughts each of us has every day. (According to studies at Stanford University, most people experience some 60,000 daily.) If the realm that Wylie represents is not linear or chronological, neither is that the one most of us inhabit. We live as much in the past – in our memories, regrets, longings and dreams – as we do in the present: history is recalled in fragments and glimpses. Wylie once explained: 'The image is arrived at through many drawings, evolving from a process of observation, personality and response: keeping something of the original subject, but hoping for a transformation into a poetic and especial "particular", free from conventional representation.'[3]

Traditional hierarchies of value are irrelevant to Wylie; in one interview, she said: 'I think the ordinary is very unordinary, in fact. It's very special and very good. And deserves respect.'[4] She's as captivated by the minutiae of daily life as she is by the grand tales of history: a painting might emerge from a sudden recollection of a checked skirt she once wore, a painting in the National Gallery, a bunch of flowers or a pair of knickers; the slumbering presences of a beloved cat or the expression of a waitress; a lush lawn and a stick of mascara, brandished like a wand. Looking at Wylie's paintings is akin to reading a history book as you walk down a busy city street: as your head fills with the stories of long-ago lives, the physical world comes crashing in, in all its immediate, marvellous dissonance.

All too aware of both the fallibility and the power of memory, the artist is enamoured of the creative potential of mistakes. 'I make them all the time,' she says.[5] 'I love crossing things out because it shows you an earlier thought. And one that you decide not to use. It shows decision-making and discrimination and thinking.'[6] In this, Wylie evokes the messy business of being human with an urgency that embraces the here and now, even as she has one eye on the past and the other on the future. How, she seems to be asking, might you represent the complexity of a life, both your own and someone else's? How can the riddle of time – as elusive as a cloud and yet powerful enough to fell the strongest of people – be visualised?

Unsurprisingly, given the erudition of her sources, Wylie's artistic influences range across centuries and countries – from Paolo Uccello and Piero della Francesca to Francisco Goya, Paul Cézanne and others. In one interview she said:

> The sort of stuff I really like is prehistoric. It is just so good. I love ancient wall painting. I do think my work possibly touches – I call it trans-temporality. [...] I hope the kind of painting I do will just go on because it's not about a blip. It's not about a fashion. It's always been there. People have always painted a flower or a mouse or a bird. [...] History is just various instances of how it was done then. Artists have always dealt visually with what they're looking at, and that's what I do.[7]

FIG. 11 Giovanni di Paolo, *St Clare Rescuing the Shipwrecked*, c. 1455–60. Tempera and gold on panel, 19.7 × 29.5 cm. Private collection

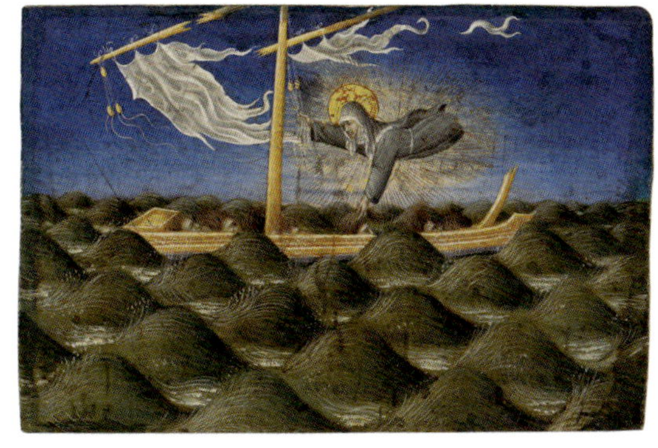

One of her favourite artists is the early Renaissance Sienese painter Giovanni di Paolo, who conjured wonderfully strange scenes in which religious fervour mingles with the everyday. In, for example, his painting *St Clare Rescuing the Shipwrecked* (c. 1455–60; fig. 11), the saint, electric with thin golden rays emanating from her body, clings to the ship's mast, her body like a kite, the rolling sea rendered like a field of green molehills. In Di Paolo's *The Creation of the World and the Expulsion from Paradise* (1445; Metropolitan Museum of Art, New York), the universe is presented as a cosmic target overseen by God, an ancient superman who flies through the air, supported by seraphim. Wylie deeply admires Di Paolo's imagination, his indifference to scale and conventional perspective and, she says, the fact that his figures 'aren't grounded'. She has also often referenced the work of the seventeenth-century

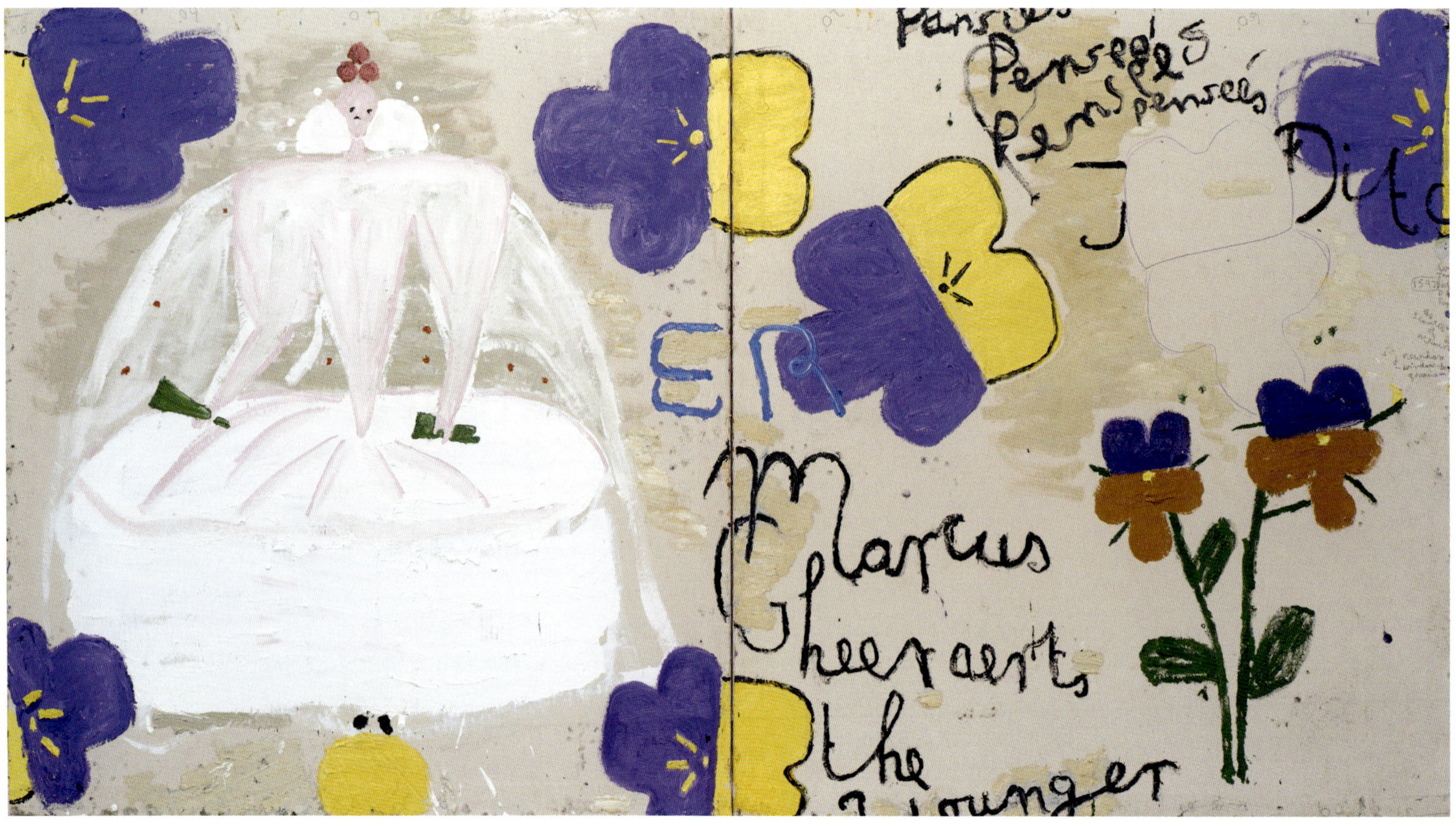

FIG. 12 *Queen of Pansies*, 2016. Oil on canvas, 183 × 333 cm (overall). Courtesy private collection and JARILAGER Gallery

Flemish artist Marcus Gheeraerts the Younger, in particular his portrait of Queen Elizabeth I (*c.* 1592; National Portrait Gallery, London), which she describes as 'stunningly beautiful'. In Wylie's homage to the artist, *Queen of Pansies* (2016; fig. 12), the queen, her head tiny, her body as lush as a wedding cake, is surrounded by enormous blooms, variations on the French word *pensées* (thoughts), and his name, scrawled in looping black paint, 'Marcus Gheeraerts the Younger'.

With her inventive non sequiturs and startling juxtapositions, much of Rose Wylie's vast body of work recalls the visions that tremble and dissolve just before you fall asleep. But there's also something very alert here: Wylie is as interested in popular culture as she is in history, and her paintings declare themselves with a crackling aliveness and curiosity. She writes to me: 'They are now.'[8]

Wylie's interests, however, are not, of course, simply limited to subject matter: she's fiercely attuned to the fresh possibilities of what paint might be able to do. She works rhythmically, scraping and pushing and pulling oil paint across unstretched canvas; staining, striking out and scumbling, constantly playing with combinations of colour, line, text and surface. How they look, and how they are. She is, she says, attracted to an 'element of the unexpected' in both her compositions and her mark-making.[9] Although there are echoes of cartoons, cave paintings, frescoes, Pompeian wall painting and Abstract Expressionism in her techniques and in her paintings, the end result is a visual language that is unique. As the curator Clarrie Wallis has observed: 'Wylie uses paint as a subversive means of expression. She prioritises "looking" over "reading", or "sensing" rather than "knowledge": the importance of pre-cognitive lived experience as opposed to conceptual thought.'[10]

One aspect of Wylie's approach to painting could be described as diaristic. She's quick to register the details of a scene: the curve of a mouth or the gesture of an arm; the startling colour of a flower; a scene from a film; an advertisement on a billboard; the shape of an opera singer's mouth; a teapot, glinting in the sun; the formation of stars; the curve of a bird's wing. But she also registers her thoughts in words, which she might combine with an image to declare a particular time or place, or to make them compositionally useful, or wilfully enigmatic. There is, of course, historical precedence in such an approach: in many medieval and some Renaissance paintings, inscriptions served various purposes, providing information about the artist, subject, date or provenance of the artwork.

Wylie likes, she says, 'the look of text and image going together',[11] and in her work, they're on an equal footing. In one interview she stated: 'writing is not about information'[12] and 'I don't care whether you can read it [...] it's the look and "being" of the painting that counts, and anyway, I paint and draw how things look and I spell how things sound.'[13] In another, she explained that she's always liked 'illustrated manuscripts where there's text and image, and also images in newspapers and magazines'. She added: 'I think writing is a method of unifying the painting. It's easier than doing a face!'[14] She is wary, however, of any sense of familiarity or complacency entering her thinking:

> I don't like things to be too familiar because you get into an easy way of doing it. So sometimes I've done Russian writing, or Persian writing, simply because it's a different shape. It has a different look to it, so familiarity goes out of the window here. I do longhand, lower case and capital, and don't mind if the spelling goes wrong. I often start in the middle of the painting and then go backwards through words, which encourages misspelling.[15]

The diptych *Dinner Outside* (2024; cat. 79) is a case in point. Like the open pages of an enormous book, the top of the left-hand painting is inscribed with the words: 'BOTH PAGES LOOKING SOUTH / FRONT AND BACK / DIARY ENTRY / AUGUST 10 2024'. In the right-hand panel, two crescent moons float in the sky, a sign of time passing: across the grey sky is written 'Getting dark'. The painting grew from a magical summer gathering attended by Wylie that was hosted by neighbours beneath the stars. Against a pale-ochre ground, the grass is suggested in groupings of three moss-green lines and the gravel in brown dots. Two women in coats gaze up at an urn, their wonder made clear in a few swift, soft lines. The ancient shape of the vessel evokes, in the simplest language possible, a universal sense of the past: that other people, in other eras, also came together to delight in the company of their fellow men and women. Below them is inscribed 'DINNER OUTSIDE', a declaration both blunt and memorialising.

A great observer of human nature, Wylie has long been fascinated by the way people socialise. When I visited her at her studio in her house in Kent in July 2025, she was in the midst of working on a large diptych inspired by the seating plans of four dinner parties (cat. 80), which she had compressed into two compositions. In the left-hand canvas, the nocturnal scene is evoked with candles, rendered in simple white lines and a yellow flame, which travel down the centre of the table. The ten guests, portrayed as floating heads on a dense, ochre-yellow ground, stare at each other across the table, their identities indicated by their abbreviations (Ann E, Captain W), hair colour and facial characteristics, such as a large forehead or sticking-out ears. At the bottom of the painting, in large black capital letters are the words SNAPSHOT OF SEATED TABLE. In the right half of the diptych, four heads of various sizes float on a dirty white ground amid ten or so tables, whose places are marked with a single initial. At the bottom of the painting are the words: '3 SEATING PLANS'. At once raw and observant, the painting is a diagram, a diary entry and, according to Wylie, an intimation, of sorts, of a Viking boat with oars – an association engendered by the characters facing each other down the line of candles. Wylie remarked that the largest head of the group was that of the waitress. She explained: 'I've given prominence not to the guests but to the workers. You know, bugger the actual dinner party guests, the workers were interesting.'[16] Wylie playfully referred to the diptych as Rothko and Rembrandt: the former, because of its blocks of saturated colour and the latter because of his famous study of about 1642 in light and shadow, *The Night Watch* – a title which could, of course, be a description of a dinner party.

During the Second World War, as a young child, Wylie partly lived in the English countryside with her family. She can remember being given a chart for aircraft recognition so that she could spot enemy planes.[17] One night, their home was bombed. Luckily, no one was killed, but certain details of the evening are still clear to the artist. She has repeatedly returned to the war, fascinated not only by the drama – both personal and global – of the events unfolding, but by the shape of aircraft and bombs. Some of her paintings on the subject include *Early Memory Series No. 2: Doodle Bug* (1998; cat. 4) and the semi-abstracted *Stealth Bomber* (2016; fig. 13), where the titular craft, painted in solid black, blocks out the sun like a sinister manta ray.

In the enormous, four-panel *Park Dogs & Air Raid* (2017; cat. 2), Wylie intertwines the personal with the political. Four dogs gambol with two ducks on a patch of scorched black earth next to a pond; the scrawled caption identifies it as the Round Pond in London's Kensington Gardens in 1940. Above this oddly cheerful scene is a serrated sky filled with Nazi bombers: above them is the caption 'AIRRAID, 2 TALBOT ROAD, BAYSWATER, LONDON, 1940', the address where Rose stayed with her Great Aunt Bella, who took her to play at the Round Pond. That the dogs are as large as the aeroplanes is telling: it's a child's memory. 'That', she says, 'is history. It's as much history as the bombing.'

In one of the most compelling of Wylie's war paintings, *Rosemount (Coloured)* (1999; cat. 3) – made on two canvases abutted together – the artist's family home, Rosemount, is pictured as a blacked-out, rough triangle in the middle of the composition, its name scrawled in red paint on its surface. (The association with blood is hard to avoid.) The painting is a map, of sorts; an aerial viewpoint denoted by the artist's single floating eye looking upwards, with thin black lines projected from the pupil towards the red outline of a 'doodlebug', headed her way. Words float

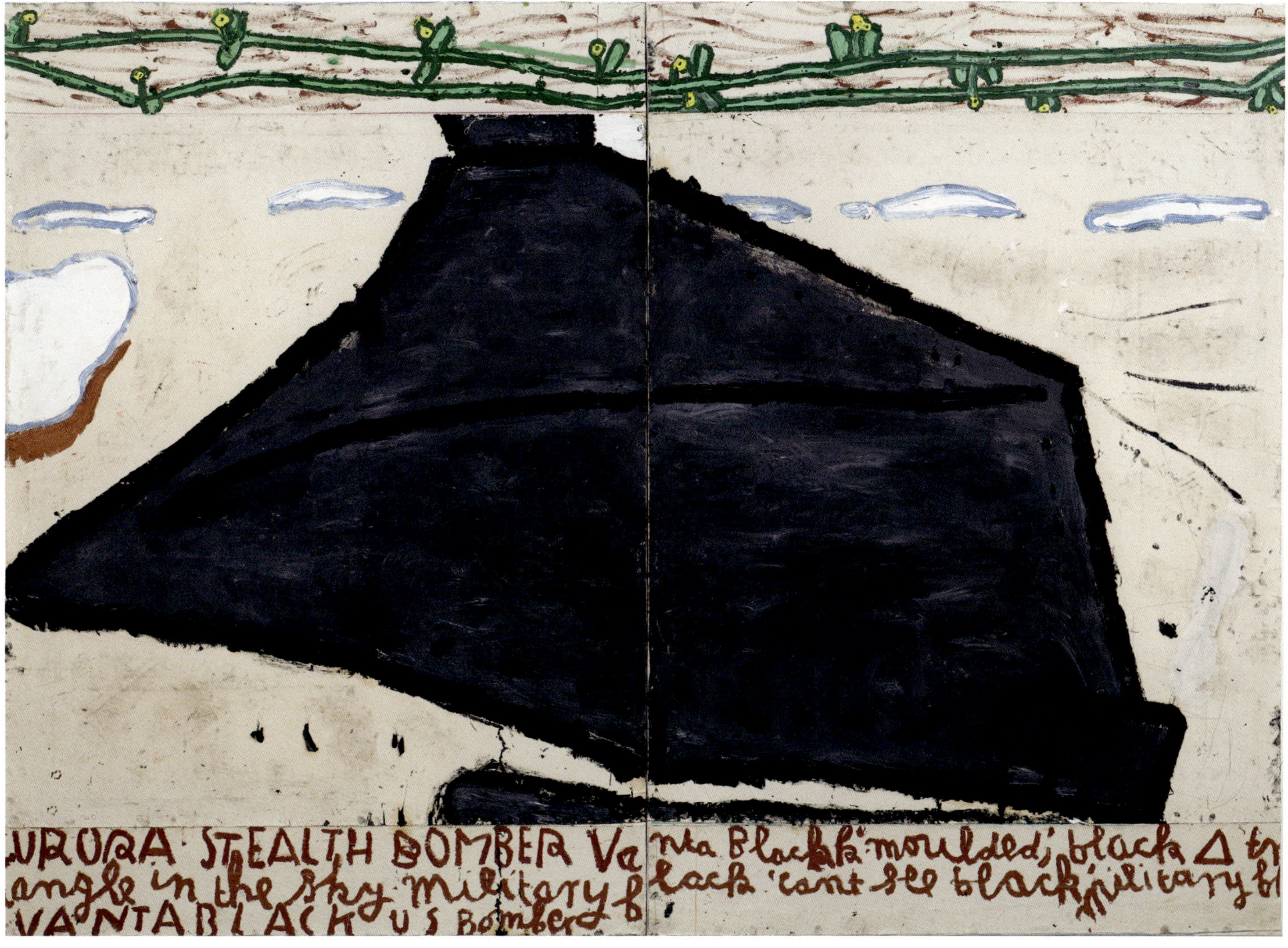

FIG. 13 *Stealth Bomber*, 2016. Oil on canvas, 238 × 336 cm (overall). La Cachepli Collection, La Paila, Colombia

across the surface of the painting: EARLY MEMORY SERIES, ALLOTTMENTS (*sic*), ELM WALK, FRUIT TREES AND VEGETABLES and more. The date is curiously written backwards: KENT 1944–40, the order in which the artist recalled the events. She explains: '1940 was when the bomb dropped. Doodlebugs are 1944. These come afterwards. So I put both dates.'[18]

Spend time with Rose Wylie's paintings and it becomes clear that painting, for the artist, is as much an act of retrieval as it is of invention. Recalling the process of recreating her wartime home, she says: 'I was thinking, how did the rooms go? I was five then and I'm now 90. So it's a long time ago. I was trying to remember, where did the chimneys go? So, I had to try to think back.' She paused. 'My memory's very poor for facts. But it's okay for my own experience.'

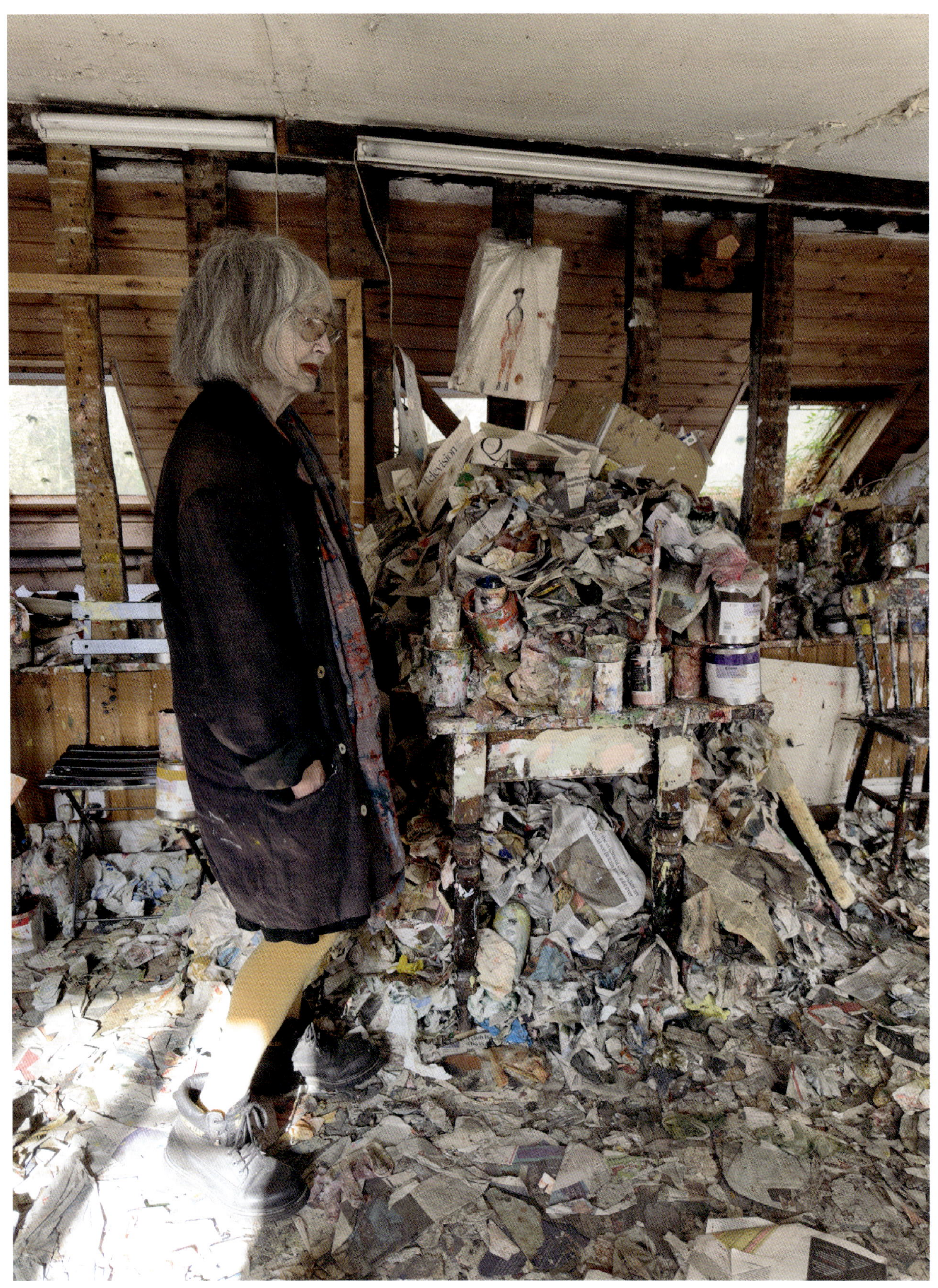

FIG. 14 Juergen Teller, *Rose Wylie, No. 19, Autre magazine, Sittingbourne*, 2024

‘Just Look at the Work!’

ROSE WYLIE IN CONVERSATION WITH FRANCES MORRIS

FM Rose (fig. 14), as an art historian schooled in the 1970s and 1980s, I was encouraged to remain at a distance from an artist’s biography. But so much of your work deals with your personal experiences, particularly your early life, that it feels difficult to remain at that remove.

RW Well, I’ve always thought that it’s quite useful to remove yourself from the life of the artist: just look at the work! That’s not a very current way of thinking, because everyone likes to look at the context, which is hugely interesting and does give you all sorts of insights, but it’s not the final thing.

FM Even so, as you’ve opened the door… in previous interviews you’ve described your childhood as Victorian. What did you mean by that?

RW Well, I was the last child of parents who lived in the nineteenth century. My father was born in 1880-something, and my mother five or six years later. They were Victorians. My father worked in India, so they were in a sense colonial, but they weren’t the colonial type.

FM And were you brought up with a set of Victorian values?

RW Yes, moral, you know: ‘Don’t push yourself forward, be modest.’ A woman should be well-mannered; she should know how to be a proper wife. That’s what I meant by Victorian: ‘Don’t adorn yourself, you shouldn’t be wearing lipstick.’

FM Hence your love of lipstick?

RW Do the thing you’re told not to.

FM At the heart of this exhibition is a series of paintings from the 1990s – almost the earliest here – that leads us yet further back, to the 1940s, in the form of pictorial memories of your earliest childhood. How did the relatively privileged youngest child of the Head of Ordnance for the whole of India end up experiencing the Blitz from under a table-top shelter in central London?

RW My brothers were at school in England, but my sisters were at school in France before the war. That’s why my mother left India, to collect them from Europe, because of the danger of invasion. My parents had a holiday house in England, in Hythe, the nearest coast to where Germany was going to invade. So my mother moved us to London, to Bayswater, where we stayed with my great-aunt. That’s where the bombs fell. My mother had gone from the risk of invasion right into the heart of the Blitz.

FM Why weren’t you evacuated?

RW She didn’t believe in it. She was quite tough. She thought children needed to be with their mothers at a certain formative time and that was important. We had a Morrison shelter, we slept under the stairs.

FM Was it exciting?

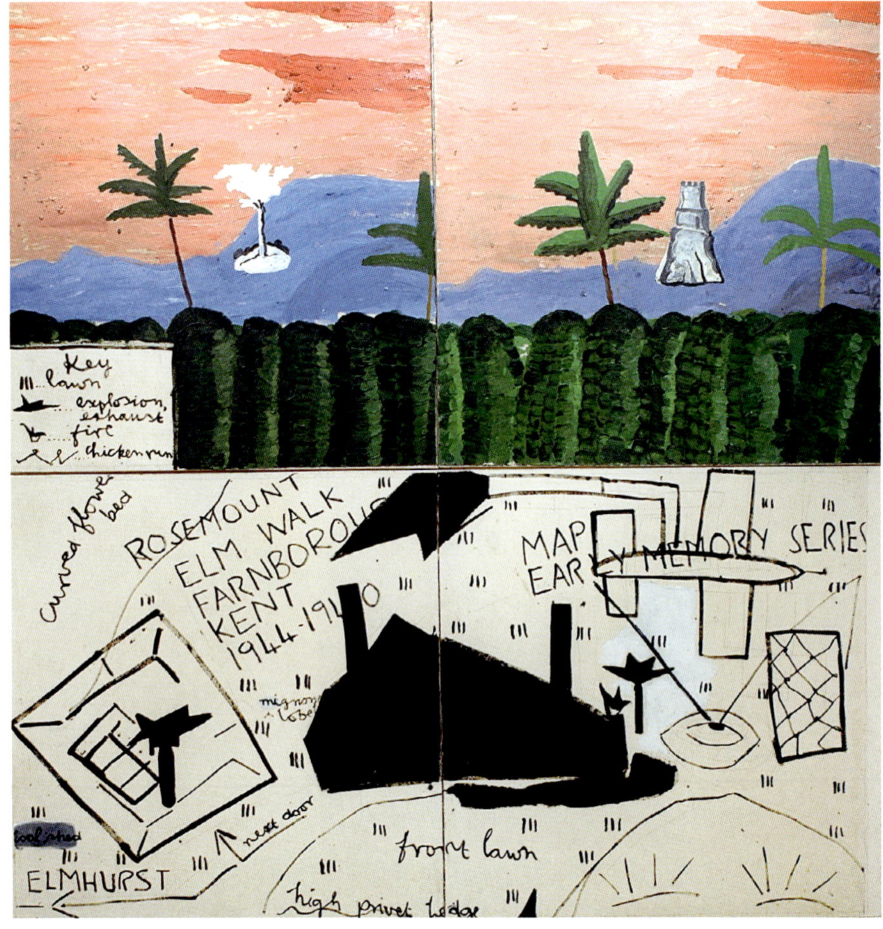

FIG. 15 *Rosemount Coffee Label*, 1999. Oil on canvas, 366 × 366 cm (overall). Courtesy private collection and JARILAGER Gallery

RW Yes, yes, yes. Gas! Gas! There were so many air raids that my sister used to note them in her diary. I didn't like the idea of being gassed. It was a horrible idea. Because of that, my mother decided to move us out of London.

FM You've painted Rosemount, the house your mother moved your family to in Bromley, Kent, on several occasions, under attack from the air, replete with bombs dropping (fig. 15 and cats 3, 45). I am curious, you have often stated that you only work with 'fond' memories?

RW Fond? I don't think memories of a bomb landing on your house are particularly fond. But they can be memories of having seen something that touches you in some way. I like things that fly, and the doodlebug is easy to draw. The fact that it's destructive actually doesn't matter to me. I like butterflies, dragonflies, angels, planes.

FM So you're not using memory to deal with trauma.

RW Probably not. It's a memory of something I've seen, which I find exciting visually. I think, blimey, that's terrific. And that's probably what I meant by 'fond'.

FM Can we talk a little bit more about your life? You've often talked about your experience of art school in the 1950s and how afterwards you delayed your painting career to focus on your children and home at a time when your peer group was forging ahead. But during those years you also pursued an impressive career as a teacher.

RW I'm not interested in teaching.

FM But you did teach in the 1960s and 1970s. Were you a terrible teacher or a good teacher?

RW I don't know!

FM Was it just a job?

RW There *were* things I liked about it. I used to like the students, talking to them about their paintings and their work. At Tunbridge Wells they were adults, and they all wanted to paint. They'd lived lives and gone to places, and seen stuff. They were wonderful. I liked the exchange between what they were doing and what I thought… I kept it open. Some people teach what's around and some people teach their own passion. I tended to teach what was around, but they probably picked up what I liked. Because I was painting and looking at work all the time, I used to do a short art-history lecture every week or so. It might be Pontormo, Titian, El Greco or somebody now. 'Now' also came into the teaching, but my lectures were more formal art history, and the students loved that. Usually, I talked about the painter I happened to be looking at the time – Cézanne, for instance.

FM So, in fact, you weren't really removed from the art world at all.

RW No, I wasn't. I was meeting artists, going to shows, looking at images in books, buying art-history books for the college, sorting through all these new books on artists. I was absolutely *in* it; I just wasn't *doing* it. It was concentrated and enriching.

FM And when you went to the Royal College in 1980, your thesis, I believe, focused on methods of teaching drawing in British art schools?
RW It was like a door opening. I was doing drawing as a student at the RCA before I started painting. I was really investigating drawing, which was hugely good, because drawing is central to what I do. I was just thinking, what is drawing? What do you expect it to do? What is it about? How do other people find it? How is it taught?
FM And was it important for the development of your own way of working?
RW Probably. I've always said that drawing is major for me. Wasn't the distinction that Florentine art was more to do with drawing, and Venetian was more to do with paint and its expression and plasticity? Probably I am more Florentine... but then I'm not, you see, because I do both: I draw *and* I use great blobs and swathes of paint. It all mixes up.
FM I'm interested that you have brought drawing centre stage in this exhibition. Can we talk more about the role of drawing in relation to your painting?
RW I'm often trying to record something that I've seen, keeping it, recording it. Actually recording is the wrong word, I want to *keep* it. Have it. Own it.
FM Where and how do you draw?
RW Everywhere. Here, for example, in the kitchen. Look, there's something on the table. I love the plates left behind after people have had dinner, I don't want to clear them away. These piles of books, I like the look of them. And in the bathroom, piles of clothes. These things just hit you. I don't know how to identify the rules of looking that make some things interesting to look at and some things not.

Drawing is spontaneous. You look around for a piece of paper because you've seen an image and you just do it there and then. You just land it. But I have also done a drawing that took nine hours! Not sitting and looking; looking, yes, but constantly changing.
FM So how does drawing intersect with your painting?
RW Painting is very difficult. Drawing is the start. But it's different to go from the drawing into the painting. The painting's runny and it can be thick; it puddles, it drips, it runs, it bumps, it jumps. You have to have impetus. Once you've got to something which is okay then you try to keep the okay bit from the drawing in the painting, which isn't always easy.
FM How do you know when a painting is working for you?
RW Well, not too much distortion, more a combination of many things: how it settles, the whole, as well, which makes it, it has touch and it touches you. I think you feel it. The painting has to *be*, it has to get to be something. I call it making it like it looks like it's all right. Which I think is what you call structure. That's a better way of putting it. It happens in the painting. Because in the drawing you haven't got the colours... I mean I often do a drawing in a coloured pencil, I like coloured pencils. But on the canvas, I do the whole thing. Filling in. I love filling in. So there's the outline and there's the colouring in. I'm often completely torn about whether to leave the original thing with the colour, whether to put a line around it or not. It becomes more primitive if you put a line around it. But do you want it more primitive? Do you want it more open? I mean, this drives me nuts. Line or not? It's an area of torture.
FM How do you sleep at night?
RW Not terribly well. It's not fun, painting. It's difficult, it's torture, torture.
FM Your finished work has such a strong formal presence. Distinctive colours, emphatic shapes, patterns, repetitions and so on. Do you see your paintings as sitting in a space between abstraction and figuration?
RW From my point of view, abstraction is wonderful but it hasn't quite got the interest that figuration has. Figuration is more difficult, it can go more wrong in a way that abstraction can't. It can be nasty, slimy, clinging, cloying, sentimental. Abstraction is freer because

it's away from depiction. You could take a lump of my painting and say, yes, that could be an abstract painting. But if I'm painting a candlestick, I want it to look like the candlestick I'm painting. I don't want it to look like *that* one or *that* one... No, and I don't want it to look like a blob. But there is also a poetic transformation about how you make it look like that candlestick. That's what's difficult.

FM Can you describe this poetic transformation?

RW It's difficult. You don't want it too close. But you want it to move. Like poetry – it becomes a new description of something that you know about. You have to progress from reality to a poetic reality. An object in a drawing can flick into something new but still has to retain its recognisability. Hard to do... it would have to sidestep banality, graphic flatness, boring repetition, it would have to get form. But then again form is a slightly problematic word for some people. There is an idea that a drawing should 'jump into form', it should not be flat, graphic – it has to have a kind of suggestive three-dimensionality about it. The line would have to be 'right', but it could be endlessly varied. I don't like the suggestion that you have to draw in a particular kind of way; I've been very against imposed drawing structures. I think you should look at something and respond. But a drawing should retain part of the original image. Then you have to decide what sort of line you're going to use, whether it's going to be thin, hard, slimy, fluffy, thick, tentative, certain... all those things come into the line. And it's not only the line, it's how the line encompasses the form that you're drawing. So, the whole of this thing all comes together to get the poetic transformation, but it has to be something new and somewhat invented.

FM It feels as if you have evolved a very personal vocabulary of forms and marks. For example, the triangle is a recurrent shape, with multiple representative roles. I see triangles everywhere in your paintings: skirts, beaks, cats' heads.

RW I do like triangles. So did Duchamp, I believe... I think it's something to do with the Trinity. But I also have squares, rectangles, circles and rhombuses. And crosses. I have the gamut. Geometry is quite interesting. I like the shape of a holly leaf too. And I love hazel leaves, which are round with a point. It's endless.

FM Could you describe your colour palette and how you make decisions about what colour to use?

RW A lot of people think colour means bright colour. But I think my colours often reflect ancient pottery and the early Renaissance. I like the colour of Fra Angelico, Piero della Francesca. I do have a very strong sense of which colours go with which.

FM Is there a colour you dislike?

RW Well, I think some are a bit more difficult. Colours like yellow ochre and black and yellowy green and pink and pale blue – they all seem to work for me more than purple and orange. I quite often have flat or flattish areas of colour, two close colours often put together, where there's a light blue and a slightly darker blue... I don't use a palette, but I do mix up colours in tins, and on the canvas. I put one on and I push them together. I have brushes which are then dipped into a different colour, and then I start to mix them up... I like shiny, and I love shiny and smooth together. Sometimes I also like it broken up or brushy as well, so it's both flat and shiny.

FM The computer screen in the room next to your studio is a mosaic of images of your paintings taken at different stages. Can you explain this process of documentation that accompanies your paintings?

RW I take pictures of the paintings when I've done something, before I change it. Once it's gone it's gone. I often have to go back to look at an earlier stage on the computer. I do this a lot. My computer's jammed full of images that record the most minute changes. I keep them all on my screen. It's immediate. I look at a painting all the time when I'm doing it. I'm in and out all the time. Before I go to bed, I look at it. I start at 12 am sometimes. I don't want to go into my studio and look at a painting if it's stuck – so I keep going at it. I have to change it.

That's obsessive, it's compulsion. Like leaving the plates on the table.

FM When did you start working with photography as part of your creative process?

RW Years ago. I used to take photographs of my paintings and then do collages. I used to do them before Hockney did what he called his 'joiners'. I mean, nobody had my paintings, nobody looked at them, they didn't get anywhere. Nobody paid the slightest attention. So, I used to photograph them and then I used to photograph the photographs, and stack them up: to give them life, give me life. To feed off them, visually.

FM What about the moving image. Film? When did you first make the connection between your painting practice and the cinematic?

RW Steve McQueen made a film, *Deadpan*, remaking that scene from Buster Keaton, do you remember, with the house falling over? I was watching it at Tate, it was in the Turner Prize in 1999. And it was marvellous. The screen was big. And I came out into another room afterwards and there were some French paintings, Légers and so on; well, they were tiny. And they were so *dull* compared with the film, the size of the film and the screen.

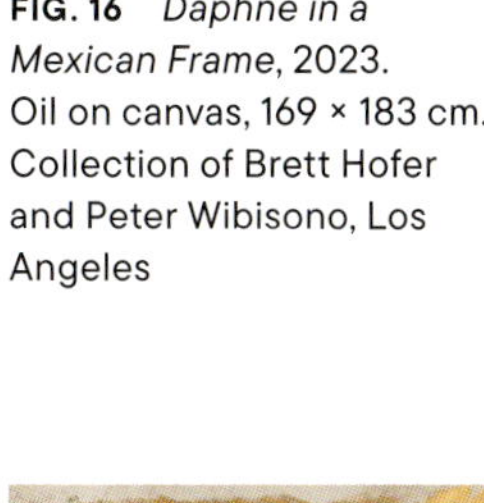

FIG. 16 *Daphne in a Mexican Frame*, 2023. Oil on canvas, 169 × 183 cm. Collection of Brett Hofer and Peter Wibisono, Los Angeles

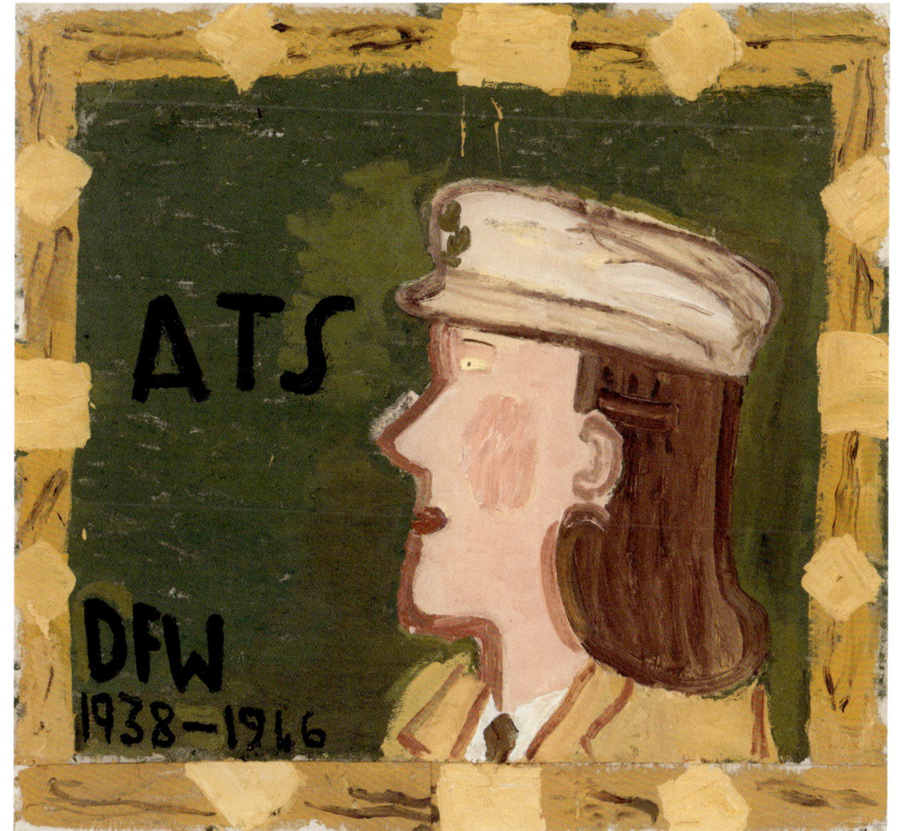

FM And you wanted to paint on that scale?

RW Yes, I did. I like a film's impact to come out in a painting. I love films. I love a big image. Which is why I also like the early Renaissance, and self-taught art.

FM Film and TV have played an important role in generating some of your visual strategies, such as cutting between disparate images, zooming in and out. But they've also provided you with a lot of visual content: epic scenes, for example, and many of your characters, movie stars like Penélope Cruz (cat. 53) and Nicole Kidman (cats 61–63 and figs 5–6), like your footballers (cat. 67), who remain recognisably themselves in your paintings. Is it important that viewers recognise the reference, or do you prefer it when the reference slips into something else – a gesture, a haircut?

RW I kicked off doing a lot of heads on oil and paper, types of head from a German theoretical book called *Der Schlüssel zum Leben* by Manfred Curry, which showed photographs of heads of people both well known and unknown. Göring, the car manufacturer Henry Ford, Ford's wife. It was a great book. I've done some works from that book, such as Pina Bausch (cat. 69), looking over her shoulder.

A popular figure is more open to reference for the audience. A lot of people know about footballers, their images are in the newspapers and on television all the time. They're accessible national interests. Wayne Rooney for example: there was something about the shape of his legs. He was so different from Peter Crouch as a physical shape. People wouldn't recognise what you'd done with a figure if you were painting someone they didn't know about, whereas with a well-known footballer, they see the image I'm presenting but they also have an image of that person in their minds.

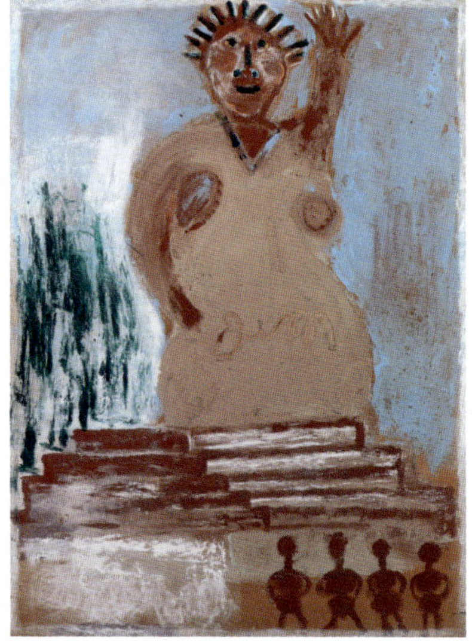

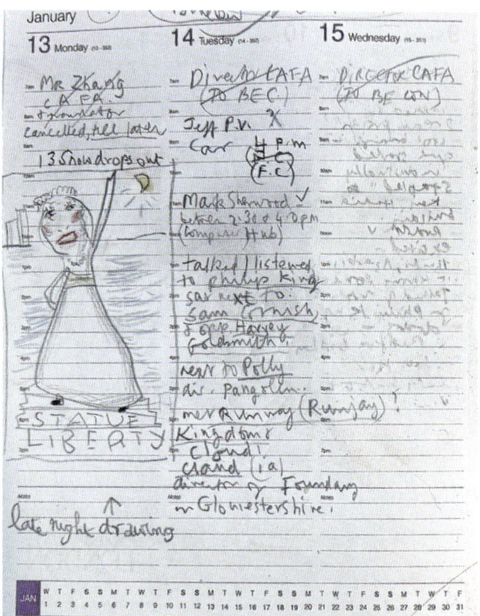

FIG. 17 Jimmy Lee Sudduth, *Untitled (Statue of Liberty)*, c. 1989. Sand, mud and paint on board, 121.9 × 91.4 cm. Gift of Orren and Marilyn Bradley and Kohler Foundation, Inc., 2015.58.21, Smithsonian American Art Museum, Washington DC

FIG. 18 *Homage to Jimmy Lee Sudduth's Statue of Liberty*, 2020. Pencil and coloured pencil on paper, 25.5 × 20.5 cm. Courtesy the artist and David Zwirner

FM You have also made a few memorable portraits of people who have been close to you. Your sisters, and your husband Roy Oxlade, towards the end of his life.

RW I've done a portrait of Daphne, my sister, twice. She was in the Auxiliary Territorial Service. I did her standing in ATS uniform with barrage balloons behind her and our house, Rosemount, in the distance. It's a sort of memory painting, a history painting. And I did a portrait of her, just her face (fig. 16), because she looks a bit like Keira Knightley. She used to have this look on her face when she thought she was really it, and I was just a nuisance little sister who'd obviously done wrong and needed to be told. This particular look, I've spotted it on Keira, the same look. They don't look alike, but there is a connection.

And the portrait of Roy (cat. 49): the eyes, they have resignation in them. They are hugely important in the work, because he was resigned; life and hope, everything had gone at that time. The eyes express resignation. But someone in the street might look at this and say, well, you know, it's not a proper drawing, it's a cartoon or whatever. They'd be wrong... also his face had got very thin. I mean there was a thinness on the temple. If you look at the drawing, there's a kind of collapsed bit. I've drawn collapse. How ever you draw collapse... I mean, how does one? But it's so like him.

FM And yet you've reiterated on many occasions that the subject matter of your paintings does not matter. Am I wrong then to find significance in a work like *Lilith and Gucci Boy* (cat. 65)? How and why did you decide to paint such a feminist icon?

RW I came across Lilith on a Babylonian tile at the British Museum (fig. 8) and I just liked her. Her face wasn't European, and she was just standing there. I thought it was a great work of art so I drew it, and then put it to one side. Later I heard Anselm Kiefer talking on TV about his painting *Lilith* and discovered she was Adam's first wife. It was a marvellous gift. The image has huge relevance in the feminist debate. It gave me a sense of exhilaration: I'd found the first feminist! I felt, wonderful, I must do a painting of this. And Adam gets into the picture through the Gucci boy, doesn't he? He just turned up by chance. I'd done a drawing of this Gucci boy; his clothes hung in such a wonderful way off his shoulders, and he had a white vest underneath, and a hairy chest. It's quite nice to have hairs, you can do little squiggles on the chest. And he was nonchalant, as models are, strolling, and he had high cheekbones and good hair. And he was current! It's no good doing antiquity all the time.

FM All the artists, genres and media you reference as pivotal in your growing databank of reference points are connected to representation and storytelling. Your copybook of sources is insatiable...

RW I love murals. I love fresco. I love Babar. There's a long list of paintings and films which I have used and countries I've been interested in: films by Quentin Tarantino, Lars von Trier, Éric Rohmer, Jane Campion, Claudia Llosa, Carlos Reygadas, Werner Herzog. And paintings by certain Indigenous and Black American artists. Asafo tribal flags from Ghana, Egyptian Hajj paintings and the Infant Jesus of Prague – a sculpture from, I think, the sixteenth century – which I did a mass of work from, and Easter Island statues.

Looking at other big artists, I have done transpositions from Cimabue, Bellini, Giovanni di Paolo, Goya, Titian. I love Rousseau. He's one of my heroes. What a great painter! So skilful in a different way. Breathtakingly so. And Guston, of course...

FM Germaine Greer described you as 'Britain's hottest new artist' in 2010. You've always looked at younger artists. Whom are you interested in now?

RW Jimmy Lee Sudduth is one. I look at the paintings and think, oh, I just love them, I wish I'd done them. He's untaught but his paintings are wonderful (fig. 17). They're not realistic; they veer off into being something completely different, an image that's completely new but that you can recognise (fig. 18). There's a renaissance in 'straightforward painting', which I love. Sam Doyle does marvellous paintings. He puts coloured lines around the outside. I love Benjamin Asante and Sister Gertrude Morgan, who did amazing pictures of angels and choirs and heads and nurses. And Frank Walter, another great artist. He painted the rim on a shark's mouth around a shark's teeth (fig. 19), and the edge is so thick. They are straightforward paintings – more like the early Renaissance – like mosaics, frescoes. That's what I love. Not Rembrandt; Rembrandt is of course marvellous but he's not my favourite painter. Noah Davis is incredible. There's an element of Manet in his work, in the use of black – which I have – and an element of El Greco, which I have too. You'll find that everyone I mention has a connection. Another one is Tschabalala Self. She has a touch of vulgarity which I like, I don't like anything refined. I've seen a sculpture of her legs. It's a flat sculpture. I do flat. It's like a stage set. I love stage sets.

FM With most artists, their work goes through a kind of trajectory. Early work, then the breakthrough moments till they get to their signature style. Looking at the work on view at the RA it feels as if *you* entered the art world fully formed.

RW Quite a long time ago, on a panel at the Royal Drawing School, William Feaver asked me, 'Rose, would you say your paintings have changed much?' I said I didn't think they had. And he said he agreed. It might change. My consciousness, my aesthetic grows.

FM I once asked you if you were driven by ambition all those years ago at art school. In response you said you remembered 'looking at a thistle and thinking what would you have to do to make it great' and that you always wanted to 'do something that connected to quality, ambition or greatness'. I think this RA show qualifies on all those counts. So what could possibly be next?

RW I'd love something to happen afterwards of great significance, but, I mean, I don't know, I have no idea.

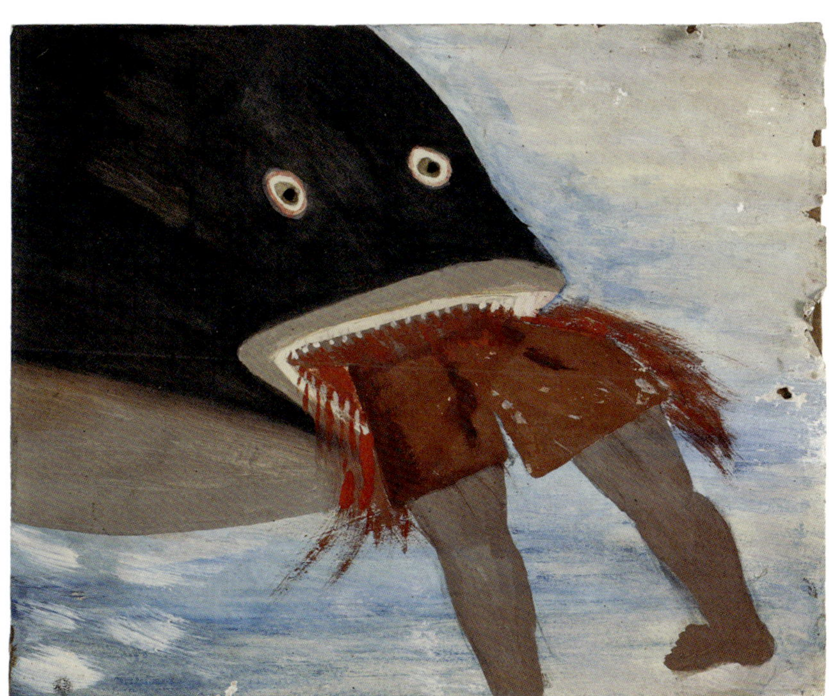

FIG. 19 Frank Walter, *Untitled (Man Eaten by Shark)*, n.d. Oil on cardstock, 20.2 × 25.3 cm

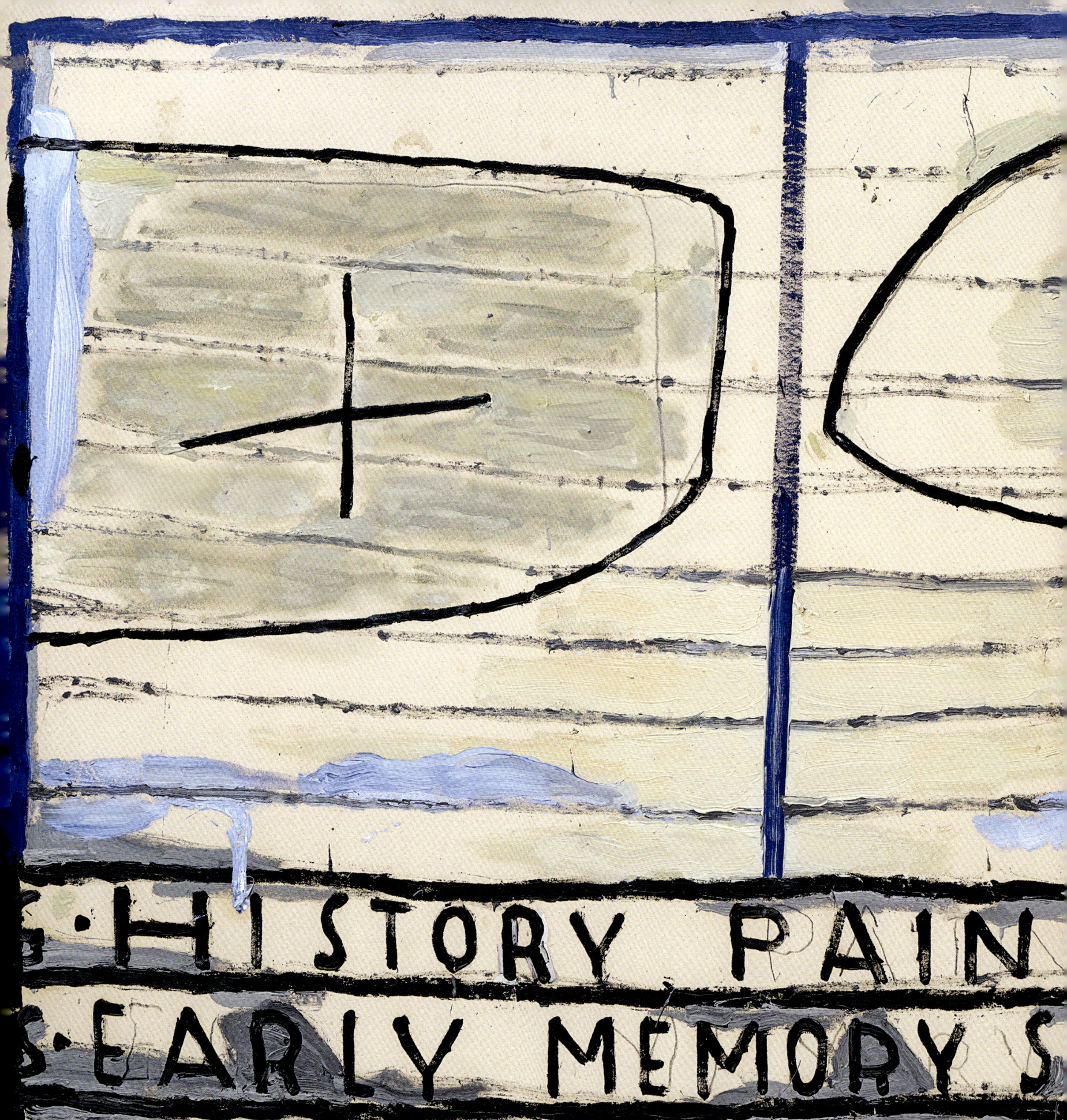
HISTORY PAIN
EARLY MEMORY S

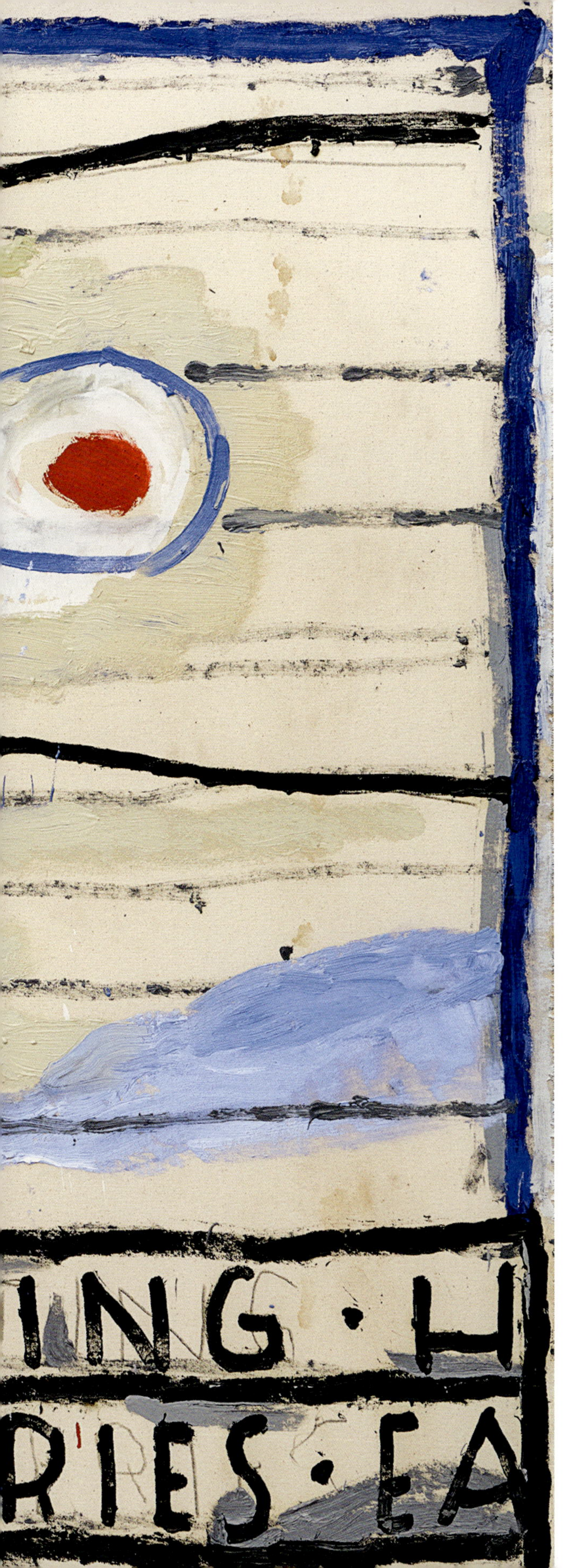

Early Memories

'It is the things I remember that I'm interested in. The memory may not be accurate but if I have a fond memory of something, the work I make gives me a chance to relate the work to the memory.'[1]

Born in 1934, Rose Wylie has early memories of living in Kent and then Bayswater in London during the Second World War. As a young child, bombing raids were Wylie's day-to-day reality. Her recollections are mixed with memories of the house she and her family lived in, Rosemount, which took a direct hit from an incendiary device that was extinguished by her sisters, alongside walks in London parks and time spent with her mother and siblings while her father worked abroad as part of the war effort. Repetition is an important part of her practice and Wylie has returned to the motif of the 'doodlebug' – Hitler's flying bomb that assaulted London in 1944 – time and time again in her drawings and paintings.

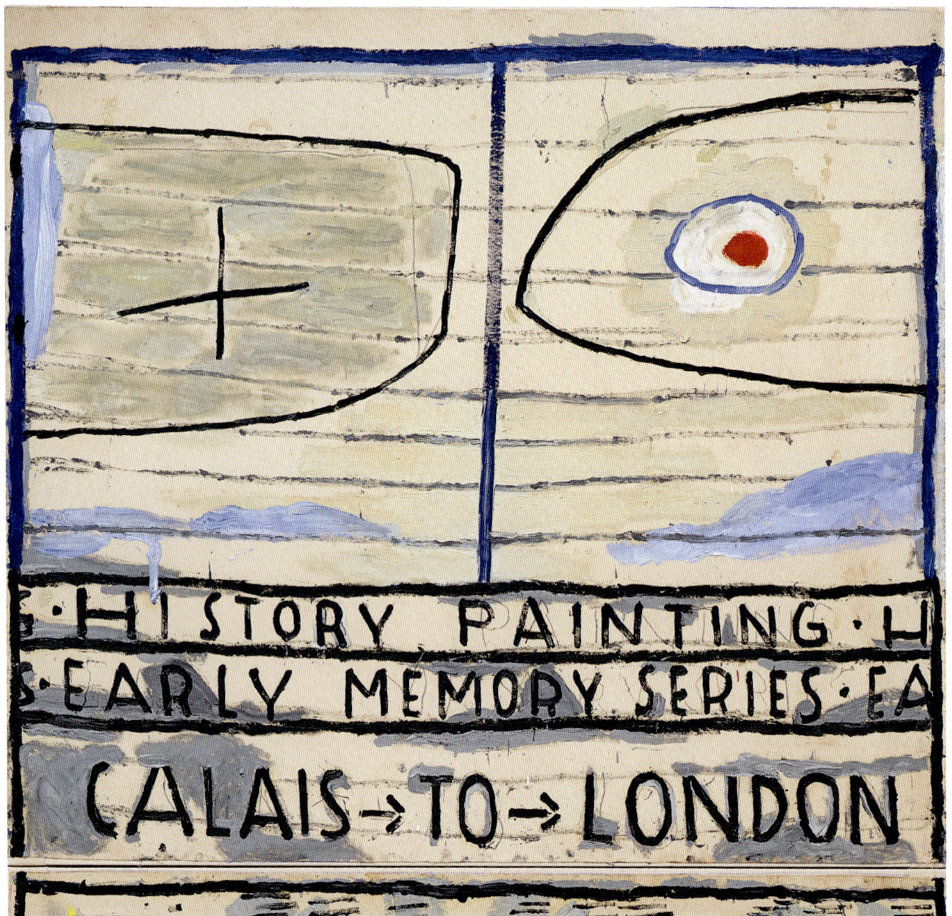

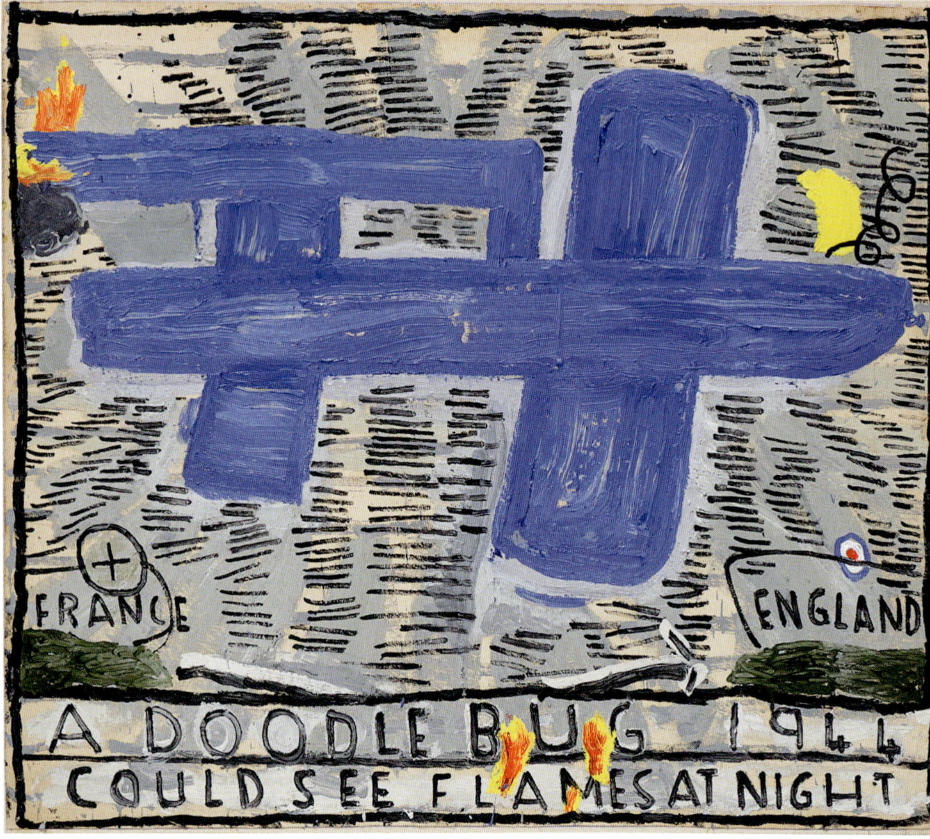

1

Wing Tips and Blue Doodlebug, 2022/23
Oil on canvas,
320.4 × 183.5 cm (overall)
Courtesy the artist and David Zwirner

2

Park Dogs & Air Raid, 2017
Oil on canvas,
393 × 331 cm (overall)
Private collection

3 *(overleaf)*

Rosemount (Coloured), 1999
Oil on canvas,
186 × 378 cm (overall)
Courtesy Vladimir Ovcharenko

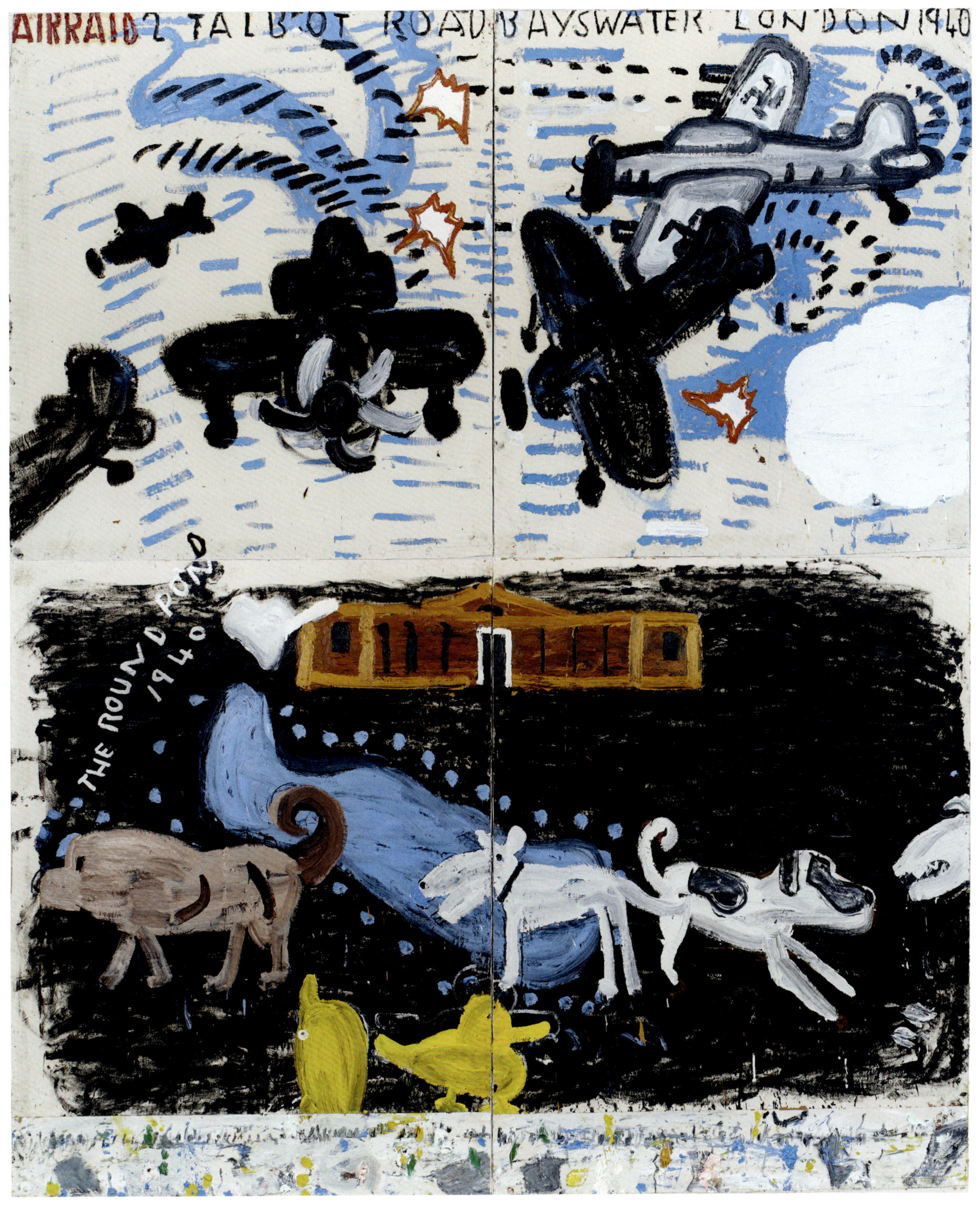
AIRRAID 2 TALBOT ROAD BAYSWATER LONDON 1940
THE ROUND POND
1940

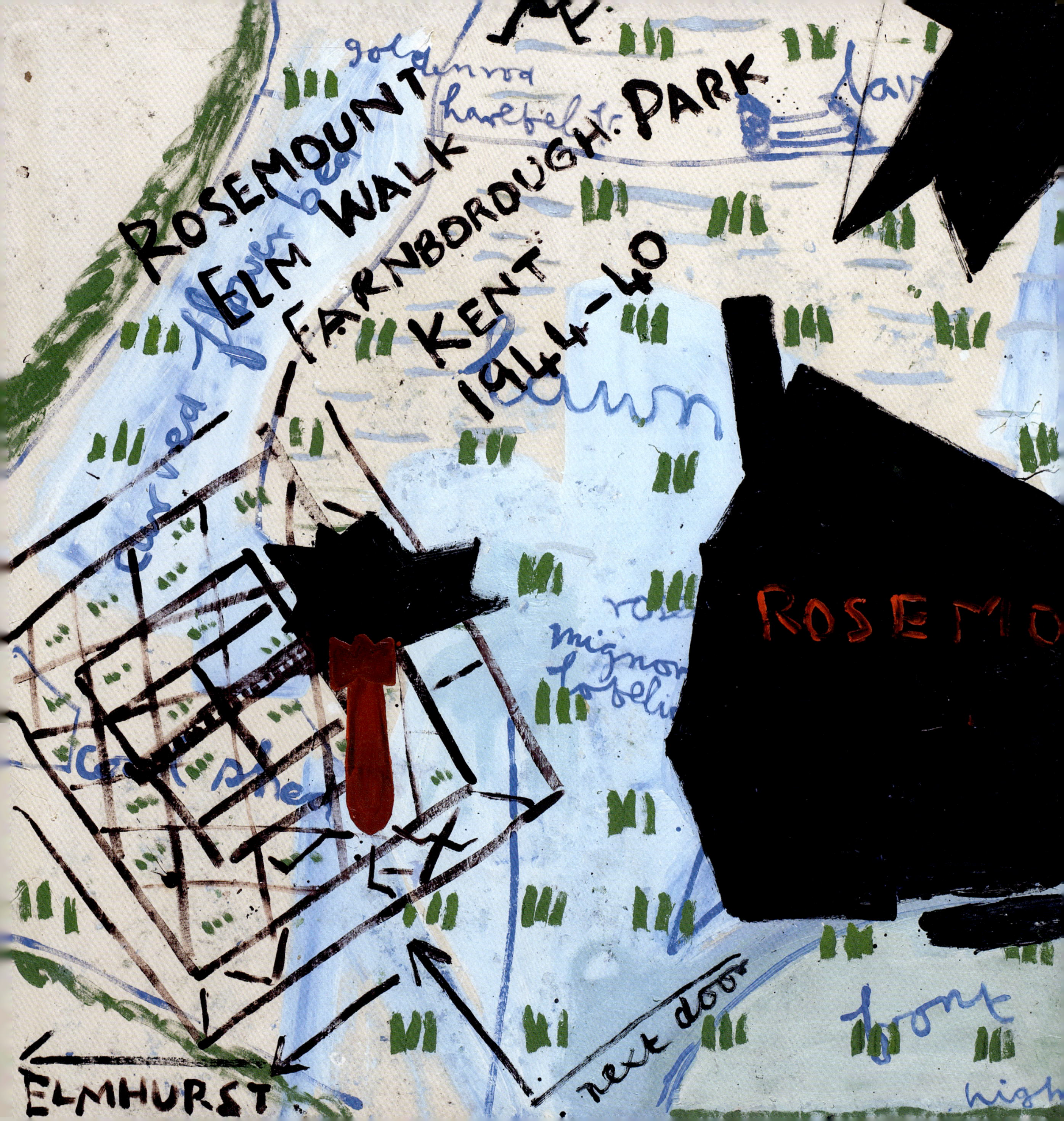
ROSEMOUNT
ELM WALK
FARNBOROUGH. PARK
KENT
1944-40
lawn
ROSEMO
mignon
front
next door
ELMHURST

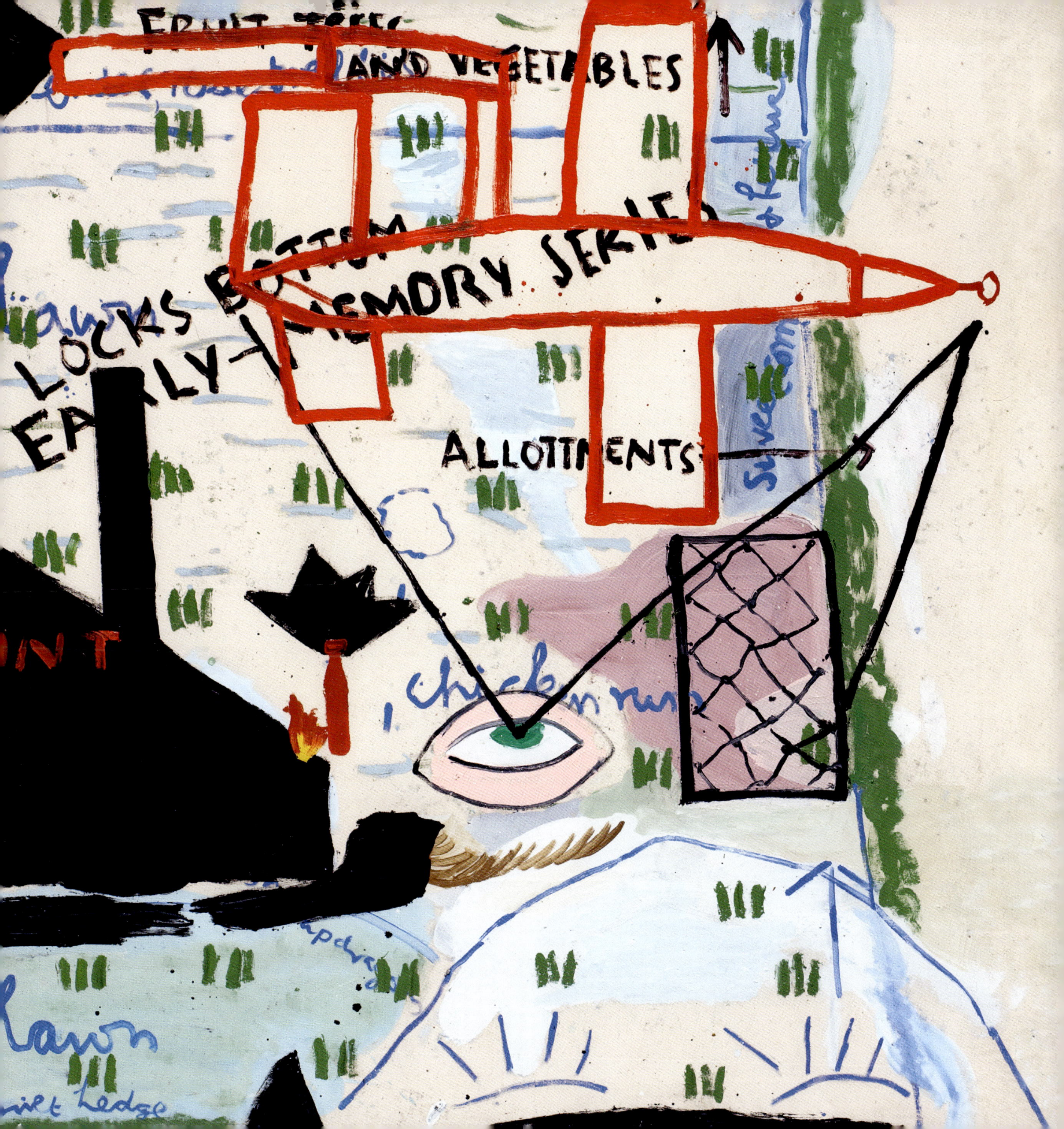
AND VEGETABLES
LOCKS BOTTOM
EARLY-MEMORY SERIES
ALLOTMENTS
chicken run
lawn

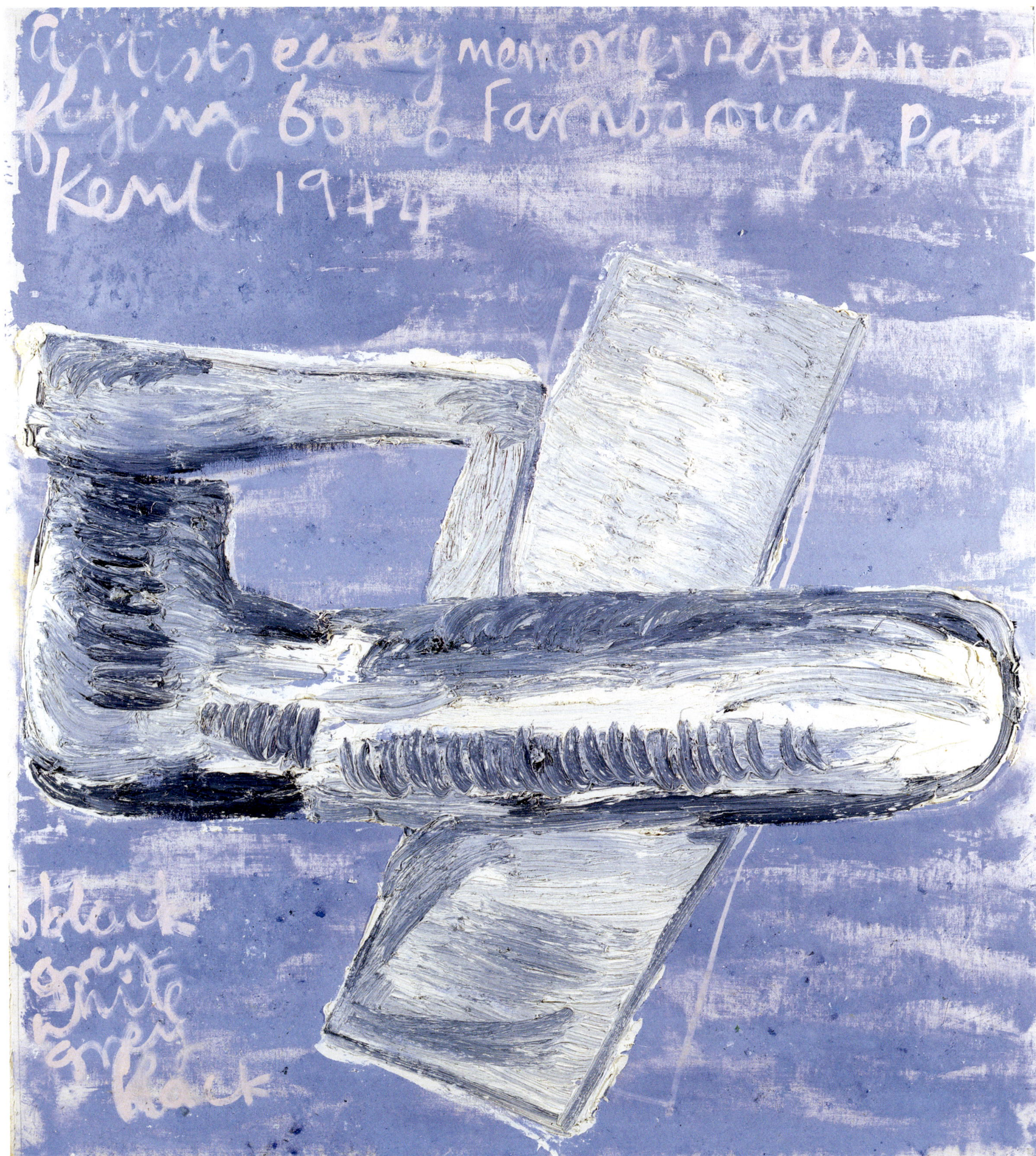
artists early memories series no 2
flying bomb Farnborough Park
Kent 1944
black
grey
white
grey
black

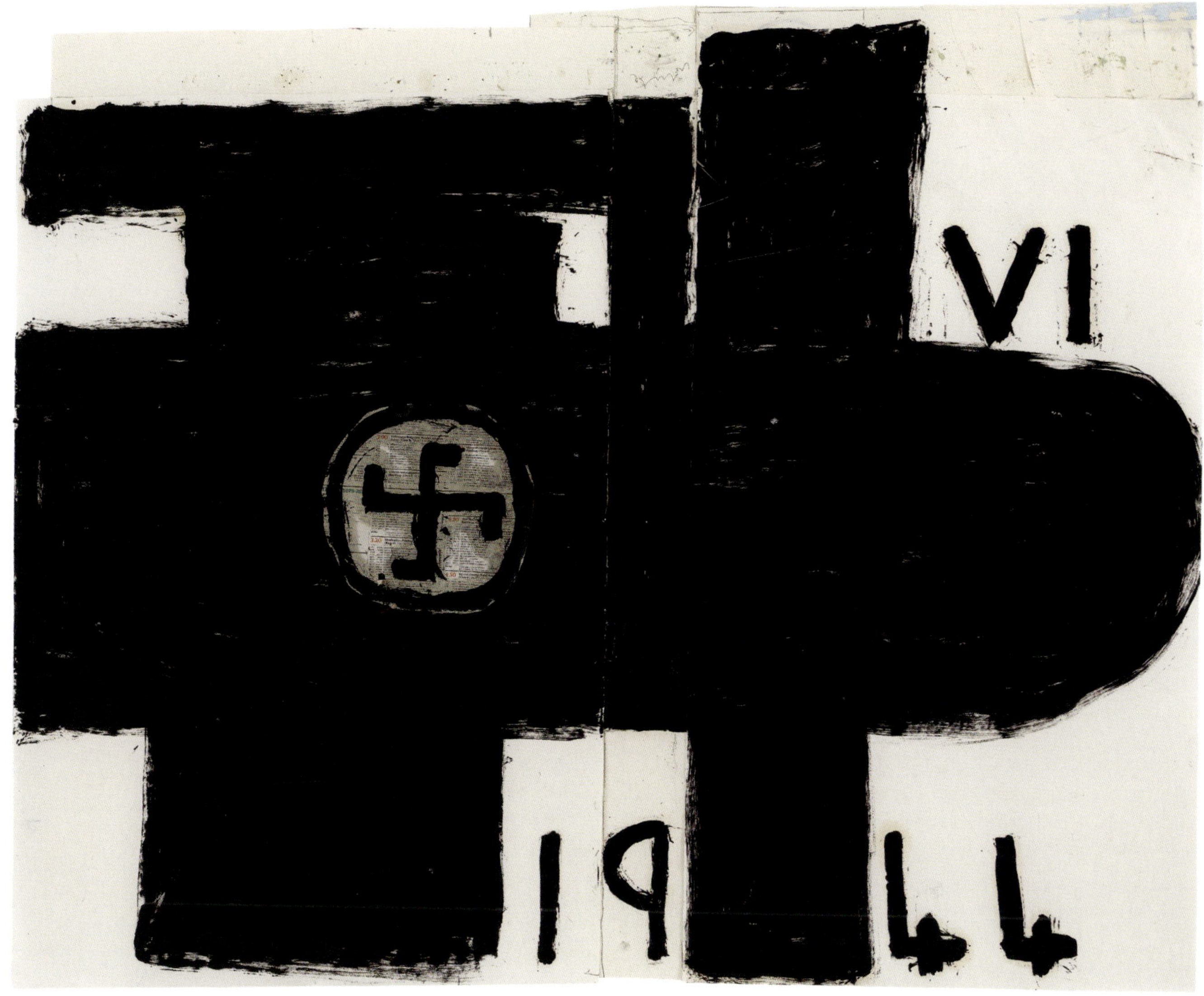

4

Early Memory Series No. 2: Doodle Bug, 1998
Oil on canvas,
181.5 × 168.8 cm
York Museums Trust (York Art Gallery)
Presented by the Contemporary Art Society, 2001

5

Black Doodlebug, 2022
Oil on paper and newspaper,
106.7 × 128.7 cm
Courtesy the artist and David Zwirner

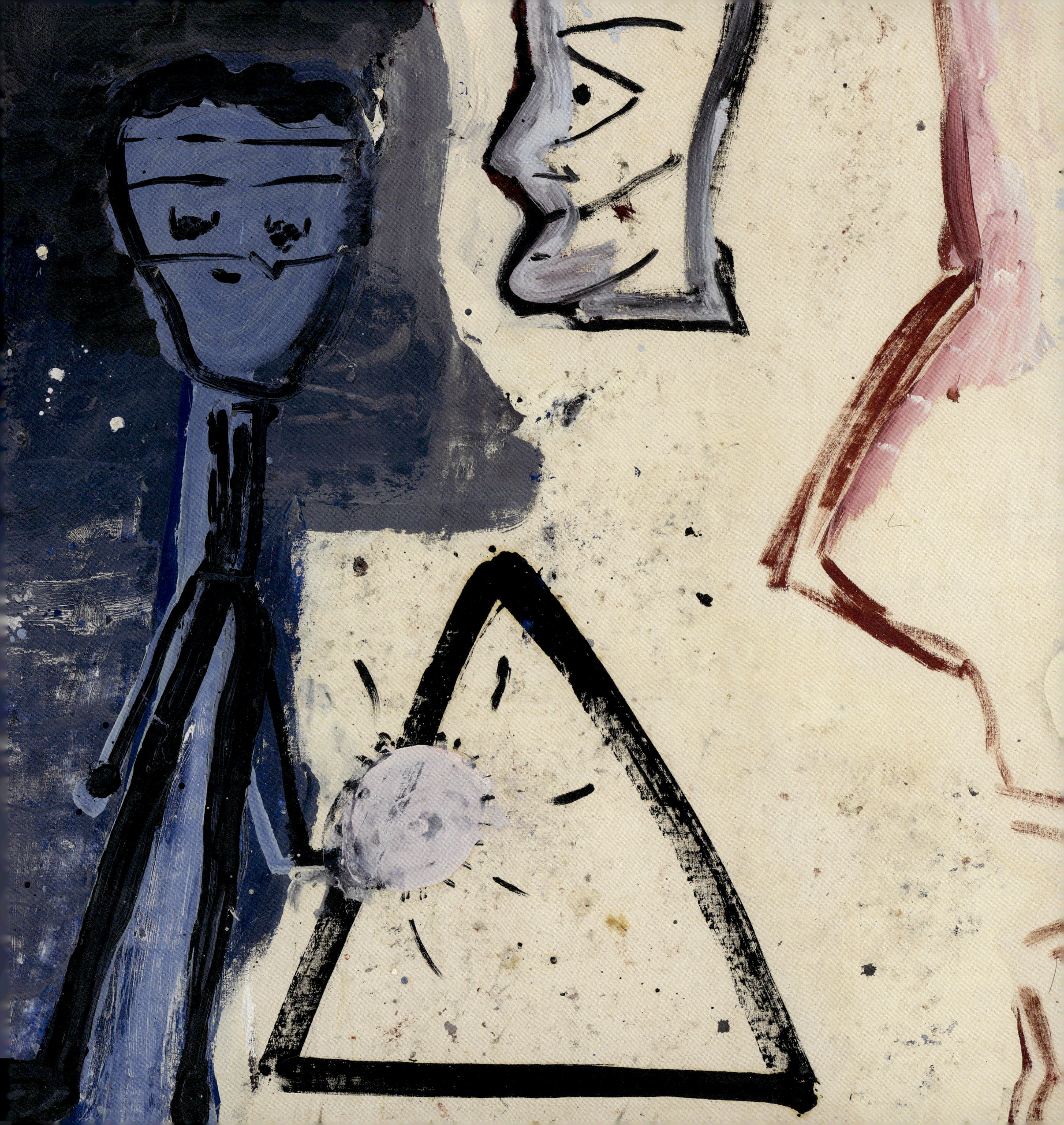

‘Transformation, synthesis and specific’

‘Wylie uses the words “transformation, synthesis and specific” to describe how she arrives at an image; she explains, “A painting is not finally what it does, or what it makes, or what it has, or what it means… it is. The painting is the meaning.”’[2]

The starting point for Rose Wylie’s paintings can come from a myriad of sources: a memory; an observed person; flora or fauna; an image encountered in print, on the internet or in a film; a favourite work from art history; or an artefact from a distant, ancient civilisation. This imagery is usually first captured in a drawing, Wylie’s daily practice of making pictorial records of an event, an encounter or an idea. Later, sometimes years later, a specific visual motif will find its way into a painting, often juxtaposed with a seemingly incongruous graphic companion or words. Through the careful process of rendering them in paint, Wylie takes these images beyond merely capturing a likeness and instead creates an arresting, original picture. *RW & Bird* (1996; cat. 11) and *RW Party Clothes (Rose Wylie)* (2016; cat. 10), painted twenty years apart, offer diverse self-portraits of the artist. In the first, the artist is reduced to a simple outline, including her 1950s-style bullet bra whose shape mirrors the beaks of the birds looming over her. In the later work, the dress’s padded shoulders emphasise another fashion style. For Wylie, it is the particularities of images that matter the most.

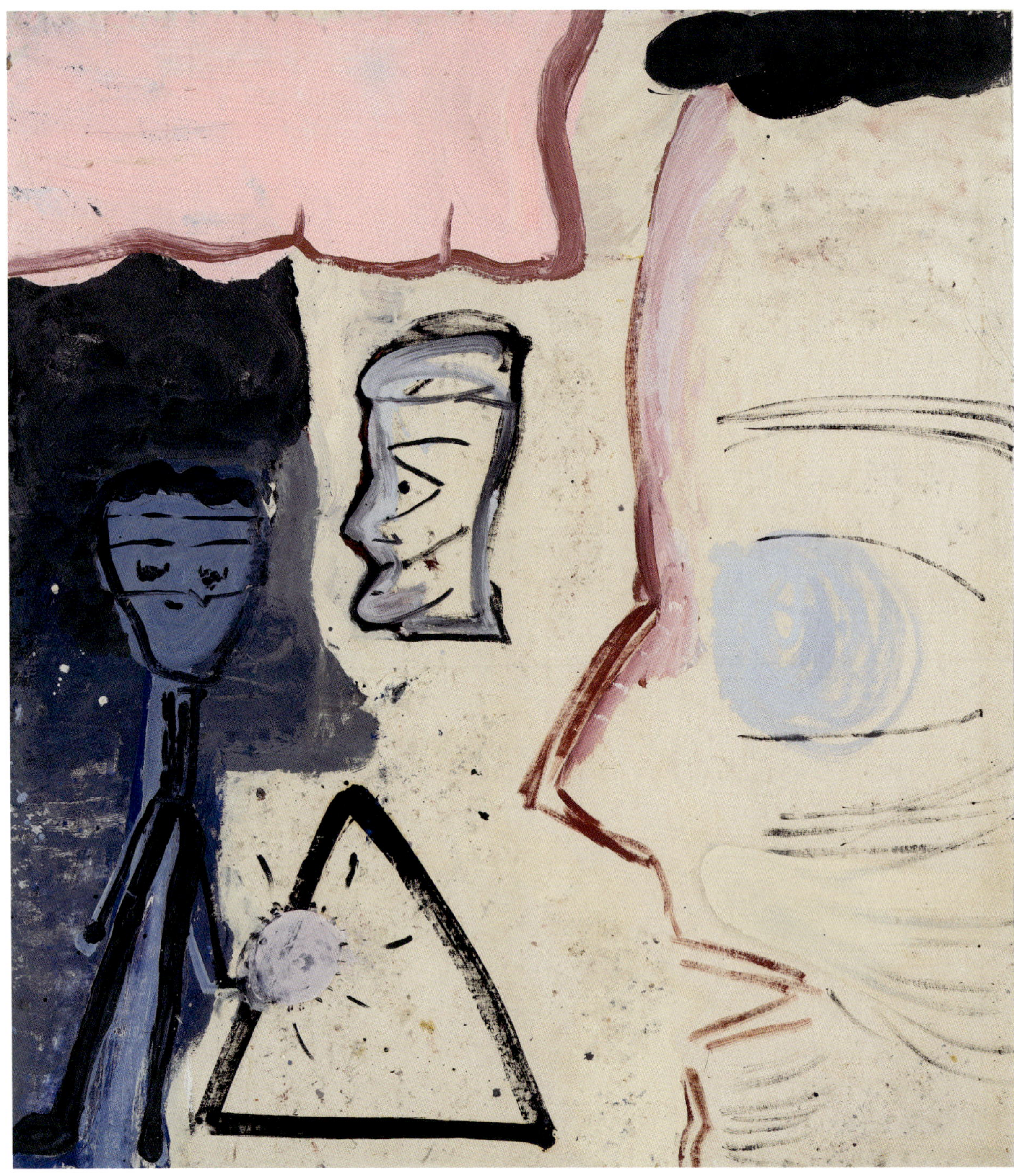

6

Henry Triangle, 1996
Oil on canvas,
183.3 × 164 cm
Courtesy the artist
and David Zwirner

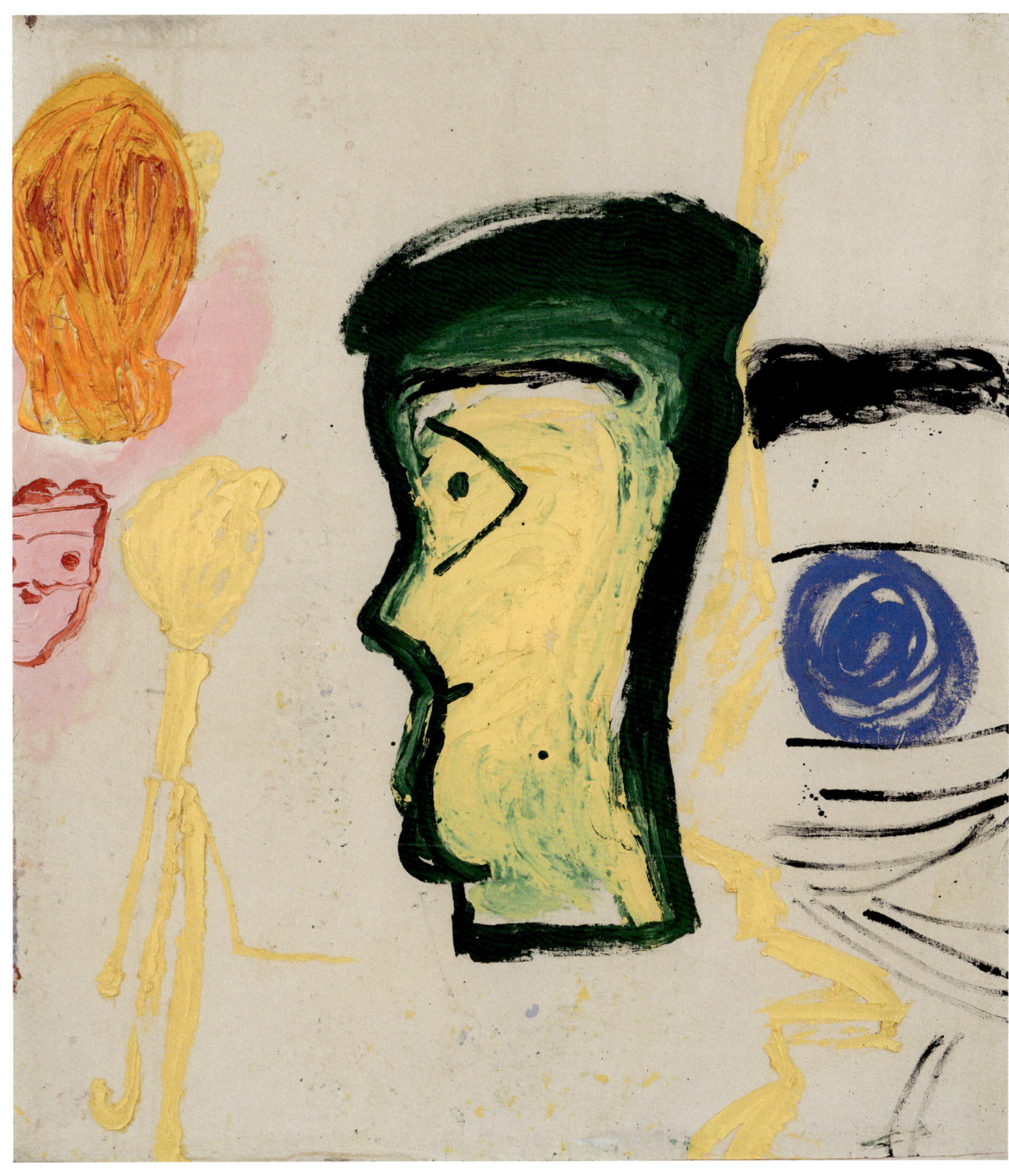

7

Yellow Henry, 1996
Oil on canvas,
184 × 166.5 cm
Courtesy the artist
and David Zwirner

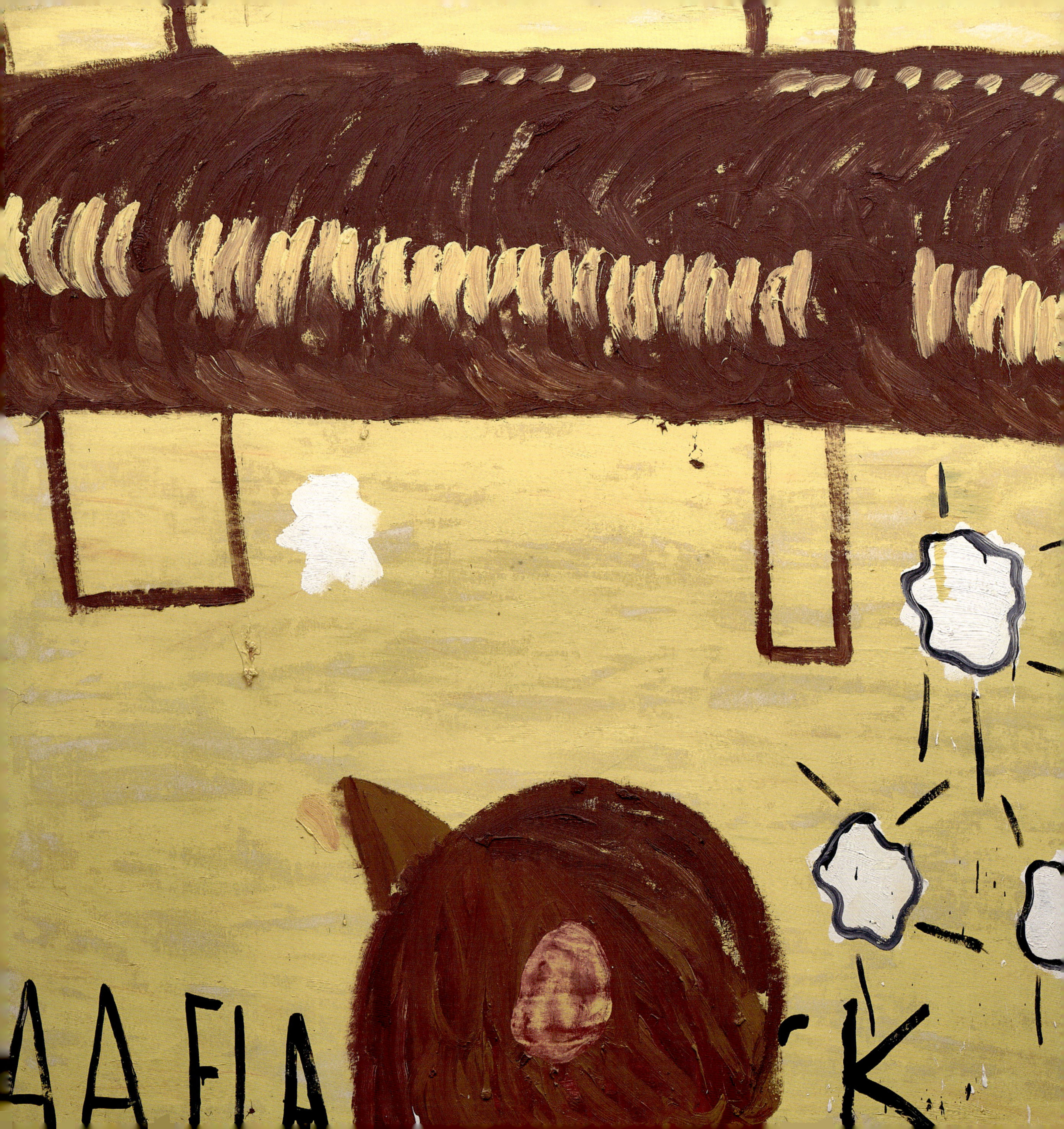

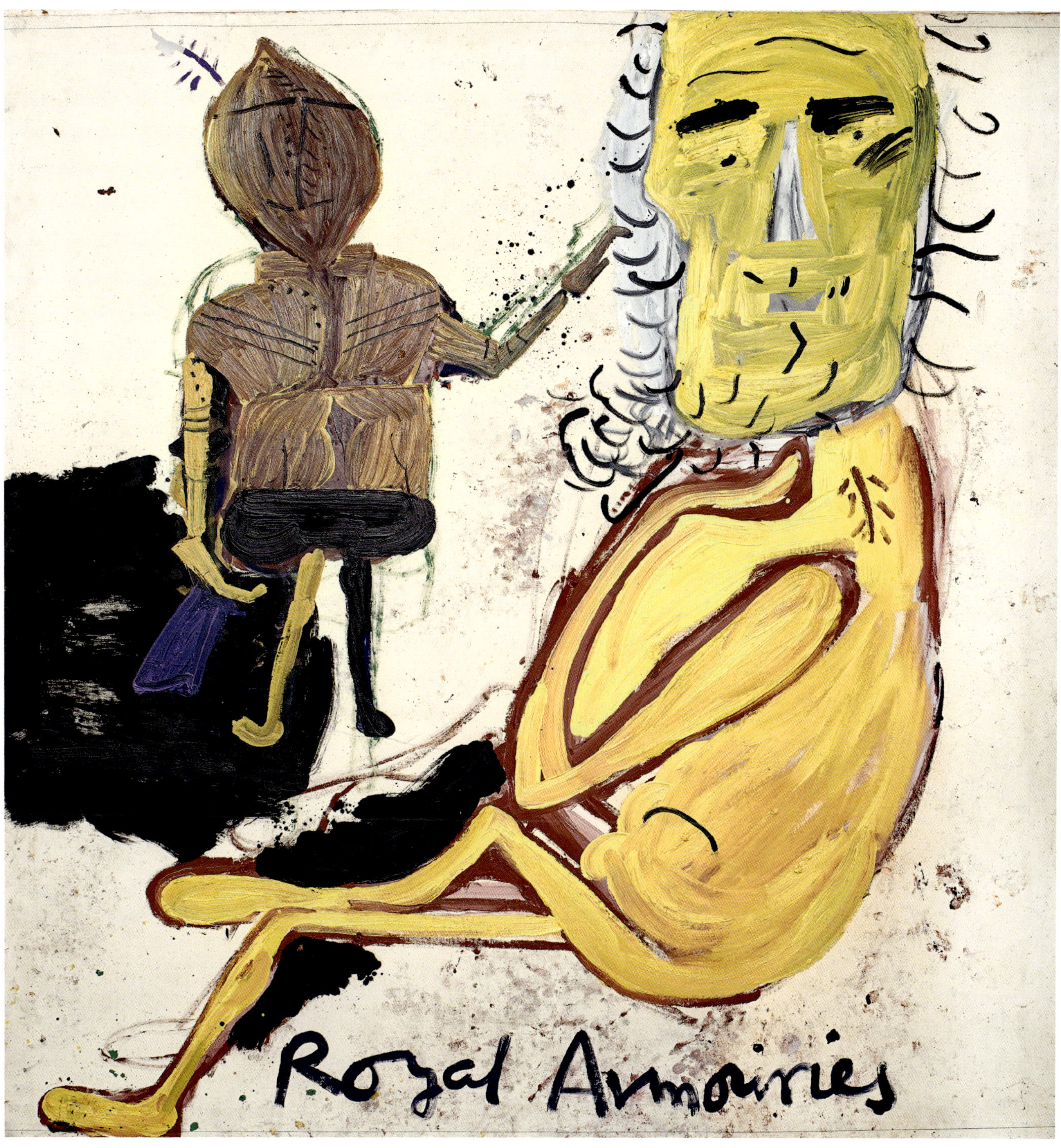

8

Ack Ack, 2003
Oil on canvas,
182.5 × 199 cm
Courtesy the artist
and David Zwirner

9

London New York, 2000
Oil on canvas,
183 × 178.5 cm
Courtesy the artist
and David Zwirner

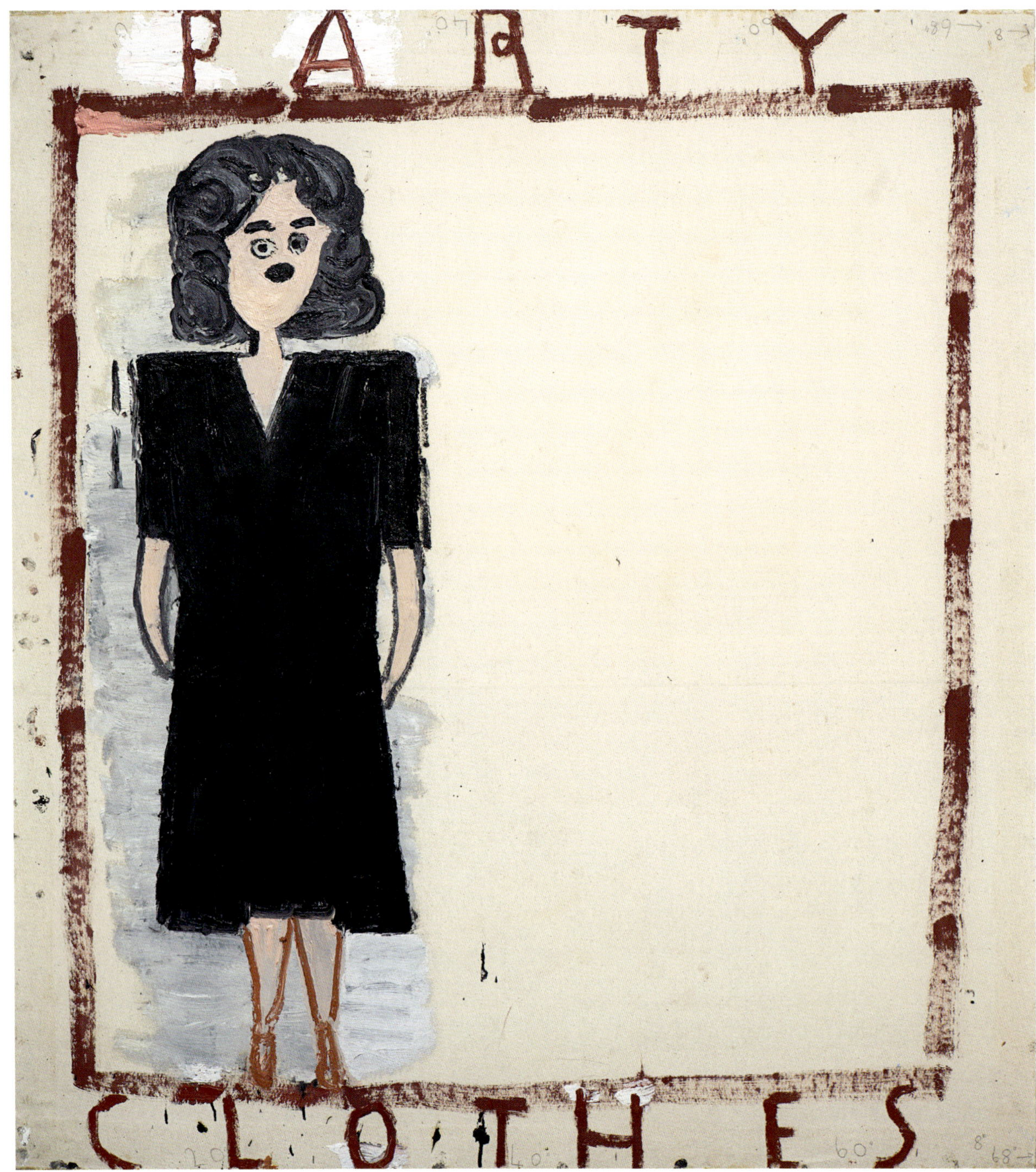

10

RW Party Clothes (Rose Wylie), 2016
Oil on canvas,
183 × 167 cm
Courtesy Luke and Louisa Oxlade

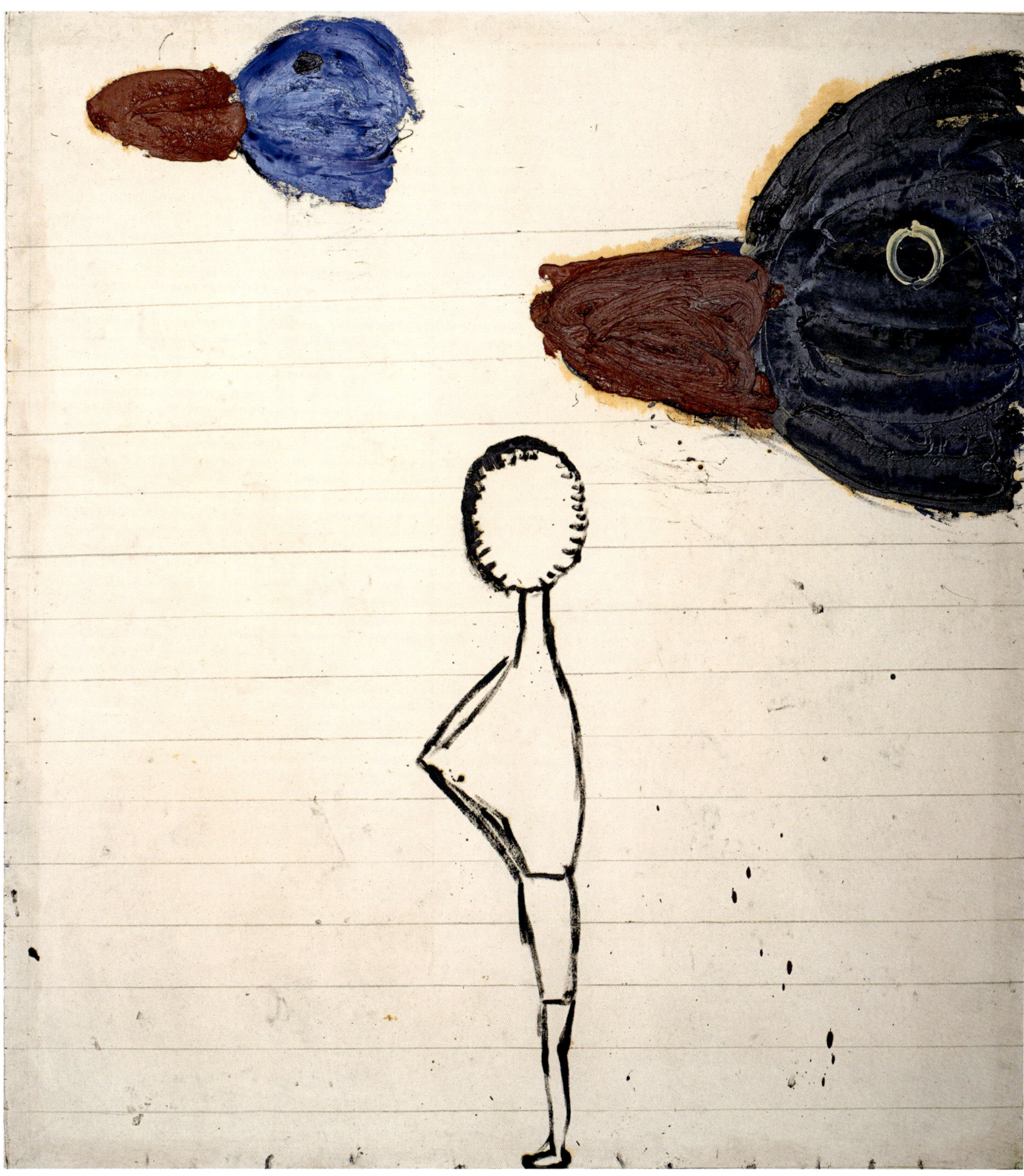

11

RW & Bird, 1996
Oil and graphite on canvas,
183 × 166.5 cm
Courtesy the artist
and David Zwirner

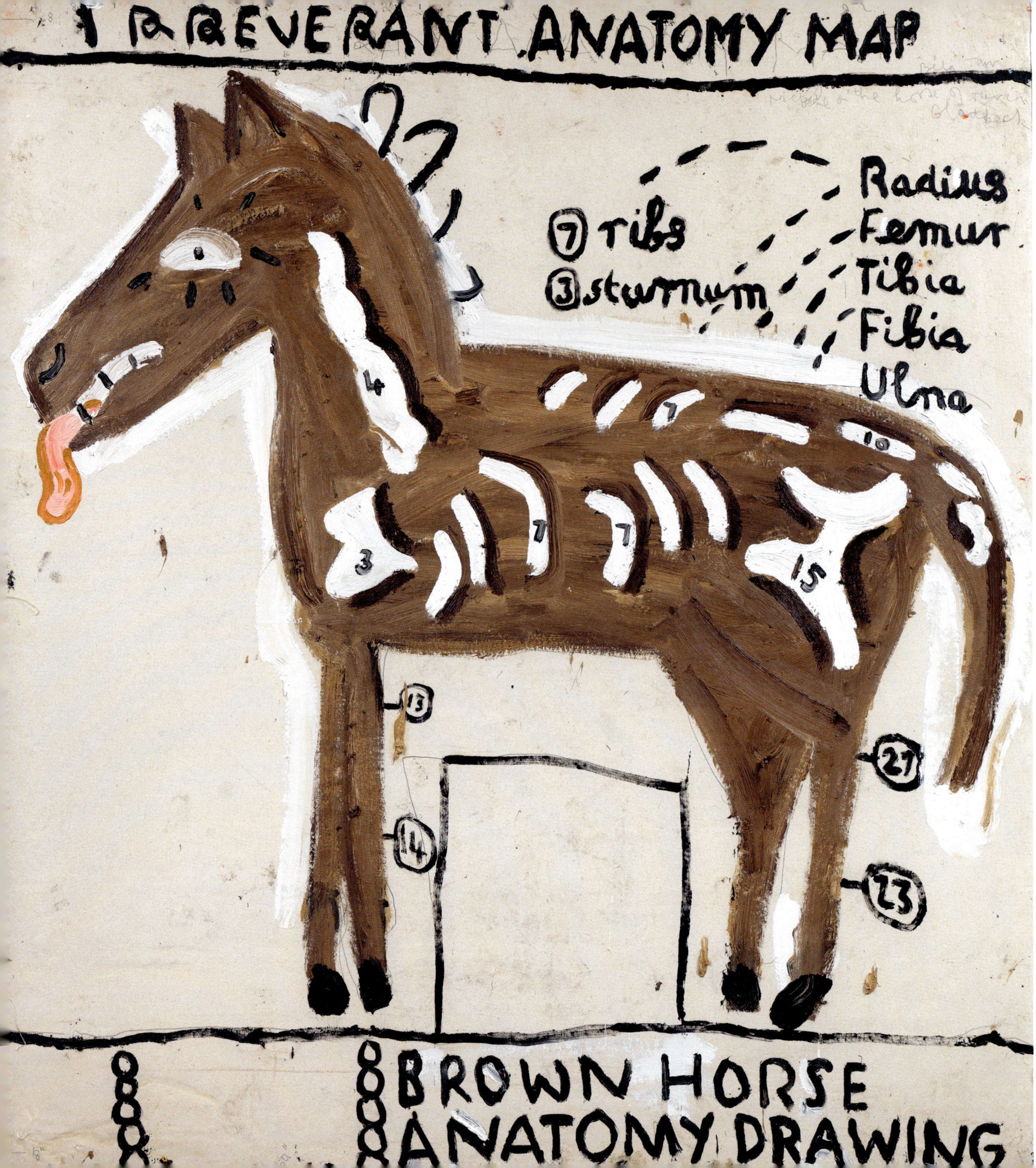

1 R REVERANT ANATOMY MAP

⑦ ribs
③ sturnum

Radius
Femur
Tibia
Fibia
Ulna

4
7
10
3
7
7
15
13
14
21
23

BROWN HORSE
ANATOMY DRAWING

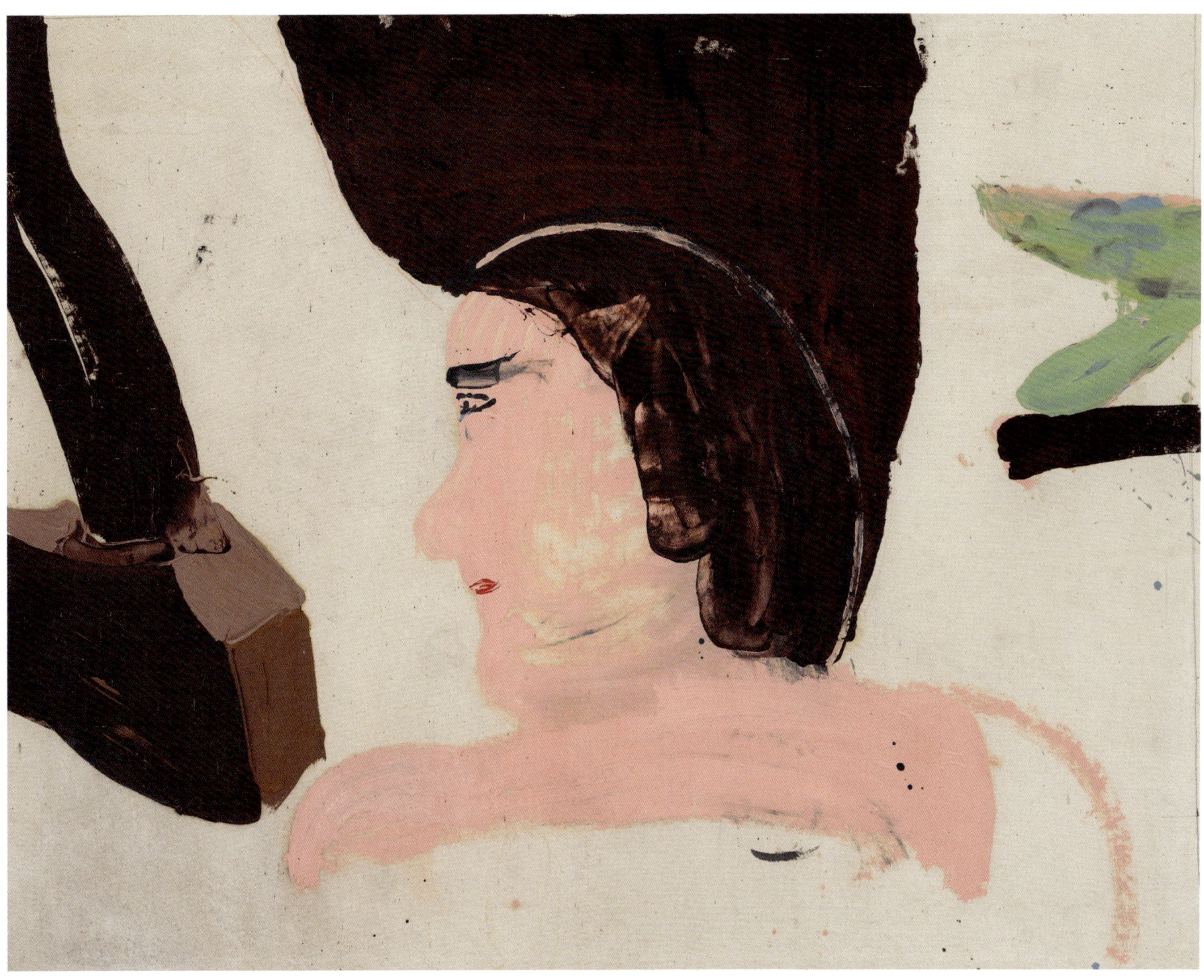

12

Irreverant Anatomy Drawing, 2017
Oil on canvas,
182 × 165 cm
Courtesy Edwin Oostmeijer

13

Actress and Axe, 1992
Oil on canvas,
120.5 × 150.8 cm
Courtesy the artist and David Zwirner

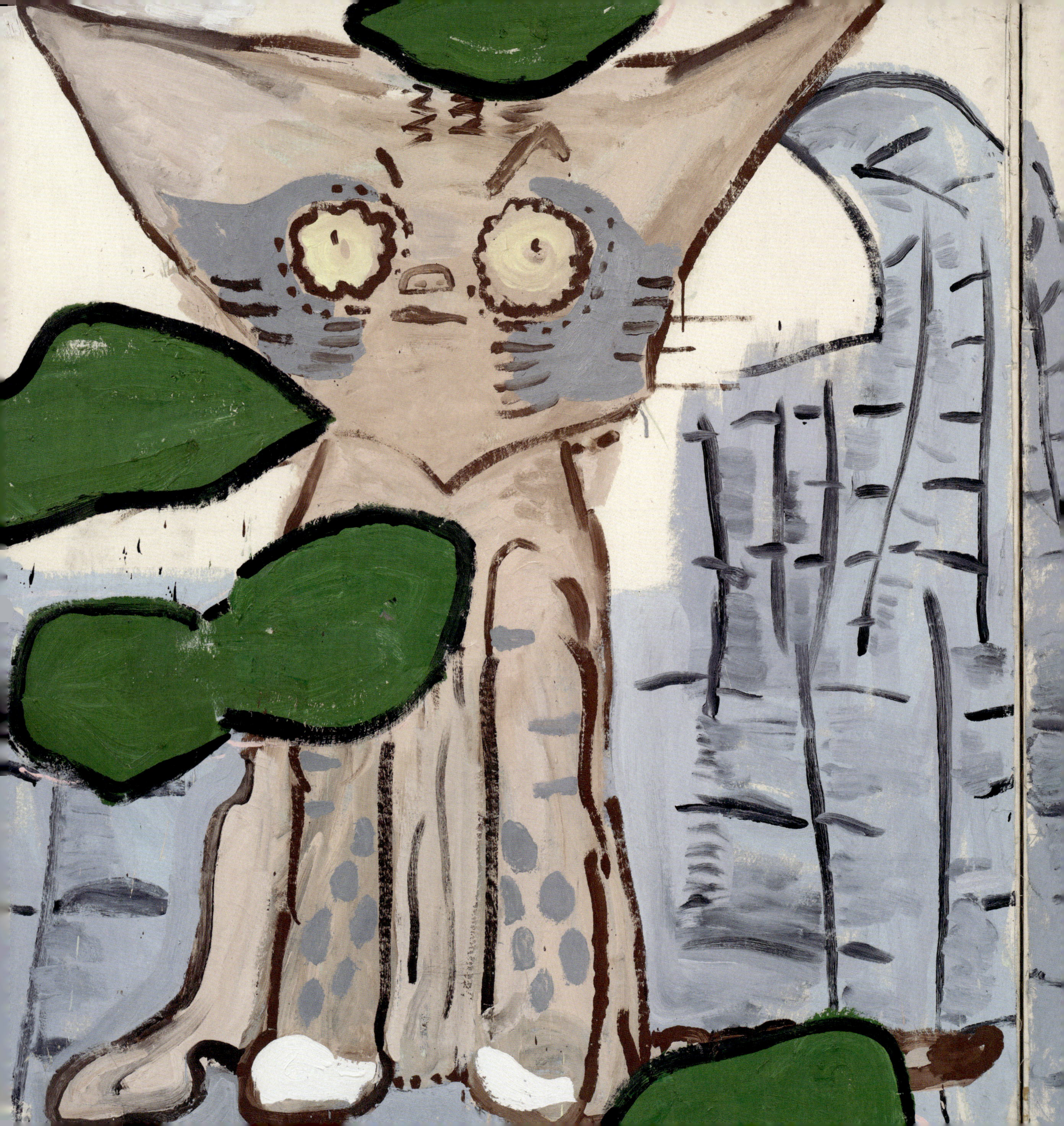

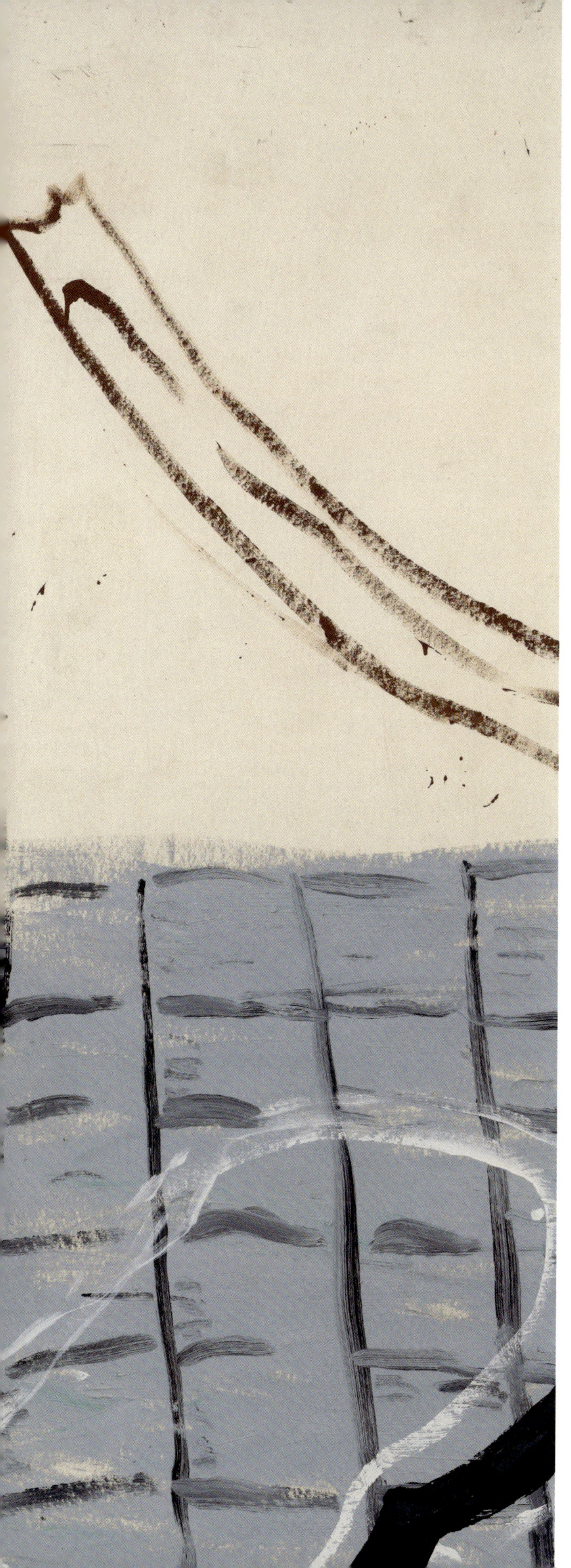

Room Project

As a young woman at Folkestone and Dover School of Art in the 1950s, Wylie studied anatomical drawing and figurative painting at a time when British neo-romantic painters dominated, and artists such as Picasso or Léger were an admired but distant avant-garde. Following a career break to raise three children, from the mid-1980s Wylie devoted herself to painting again, establishing a studio in her Kent house where she still works today. *Room Project* (2002–03; cats 14–17) reveals Wylie's voracious ambition to create large paintings that present their own playful world, here populated by cats, paper dolls, Olympic swimmers and the artist wearing a favourite checked skirt. The year after their creation, these four paintings were selected for East International at Norwich Gallery, where they received significant attention from the art world.

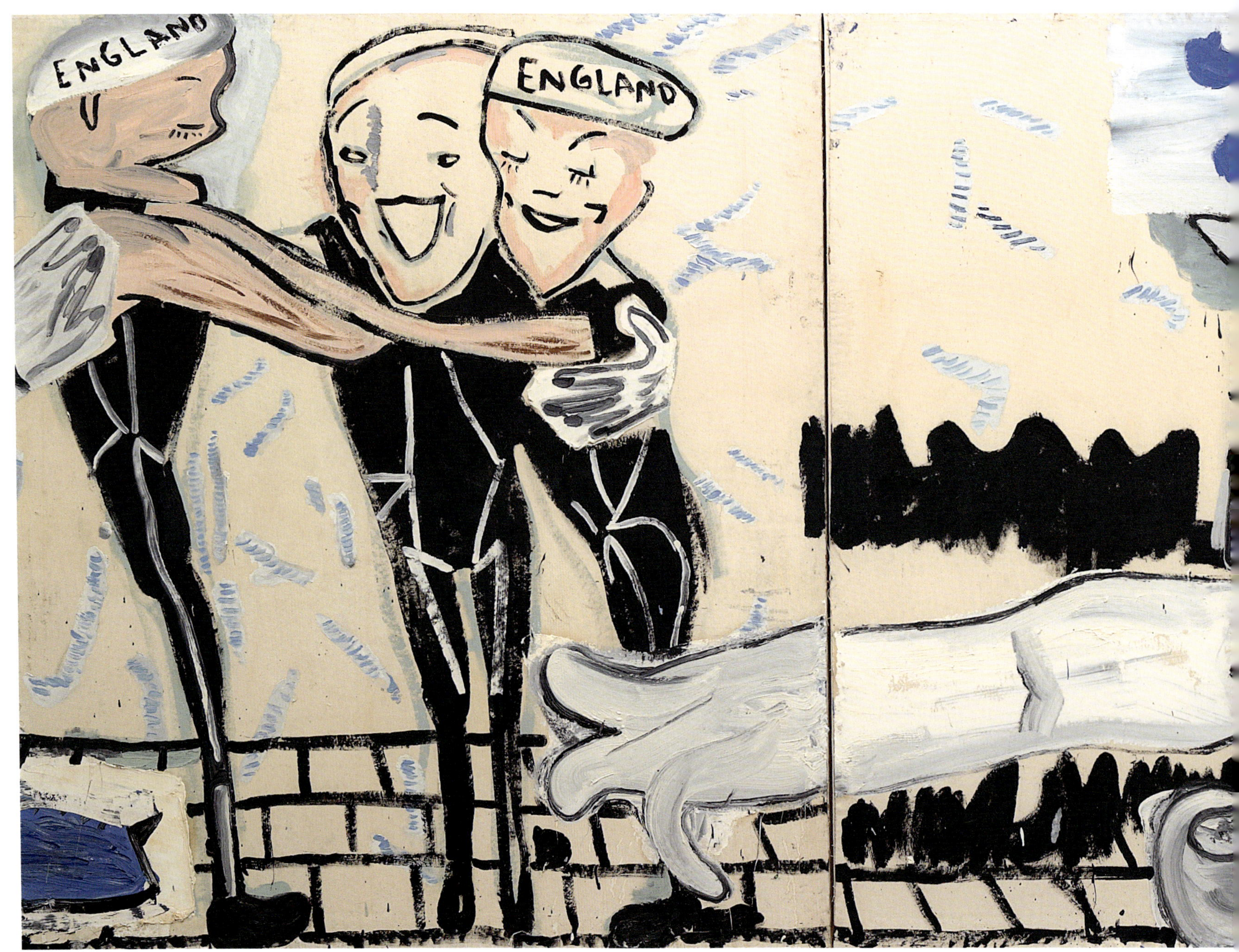

14

Swimming with Cats (Blue Twink), 2002
Oil on canvas,
183 × 503 cm (overall)
Courtesy the artist
and David Zwirner

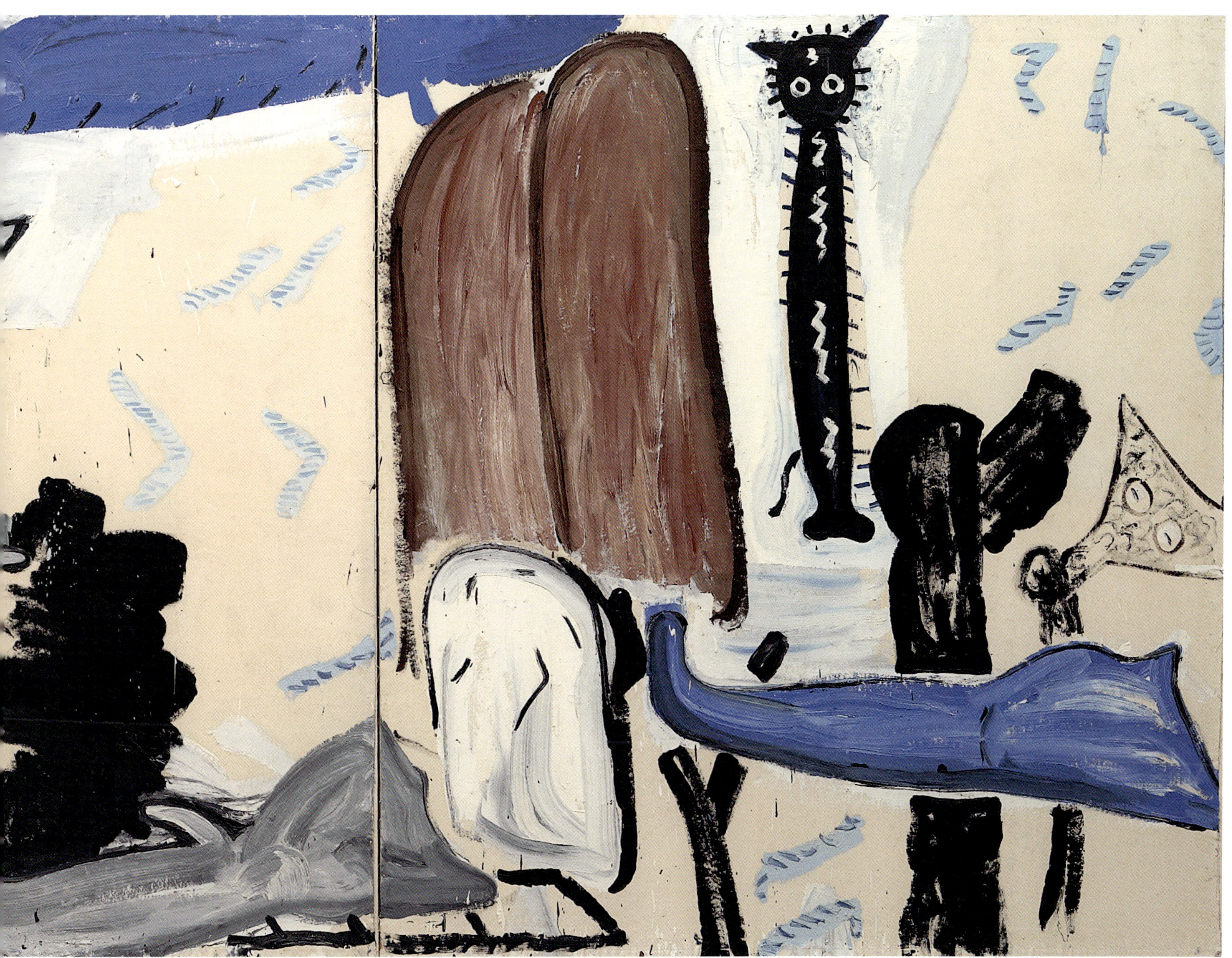

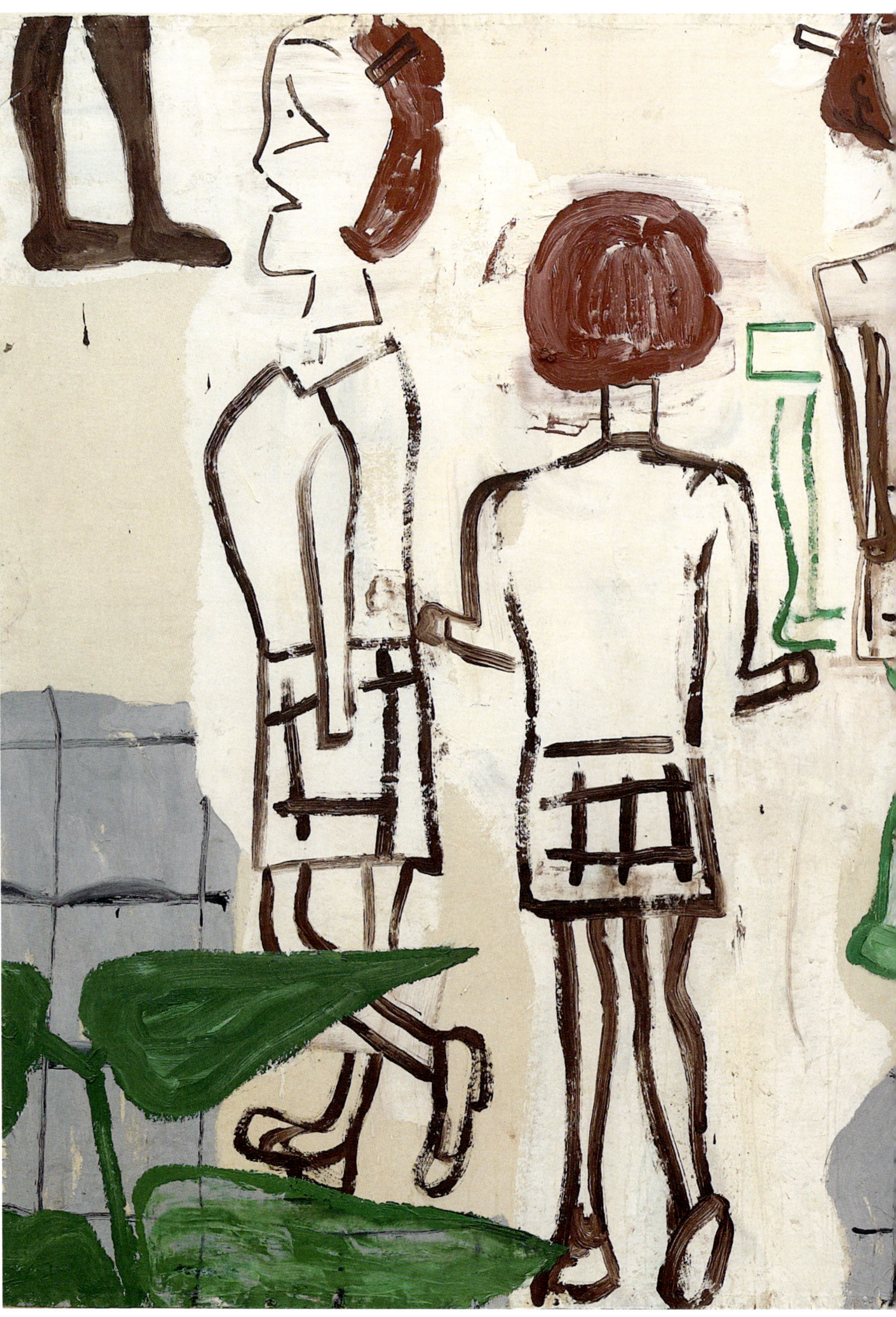

15

Wearing a Check Skirt, 2002
Oil on canvas,
183 × 330.5 cm (overall)
Courtesy the artist
and David Zwirner

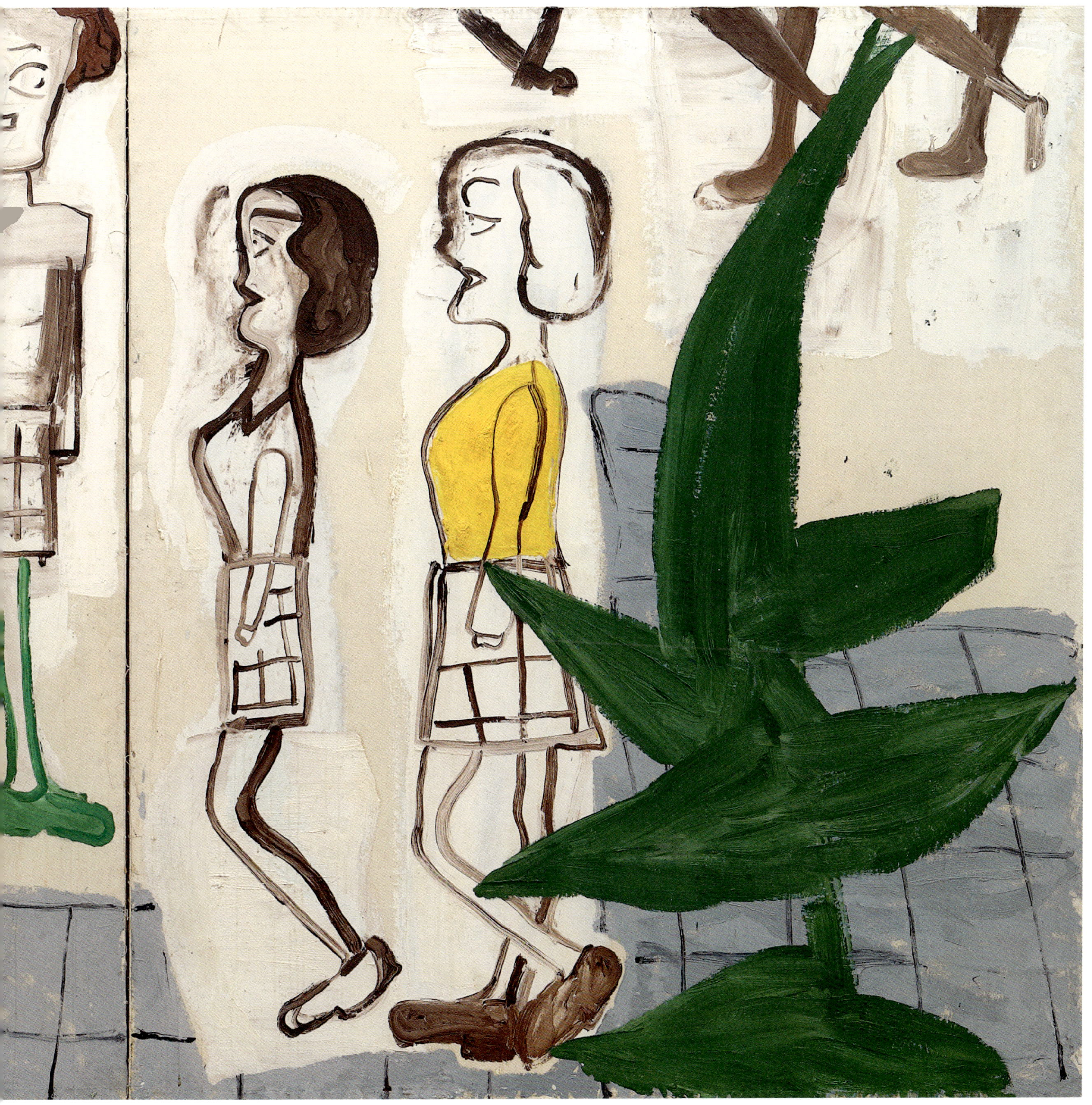

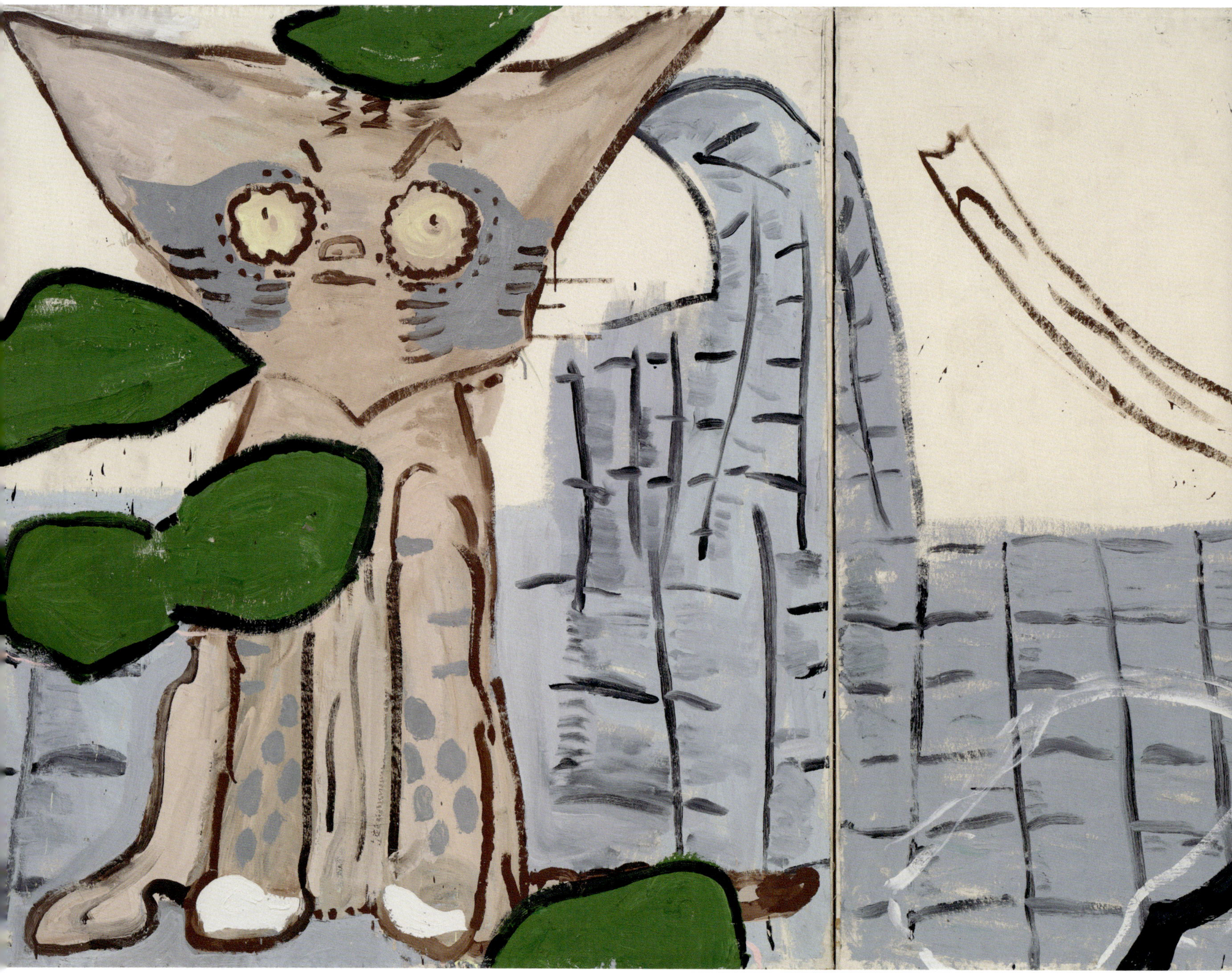

16

Red Twink and Ivy, 2002
Oil on canvas,
183.5 × 504 cm (overall)
Courtesy the artist
and David Zwirner

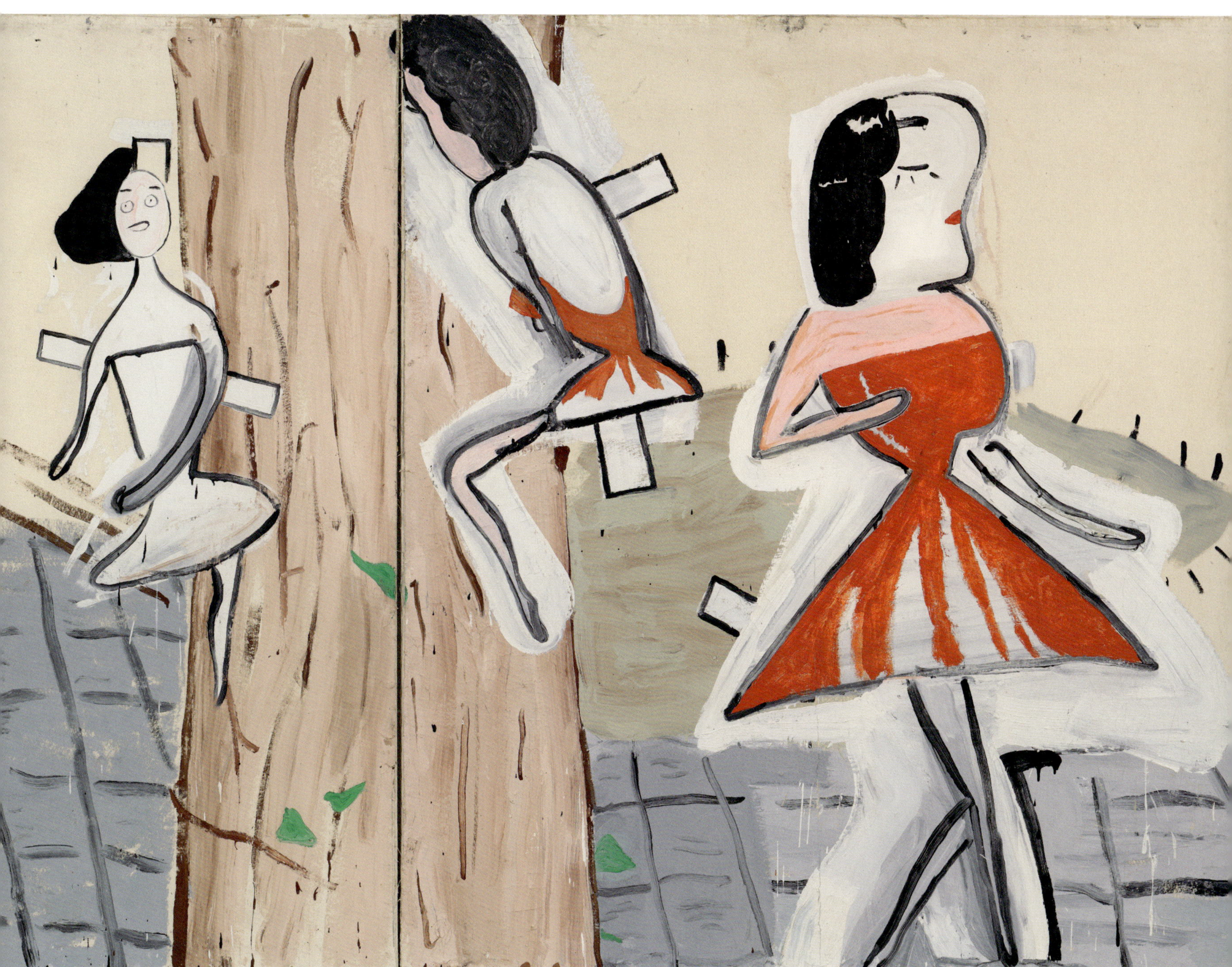

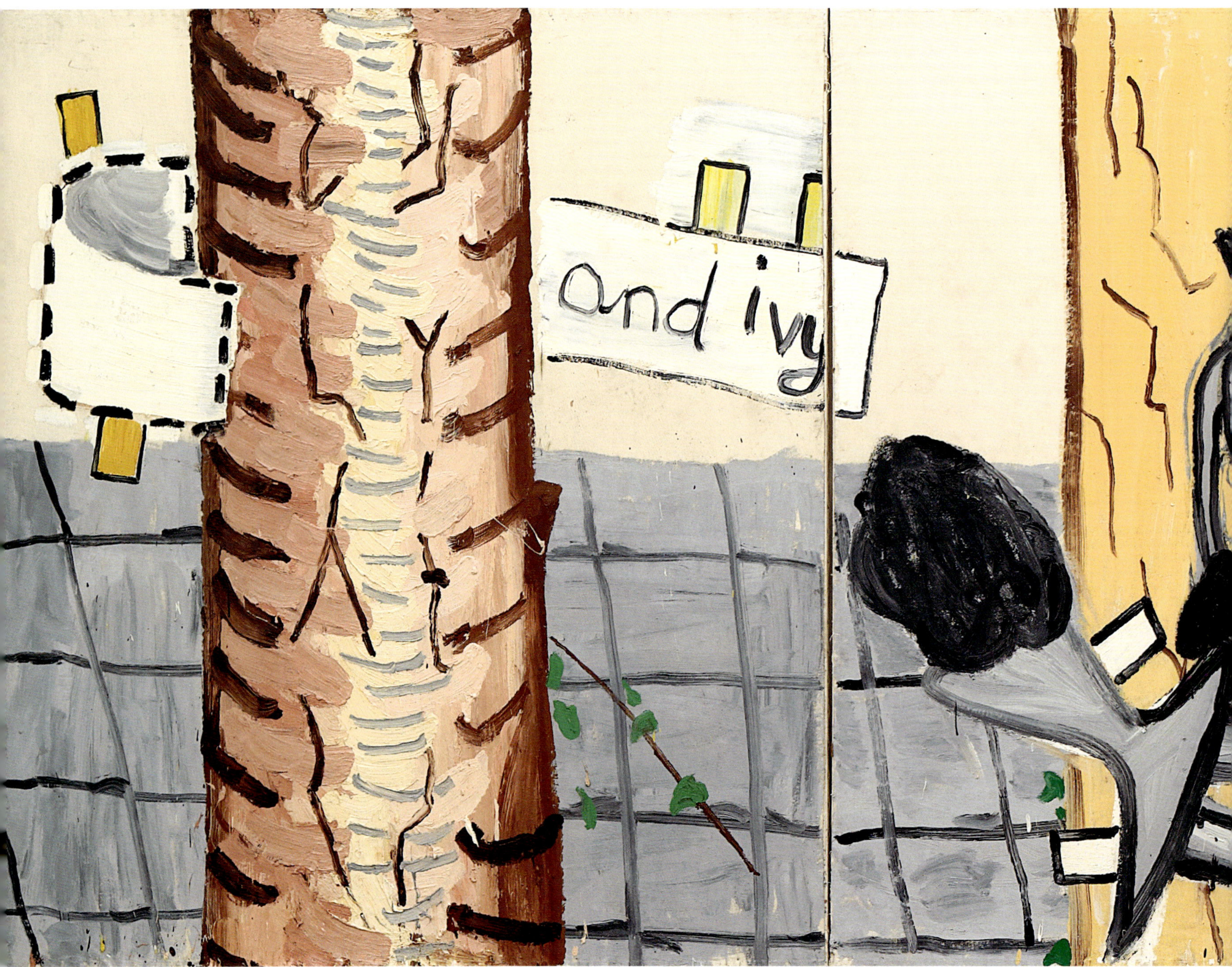

17

Green Twink and Ivy, 2003
Oil on canvas,
182.5 × 499 cm (overall)
Courtesy the artist
and David Zwirner

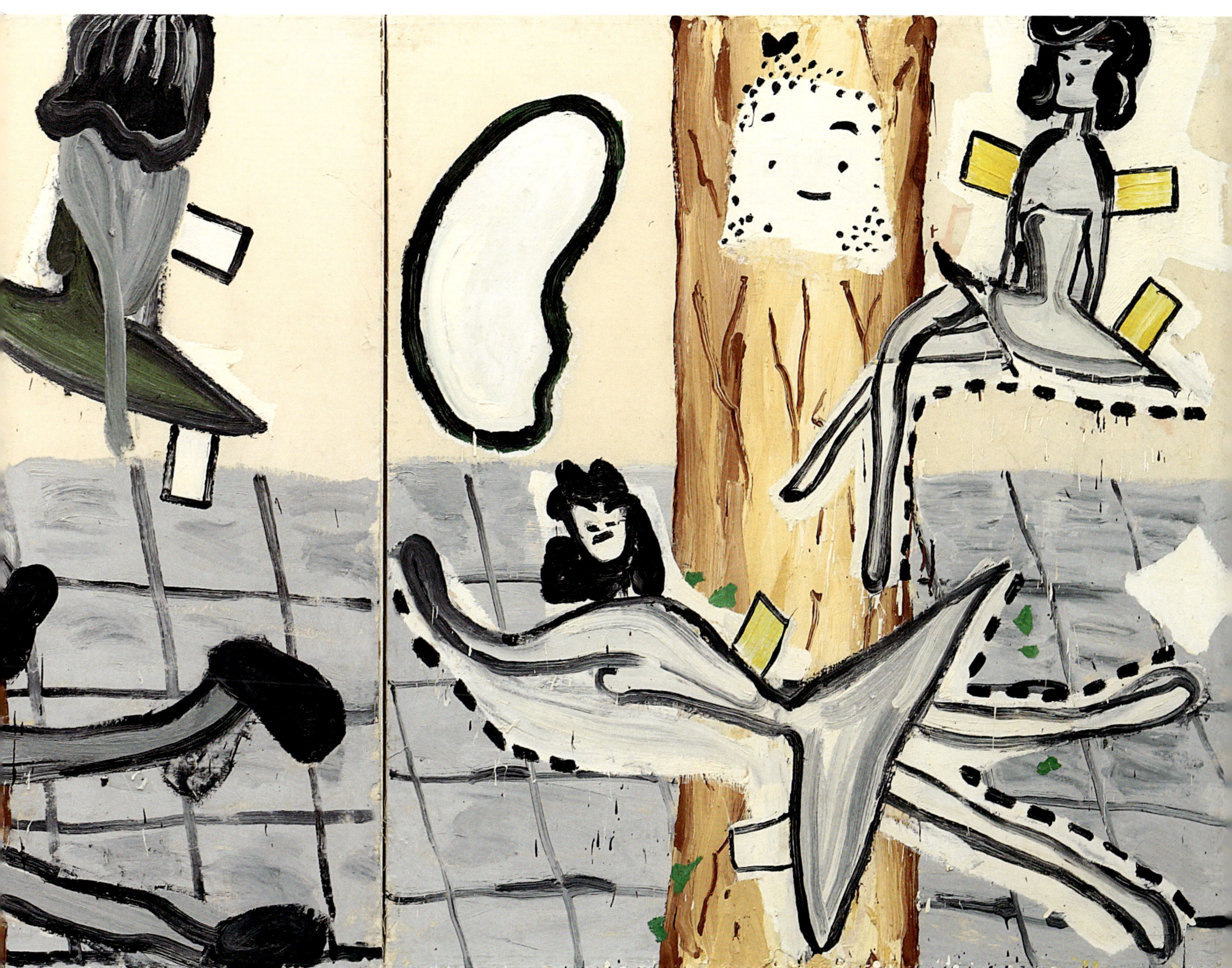

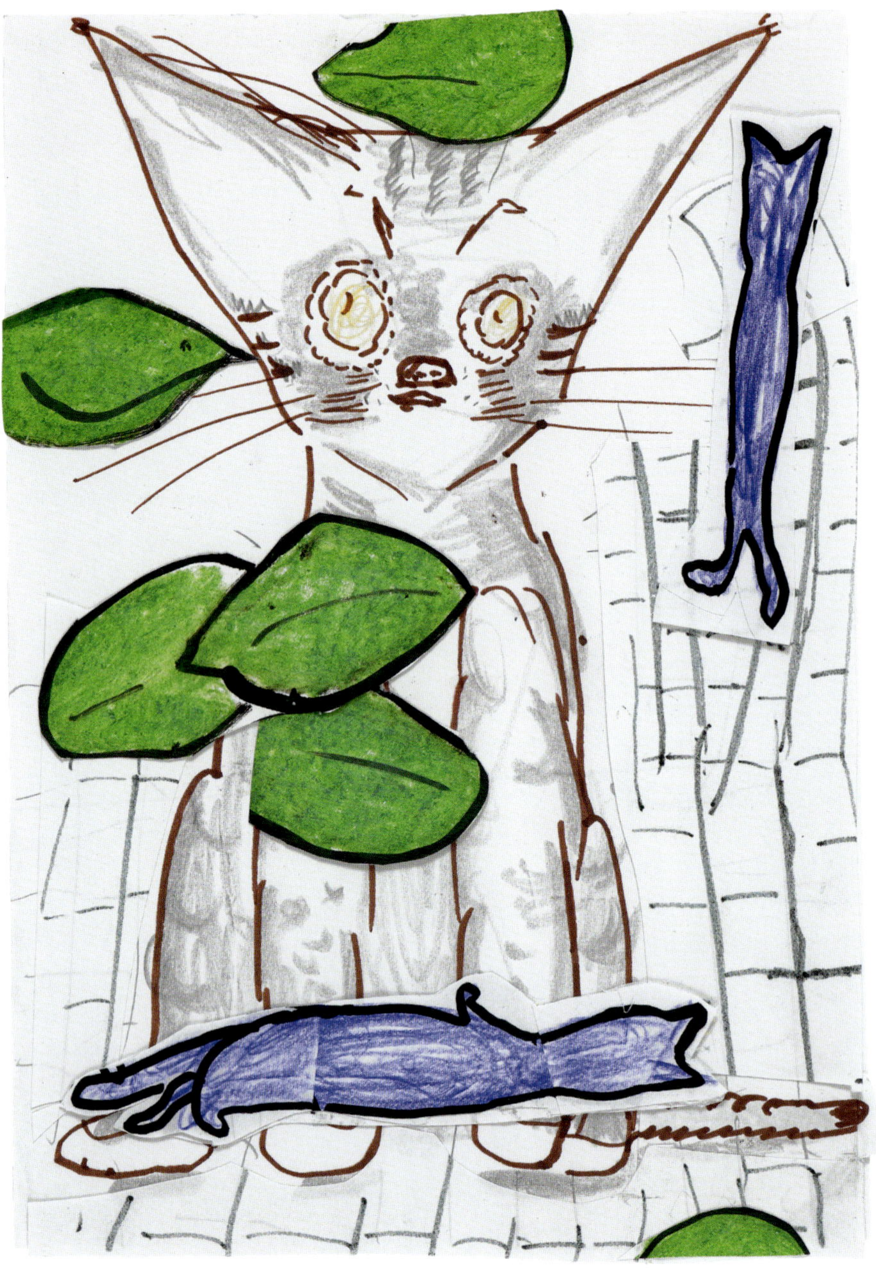

18

Bunt and Japonica Leaves, Study for Red Twink, 2002
Ink, graphite and coloured pencil on paper, 30.2 × 21.6 cm
Courtesy the artist and David Zwirner

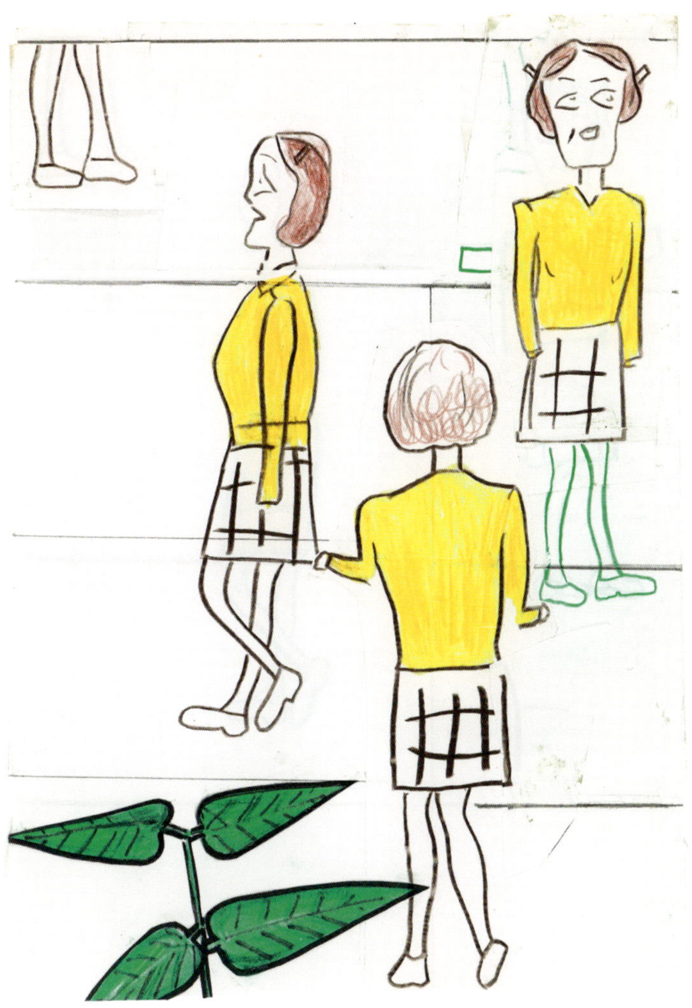

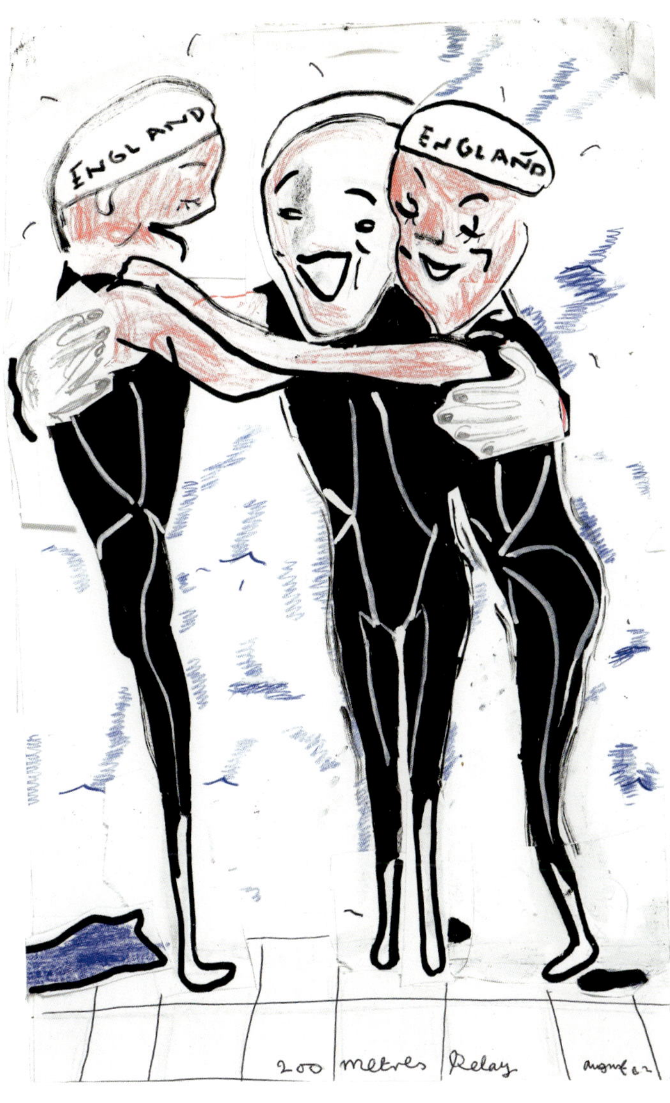

19

Yellow Twink (and Clematis), 2001
Marker, coloured pencil and collage on paper, 29.7 × 21 cm
Courtesy the artist and David Zwirner

20

200 Metres Relay, 2002
Ink and coloured pencil on paper, 33.8 × 26.1 cm
Courtesy the artist and David Zwirner

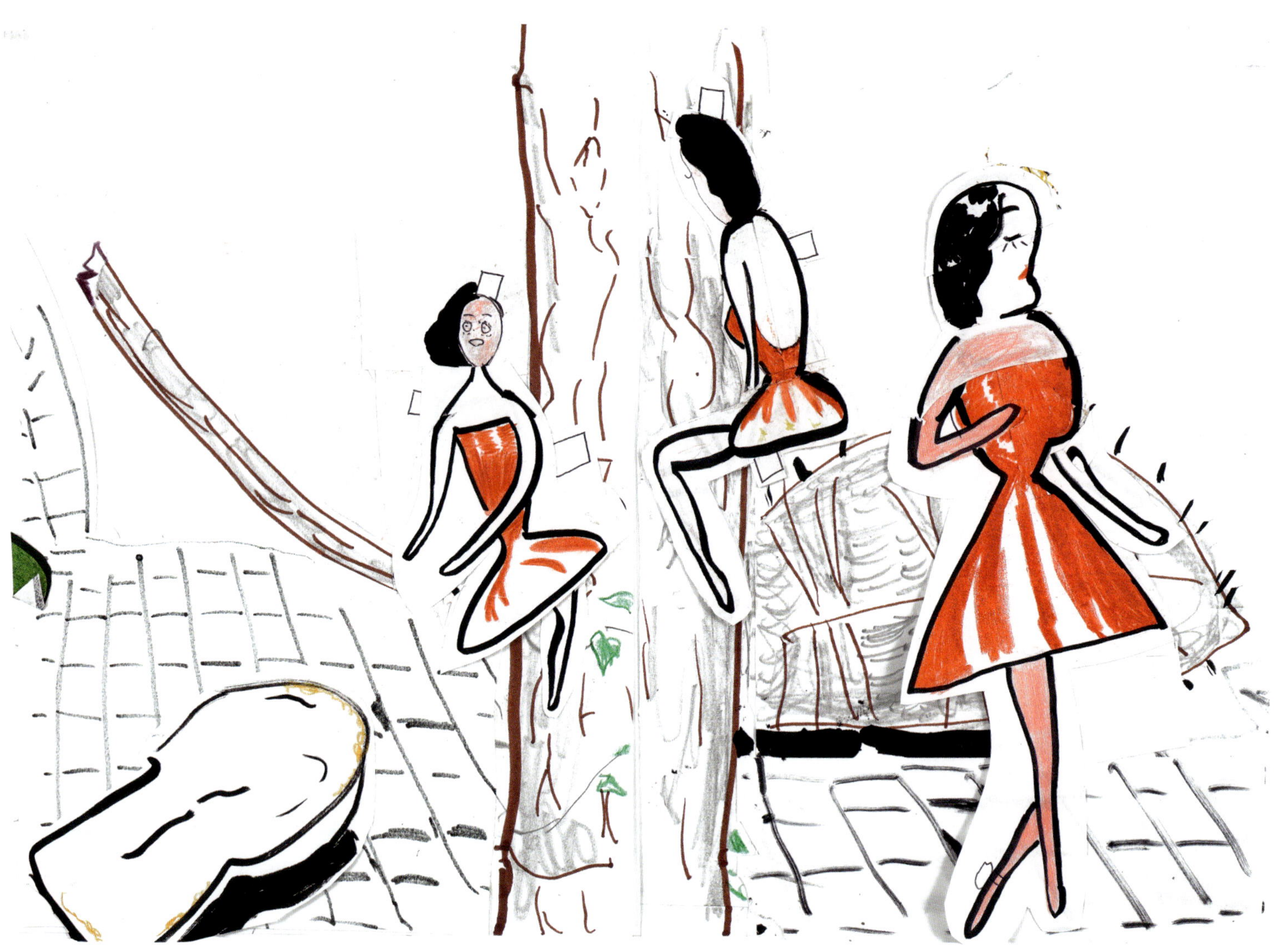

21

Study for Red Twink, 2002
Graphite and coloured pencil
on paper, 31 × 42.5 cm (overall)
Courtesy the artist
and David Zwirner

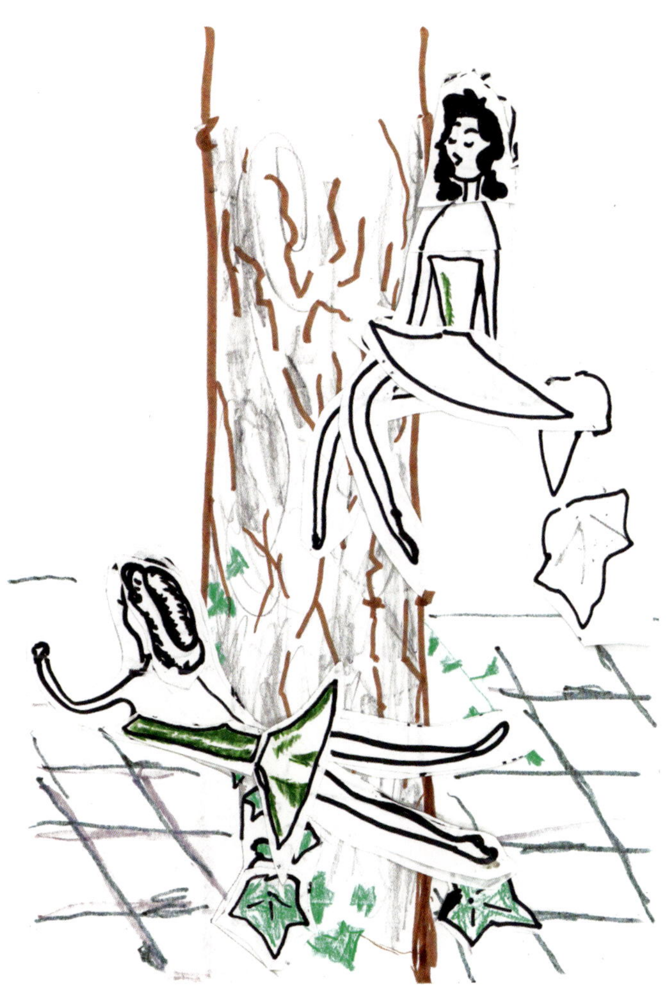

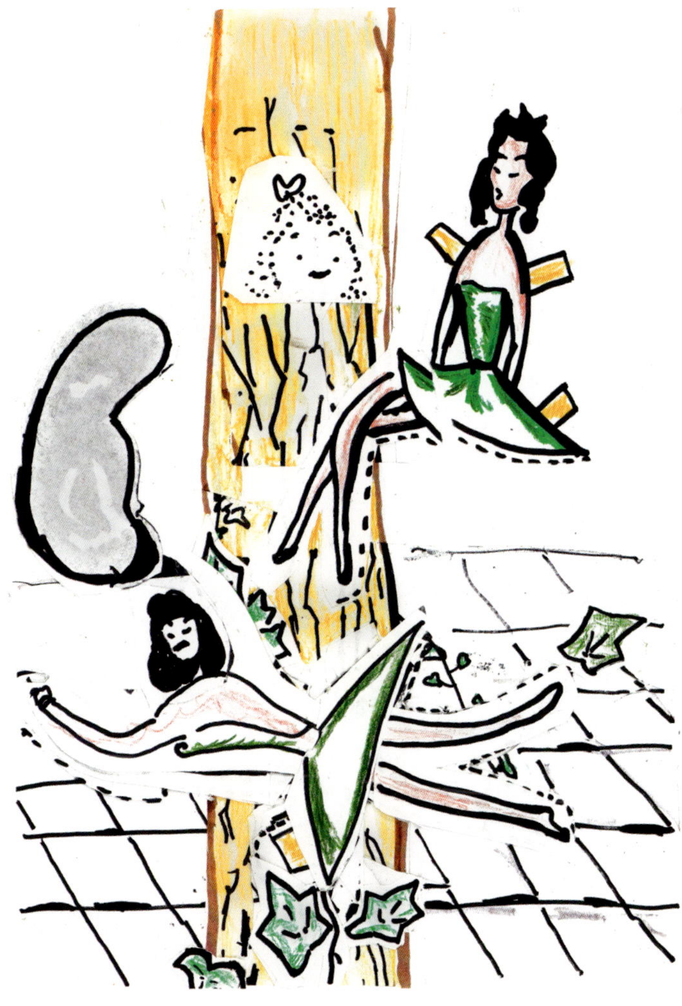

22

Twink, 2001
Marker, coloured pencil and collage on paper,
29.7 × 21 cm
Courtesy the artist and David Zwirner

23

Green Twink, 2001
Marker, coloured pencil and collage on paper,
30.2 × 21.7 cm
Courtesy the artist and David Zwirner

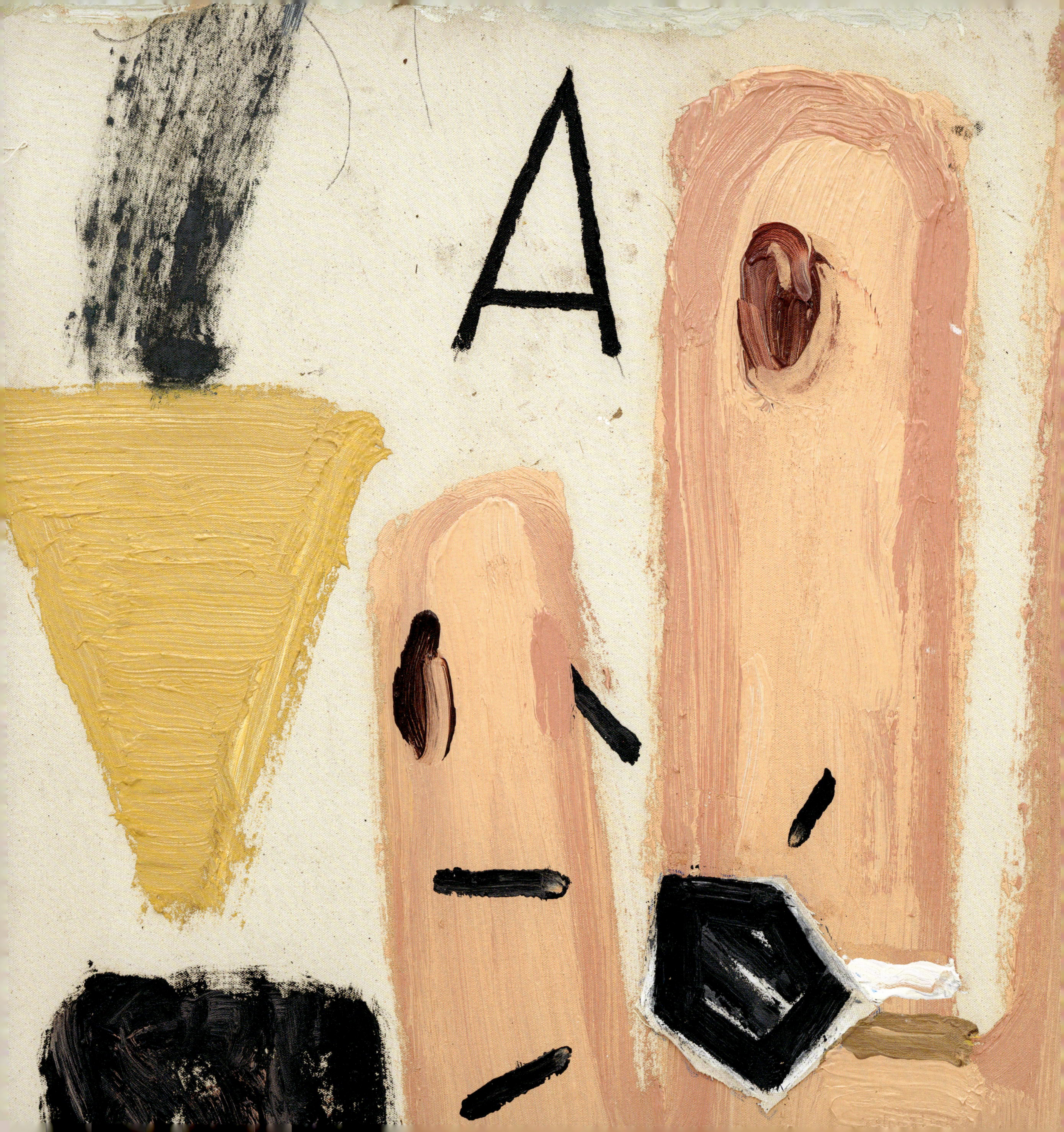
A

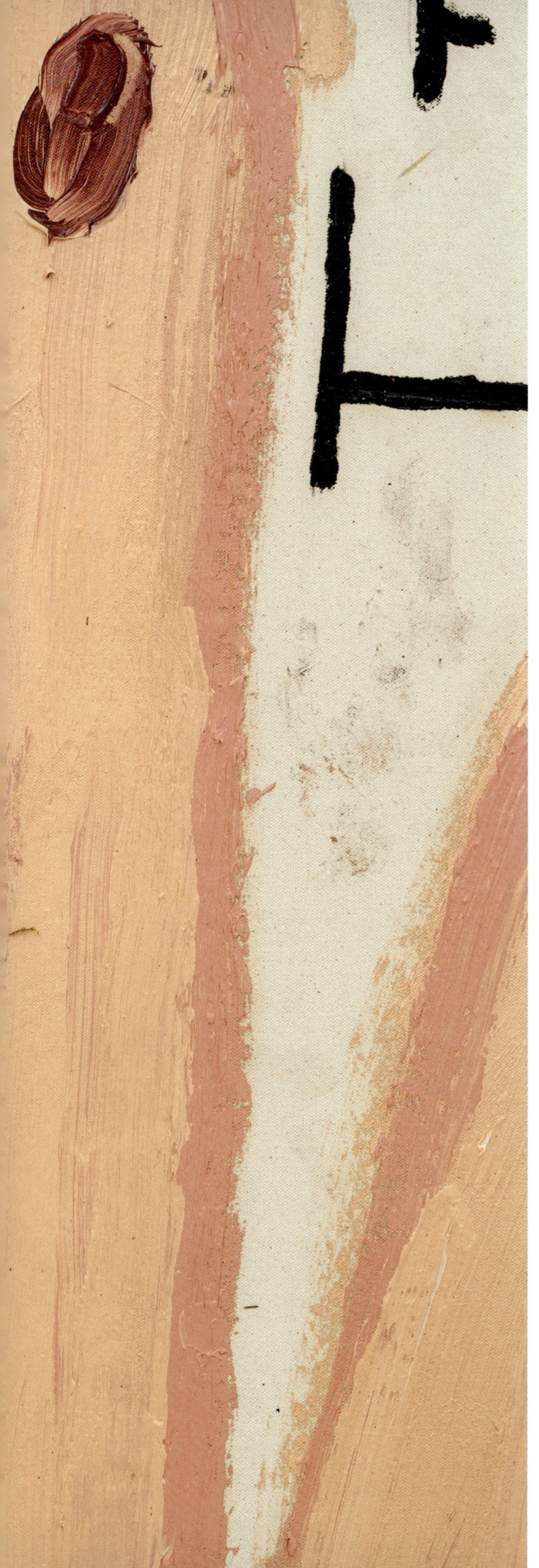

Hand: Drawing as Central

'You follow up leads, and then you can suddenly be arrested by an image. I think that's wonderful. And that's what I tend to draw. I don't care if it's related to the history of art, or if it's a ready-made object, or a person, or an animal. I constantly draw them on little bits of paper. It's mixed, it has to do with chance.'[3]

For Rose Wylie, 'drawing is central', as she has declared both in her painting *HAND, Drawing as Central* (2022; cat. 24) and in interviews. Having written her MA dissertation at the Royal College of Art in 1981 on the language of drawing and its tuition in English art schools, Wylie's knowledge of the discipline is extensive. But her approach is not academic. She draws every day on A4 paper, large sheets or available scraps, using graphite, coloured pencils, ink or watercolours. These drawings can be complete works in themselves, or a drawn diary record. A vast memory bank of visual references, Wylie's ever-growing collection of thousands of works on paper reveals her insatiable curiosity and awareness of the world around her, from her immediate surroundings – objects lying around the house or the wildlife in her garden – to diverse interests made accessible through the proliferation of images and information on the internet and in print. Some drawings are worked and reworked over a period and become meticulous studies for a painting.

24 *(overleaf)*
HAND, Drawing as Central, 2022
Oil on canvas,
184 × 402 cm (overall)
Stedelijk Museum voor Actuele Kunst, Ghent

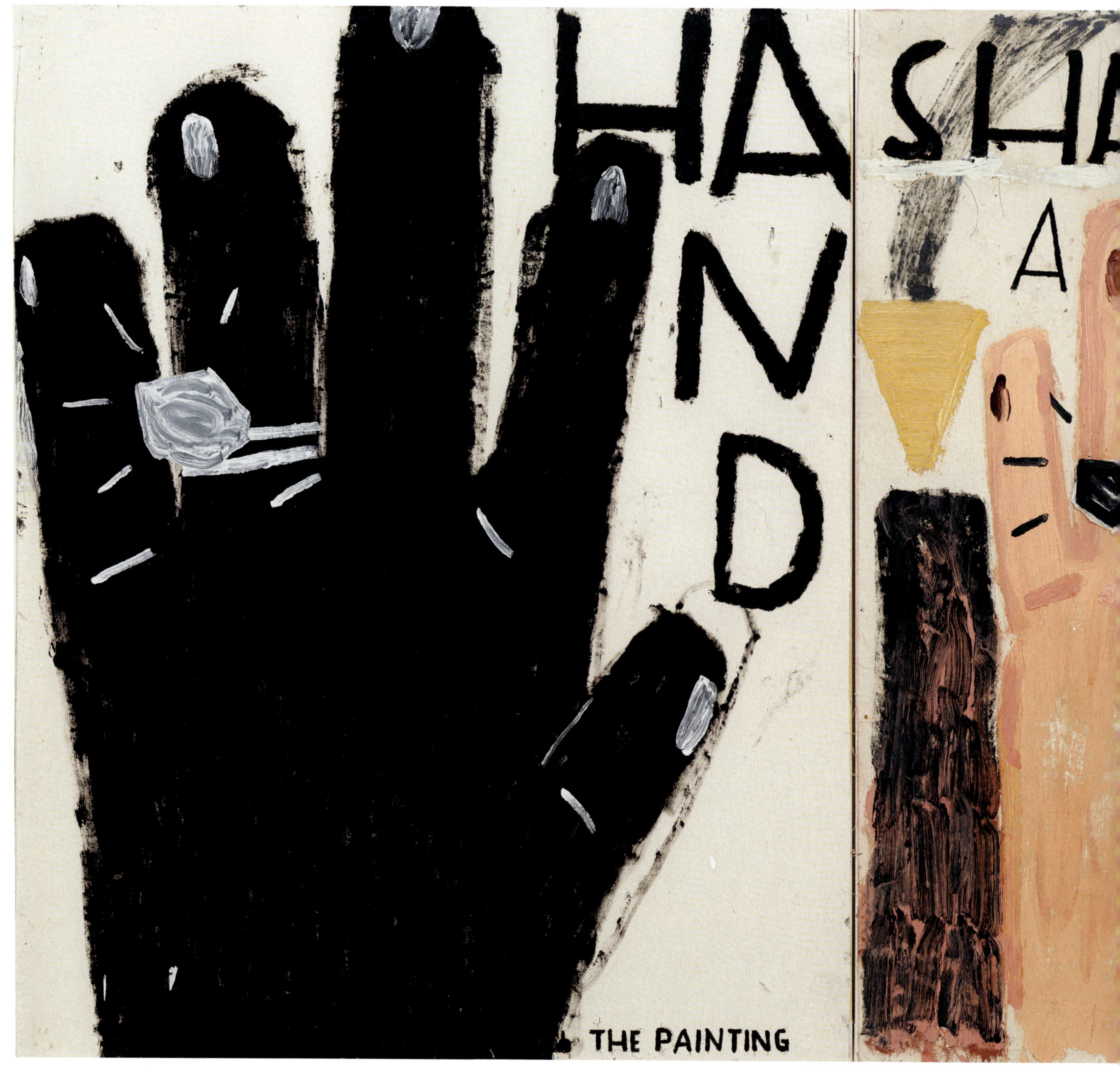
HA
N
D
SHA
A
THE PAINTING

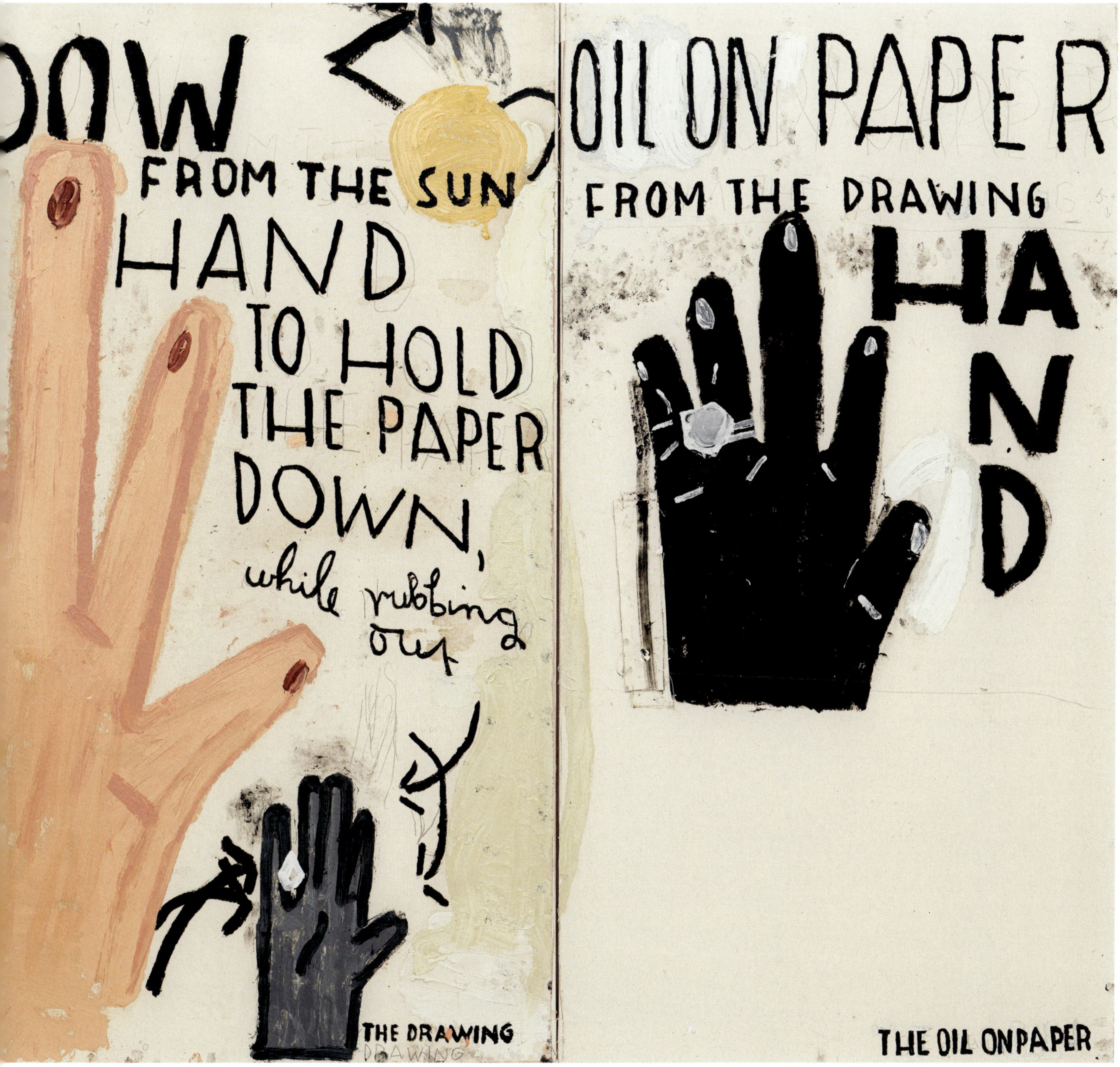

DOW
FROM THE SUN
HAND
TO HOLD
THE PAPER
DOWN,
while rubbing
out
THE DRAWING

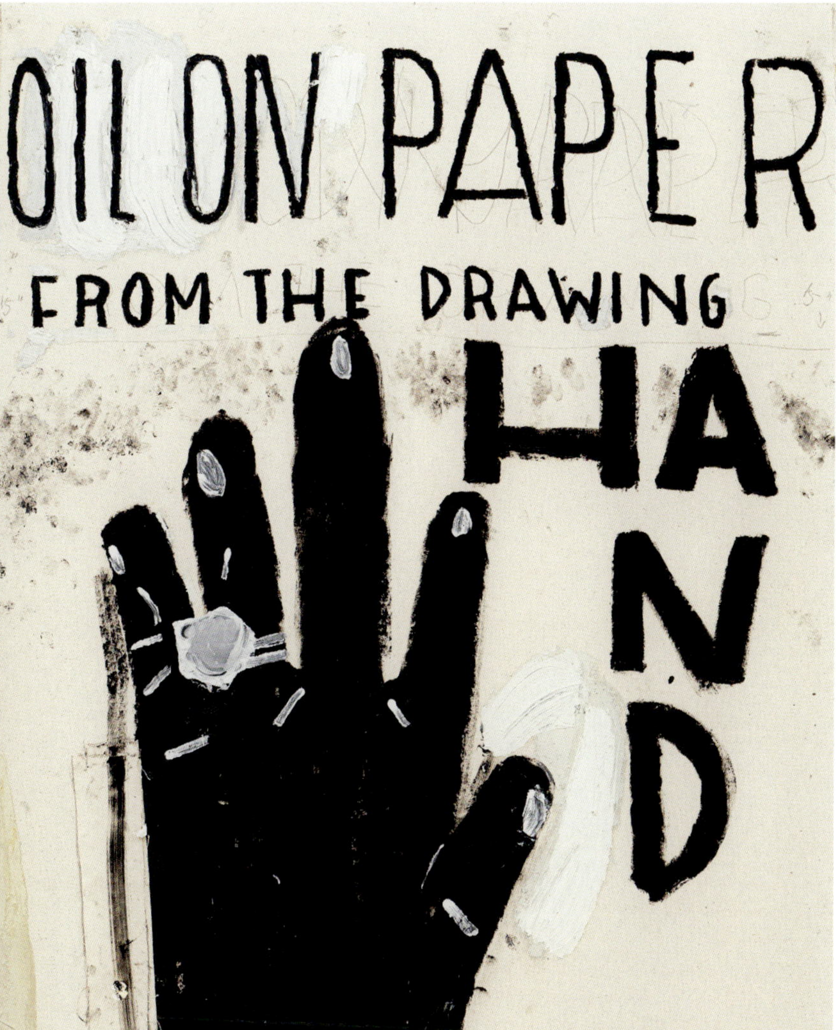

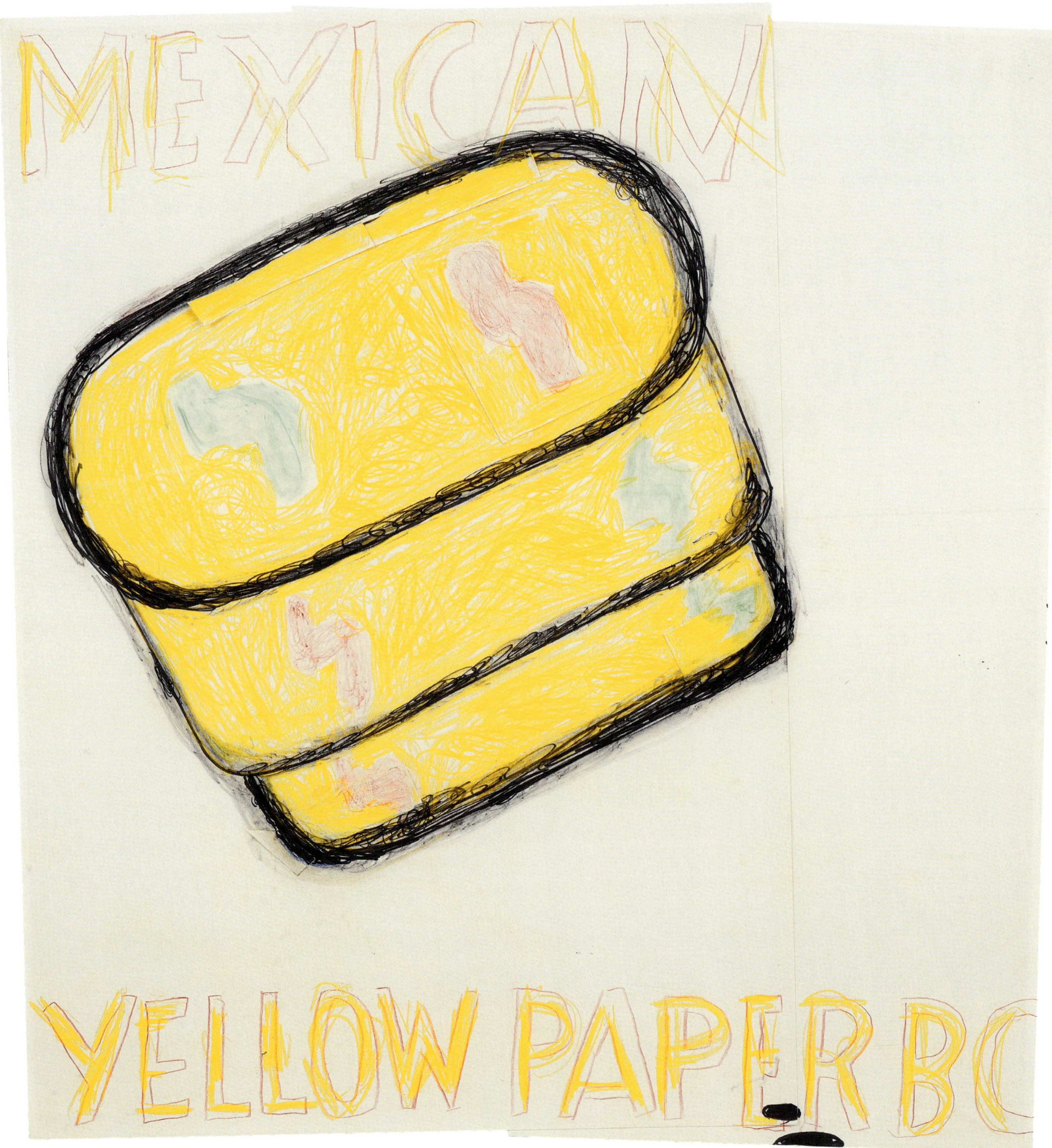
MEXICAN
YELLOW PAPER BO

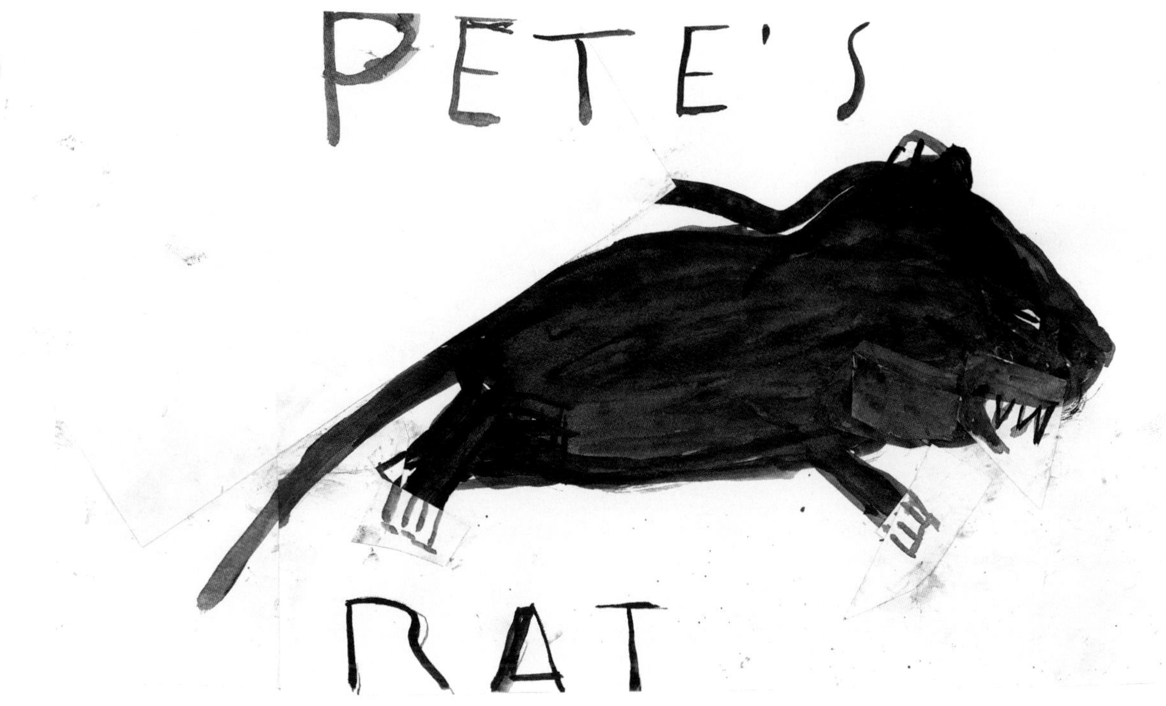

25

Yellow Mexican Box, 2019
Marker, coloured pencil and collage on paper, 97.1 × 93.5 cm
Courtesy the artist and David Zwirner

26

Pete's Rat, 2019
Watercolour on paper, 21 × 38.7 cm
Courtesy the artist and David Zwirner

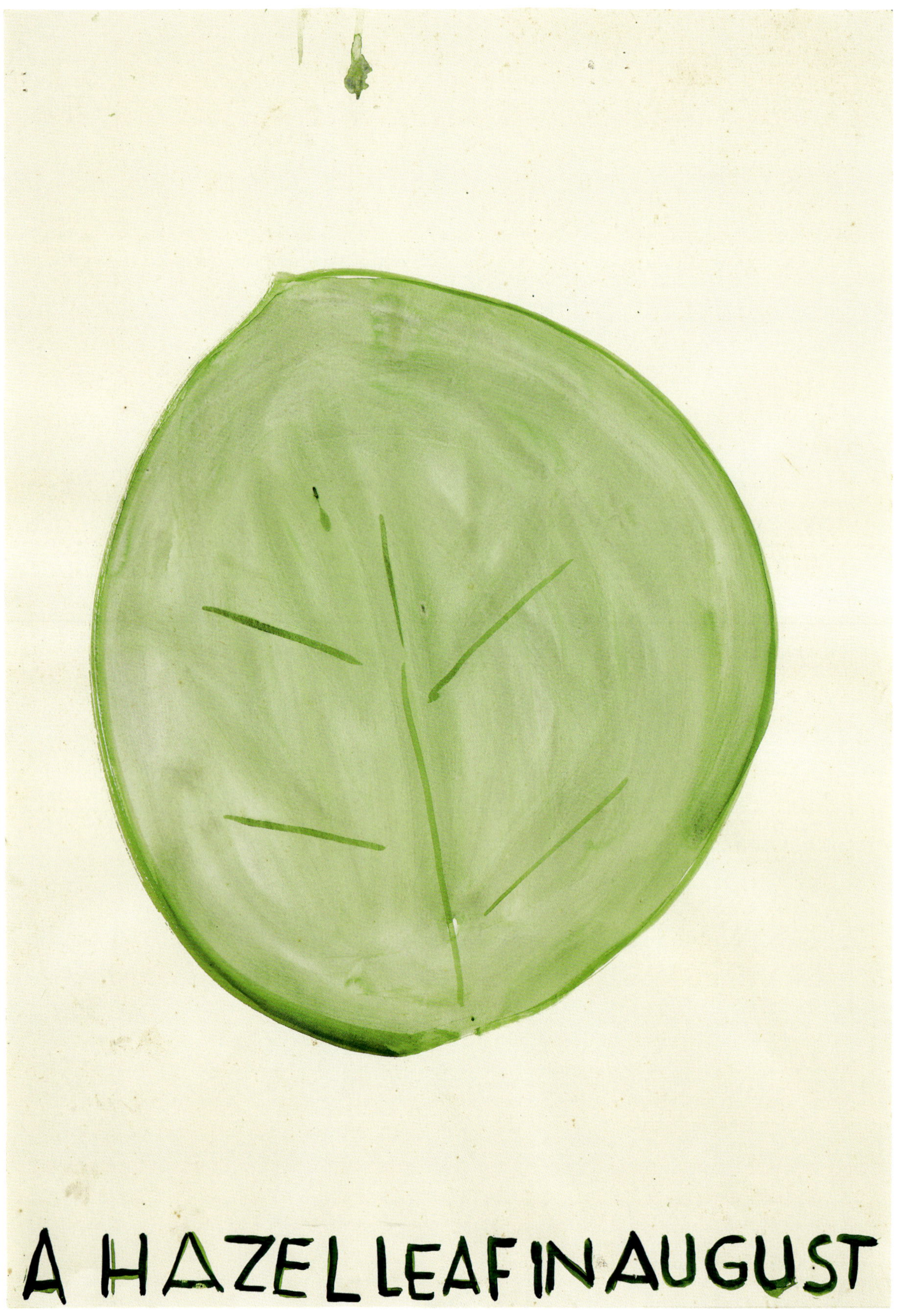

27

Hazelnut Leaf, 2017
Watercolour on paper,
84 × 59.5 cm
Courtesy the artist
and David Zwirner

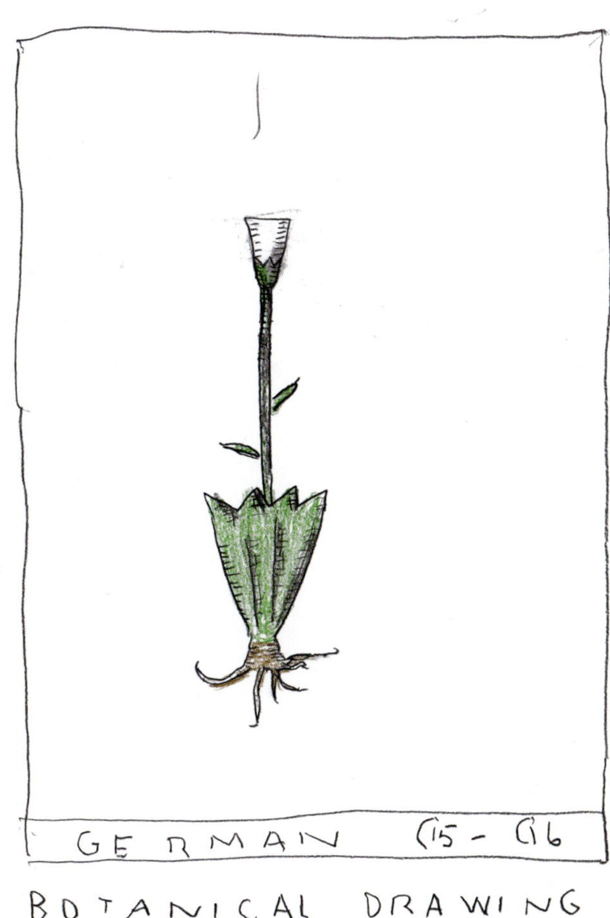

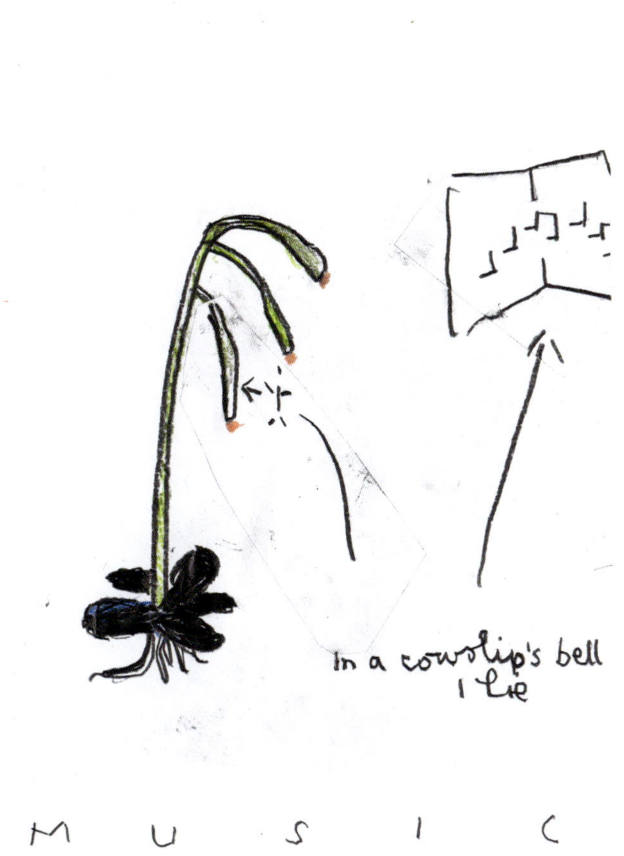

28

German Botanical Drawing, 2016
Coloured pencil on paper,
29.7 × 21 cm
Courtesy the artist and David Zwirner

29

In a Cowslip's Bell with Music, 2020
Graphite, coloured pencil and collage on paper,
29.7 × 21 cm
Courtesy the artist and David Zwirner

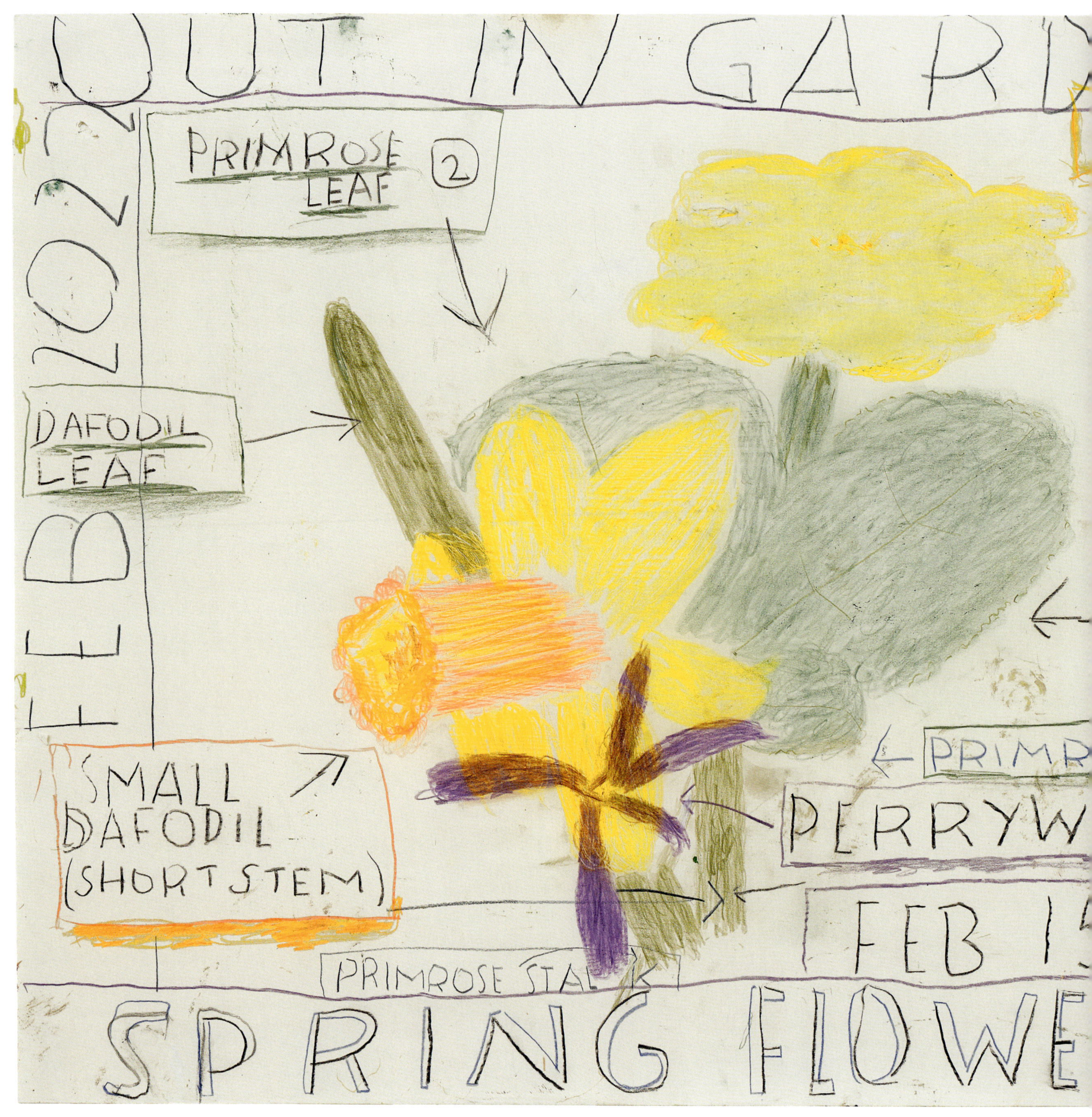
OUT IN GARD
FEB 2022
PRIMROSE LEAF
2
DAFODIL LEAF
SMALL DAFODIL (SHORT STEM)
PRIMROSE STALK
PRIMR
PERRYW
FEB 1
SPRING FLOWE

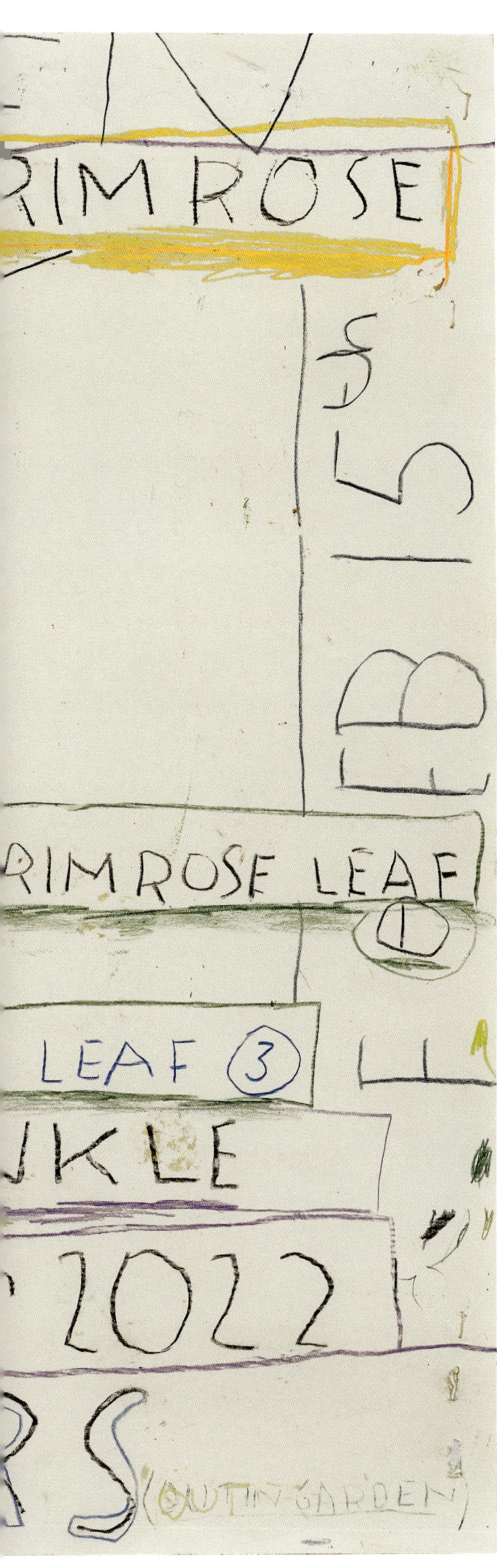

30

Out in Garden Now, Feb 5th, 2022, 2022
Graphite and coloured pencil on paper,
73.5 × 98.2 cm
Courtesy Brian Garish

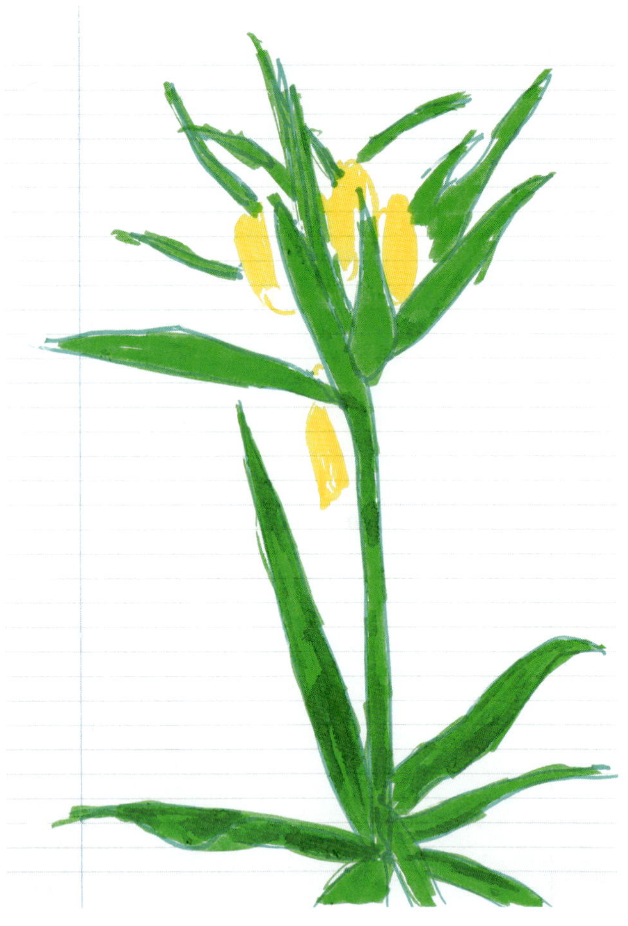

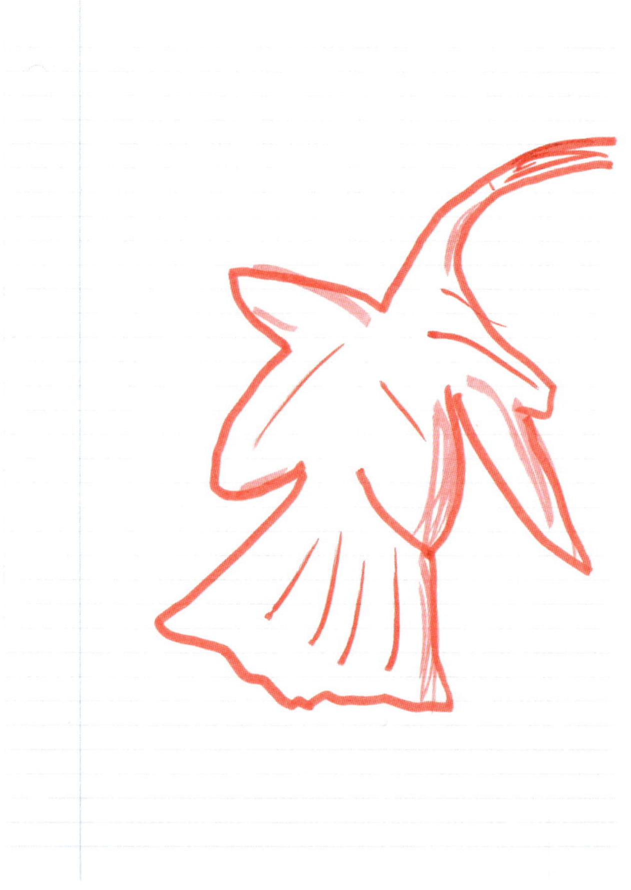

31

Crown Imperial (From the Garden), 2015
Marker on lined paper,
29.7 × 21 cm
Courtesy the artist
and David Zwirner

32

Yellow Daffodil, 2015
Marker on lined paper,
29.7 × 21 cm
Courtesy the artist
and David Zwirner

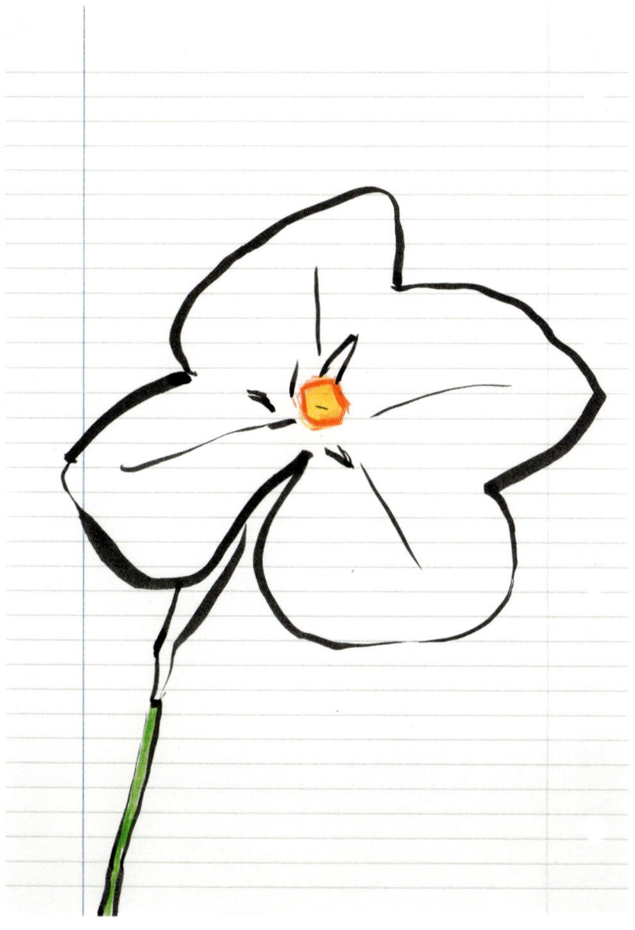

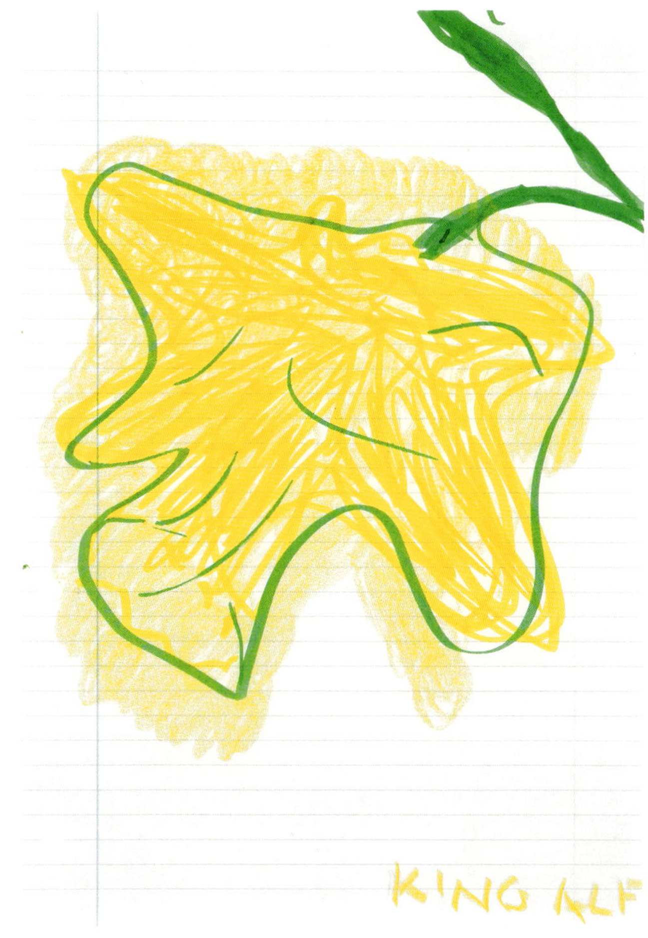

33

Pheasant Eye Narcissus, 2015
Marker and coloured pencil on paper, 29.7 × 21 cm
Courtesy the artist and David Zwirner

34

King Alfred, 2015
Marker and coloured pencil on lined paper, 29.7 × 21 cm
Courtesy the artist and David Zwirner

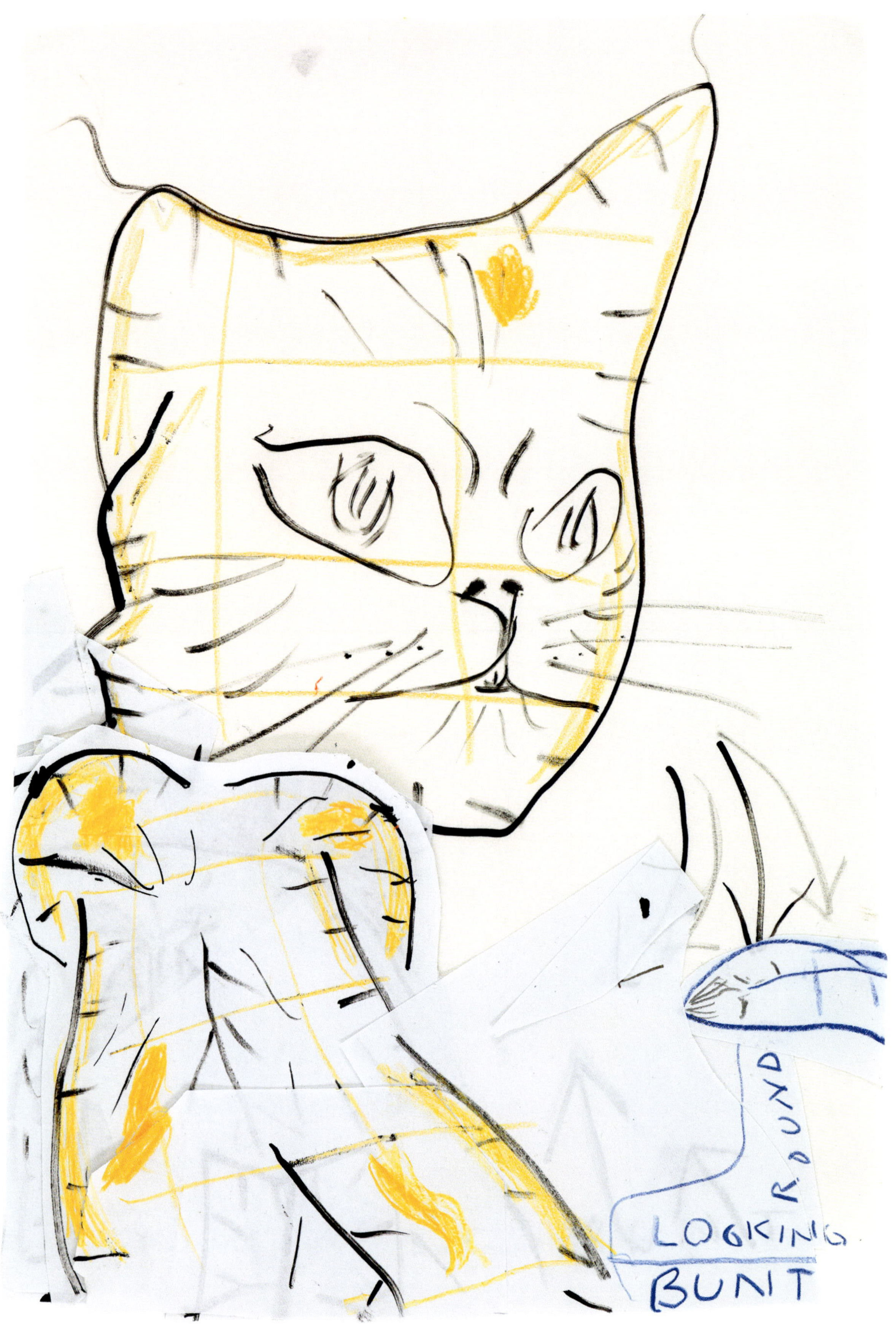

35

Bunt Looking Round, 2002
Marker, coloured pencil
and collage on paper,
32 × 22 cm
Courtesy the artist
and David Zwirner

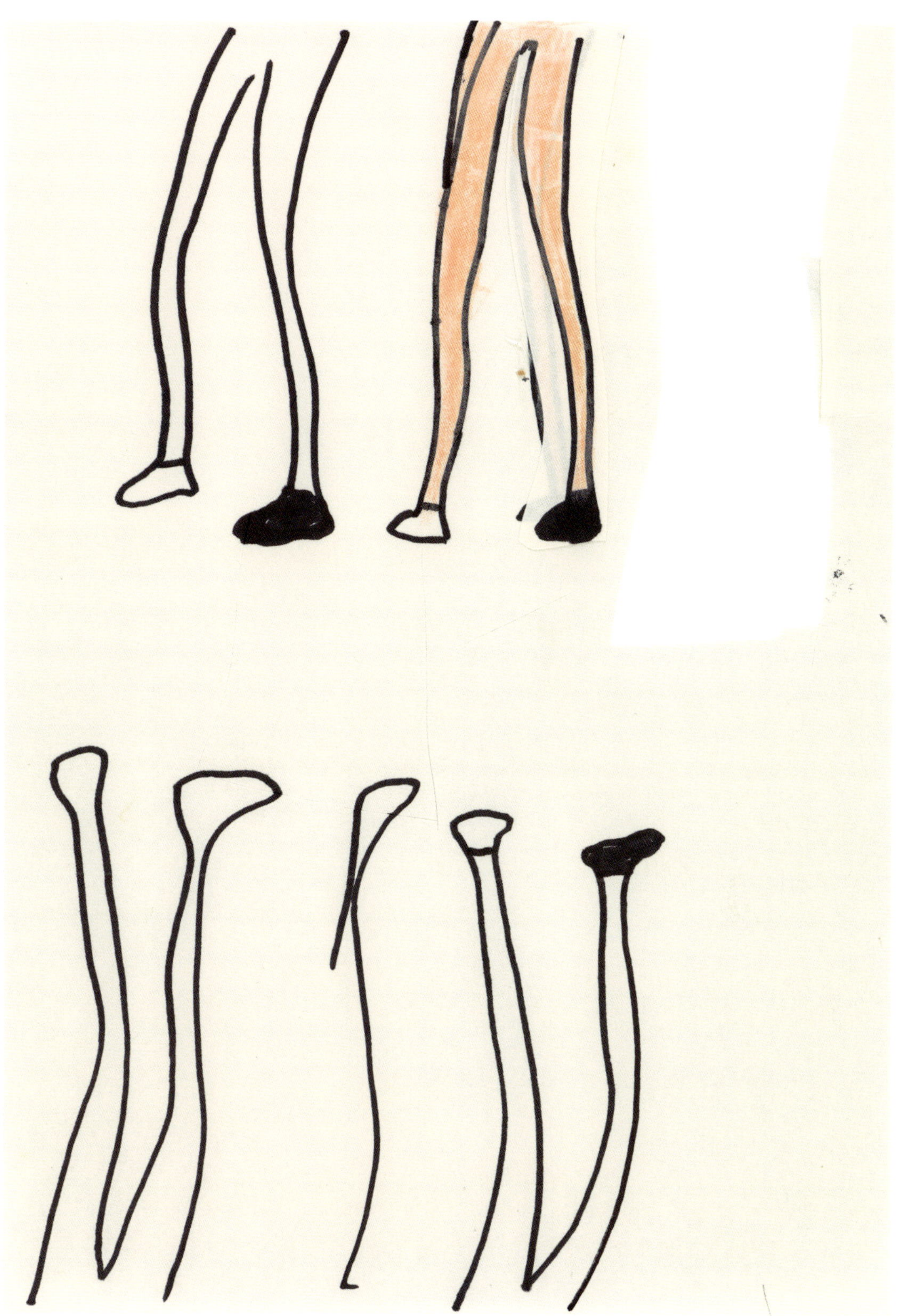

36

Legs, 2001
Marker and coloured pencil
on paper, 29.7 × 21 cm
Courtesy the artist
and David Zwirner

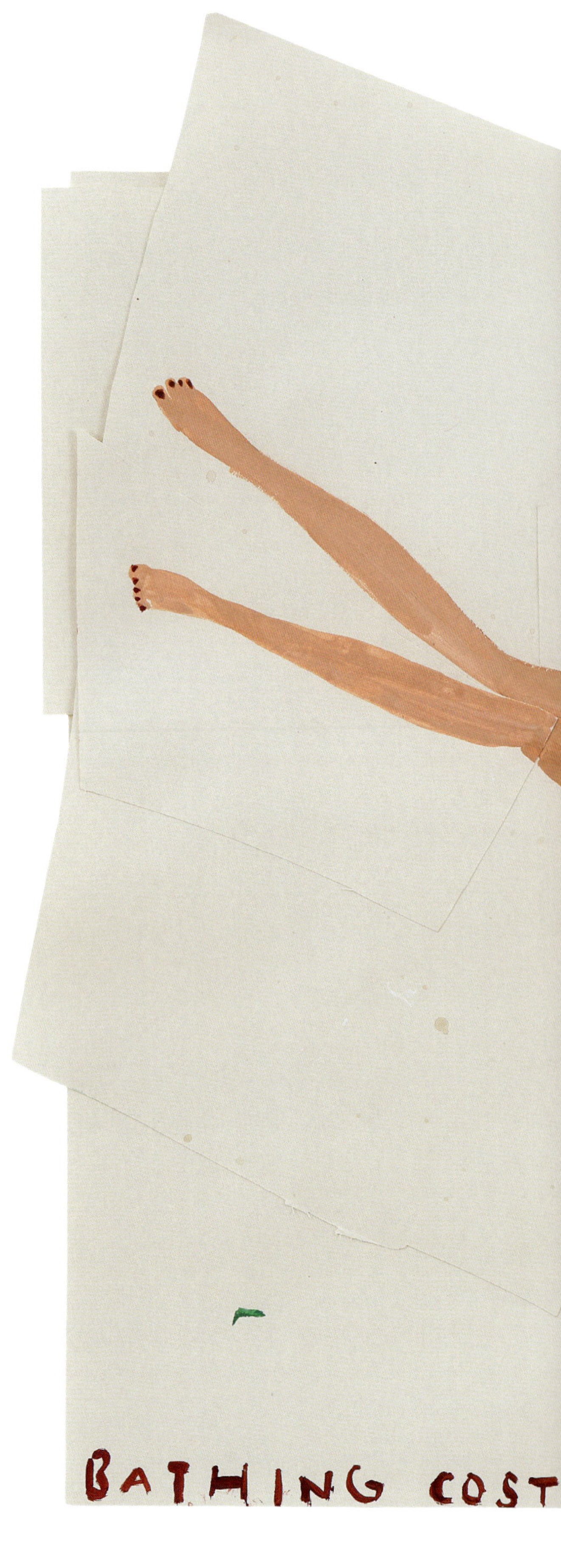

37

Reclining Figure, 2010
Watercolour and collage
on paper, 59 × 86 cm
Courtesy the artist
and David Zwirner

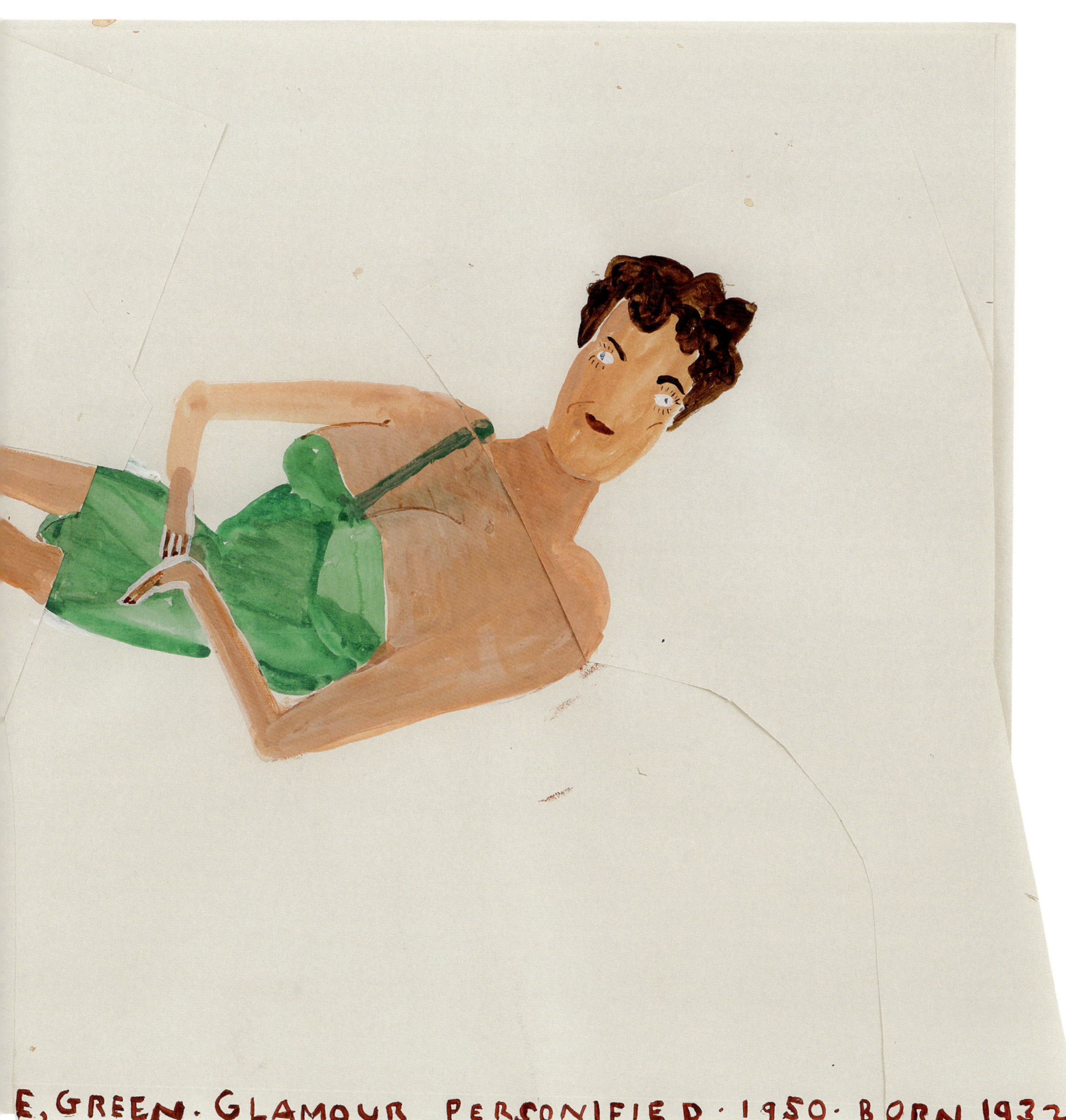
E, GREEN. GLAMOUR PERSONIFIED. 1950. BORN 1932

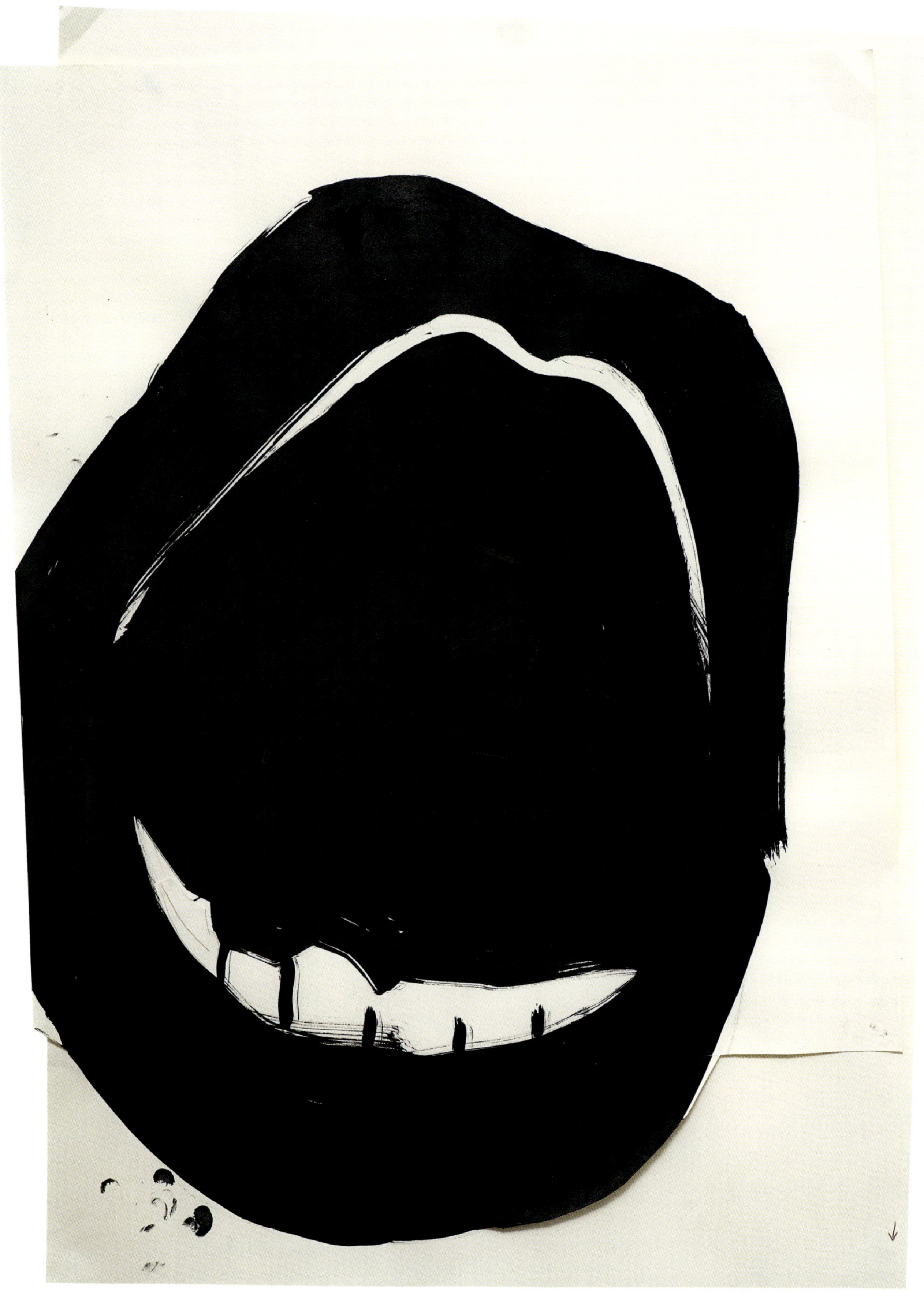

38

Bottom Teeth, Self-Portrait, 2016
Ink and collage on paper, 84 × 63.5 cm
Courtesy Sven Petersen and Holly Frean

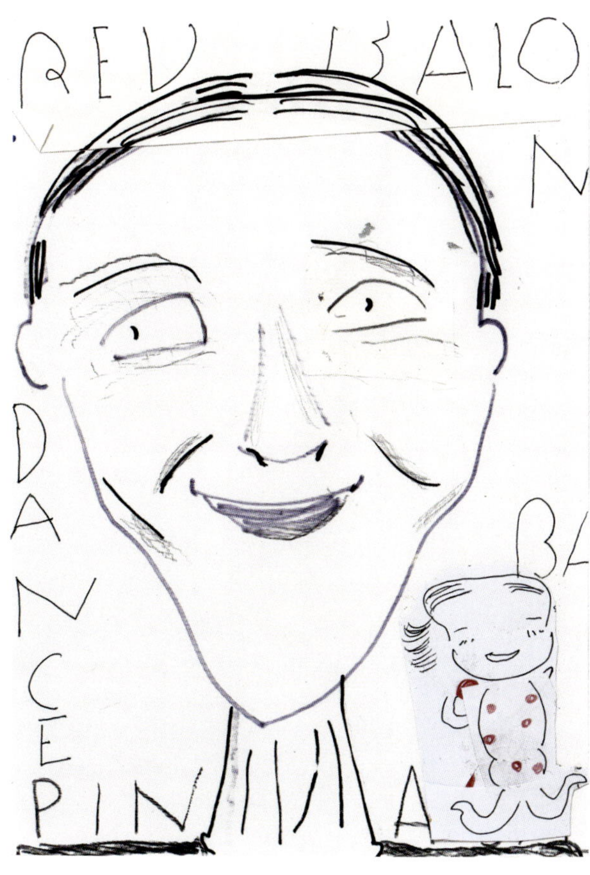

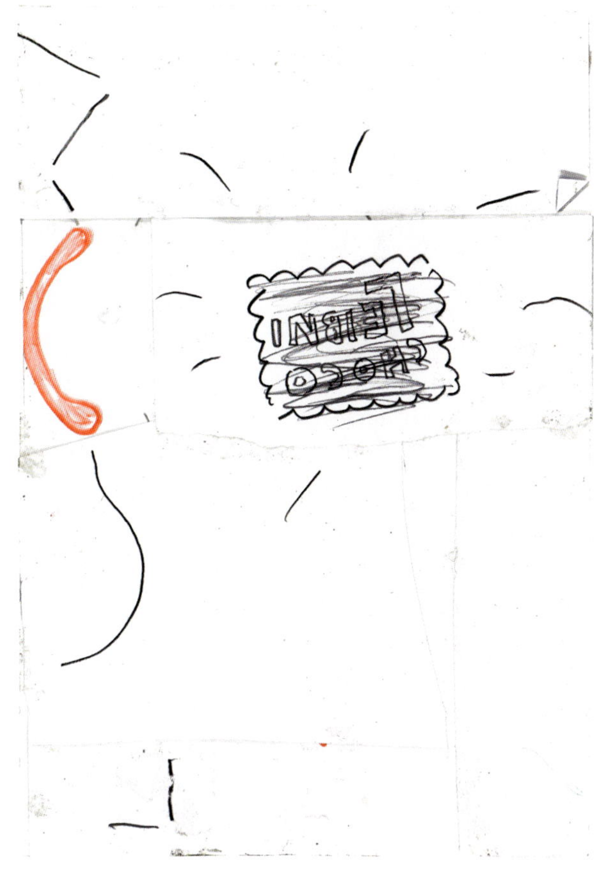

39

After P B, with Balloon Outfit, c. 2015
Marker, graphite, coloured pencil and collage on paper, 29.7 × 21 cm
Courtesy the artist and David Zwirner

40

Choco Leibnitz (Self-Portrait), 2006
Graphite, coloured pencil and collage on paper, 30 × 21 cm
Courtesy the artist and David Zwirner

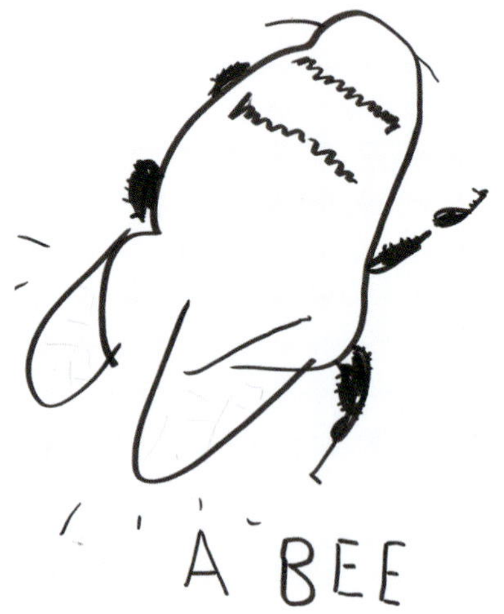

41

A Bee, 2000–02
Ink and collage on paper, 29.7 × 21 cm
Courtesy the artist and David Zwirner

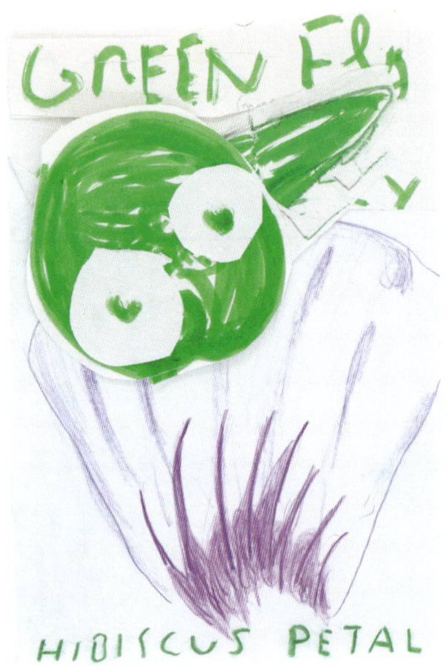

42

Hibiscus and Greenfly, 2002
Marker, coloured pencil and collage on paper, 29.7 × 21 cm
Courtesy the artist and David Zwirner

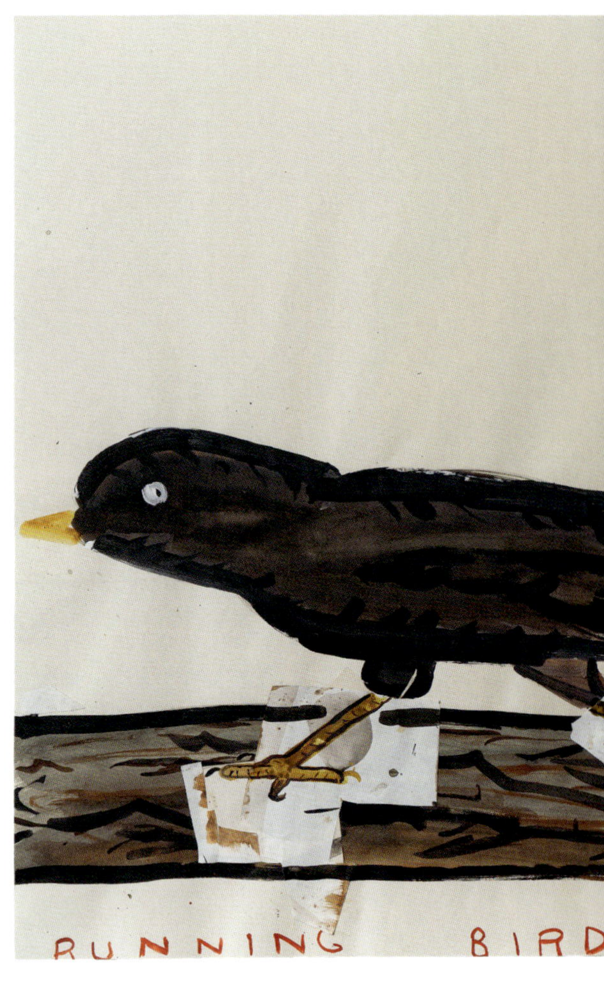

43

Running Bird and Silver Birch, 2007
Watercolour, ink and collage on paper, 84 × 118 cm
Courtesy private collection and JARILAGER Gallery

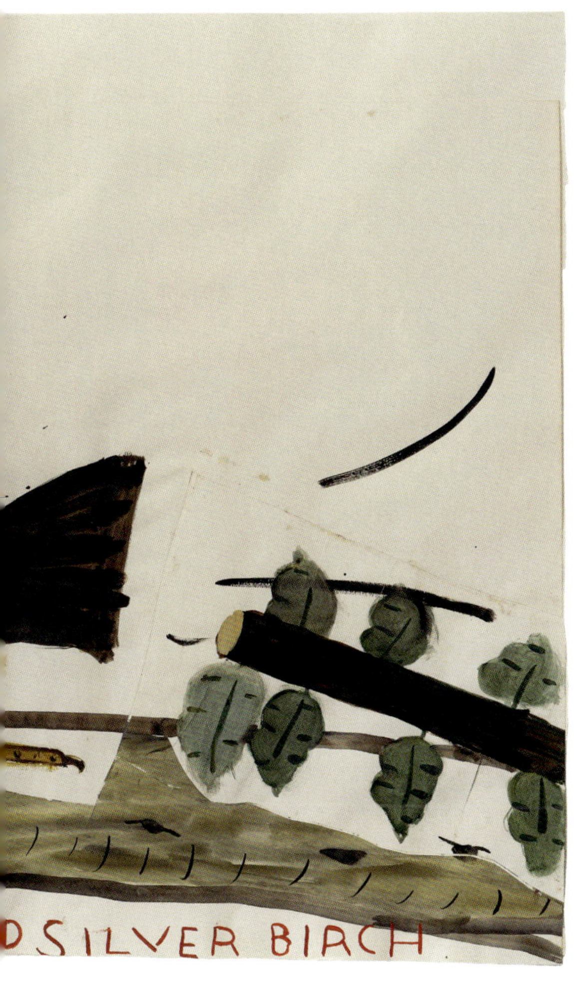

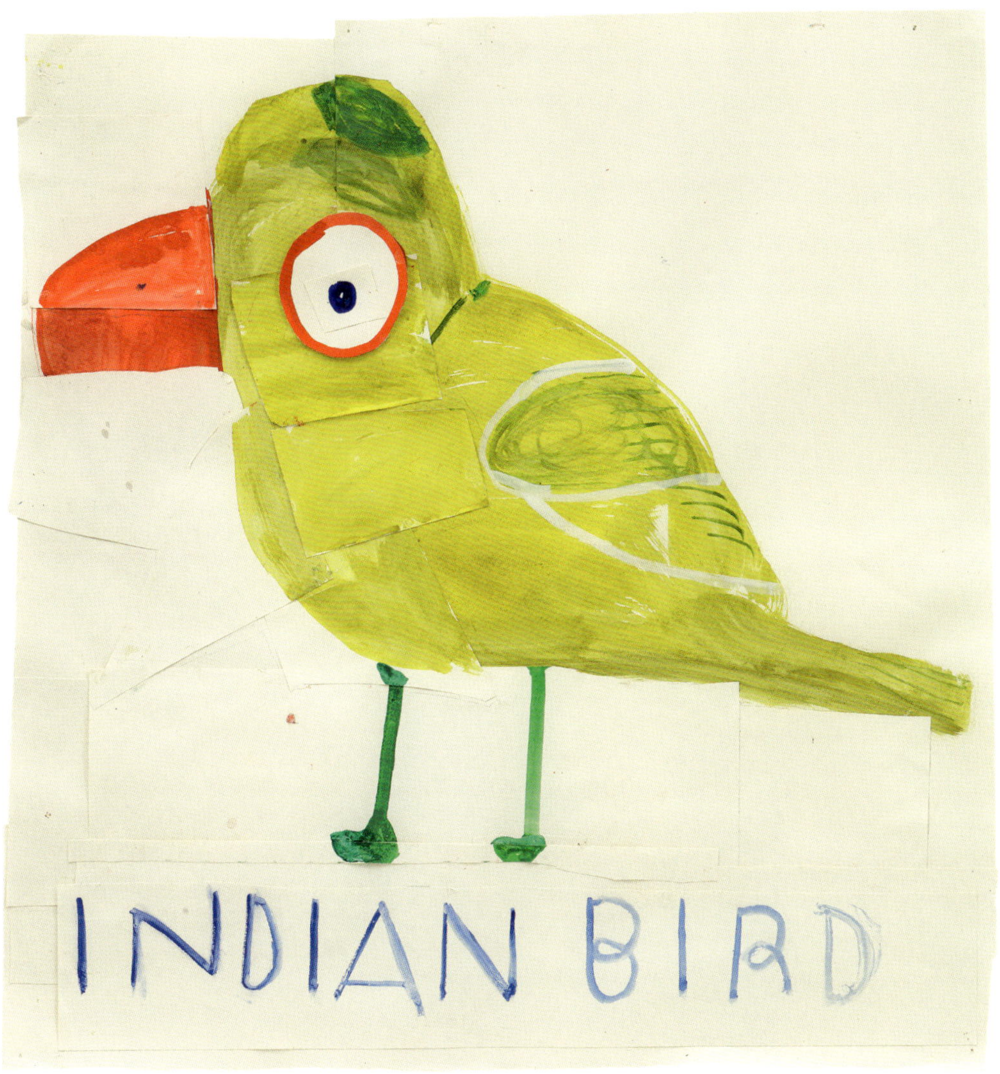

44

Indian Bird, 2013
Watercolour and collage on paper, 93.5 × 91.5 cm
Courtesy Brett and Julia Frankle

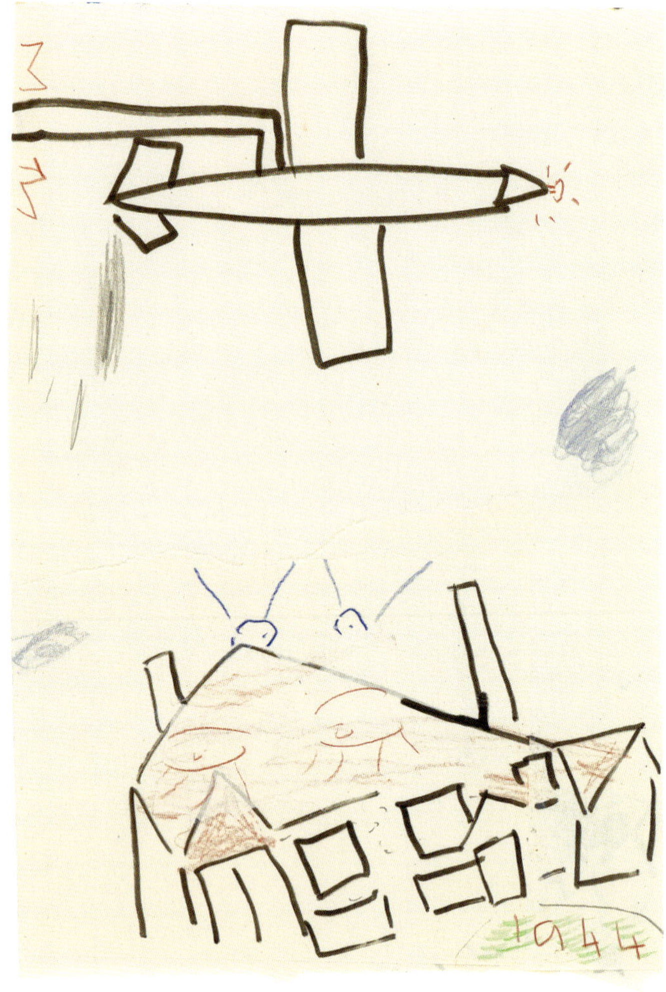

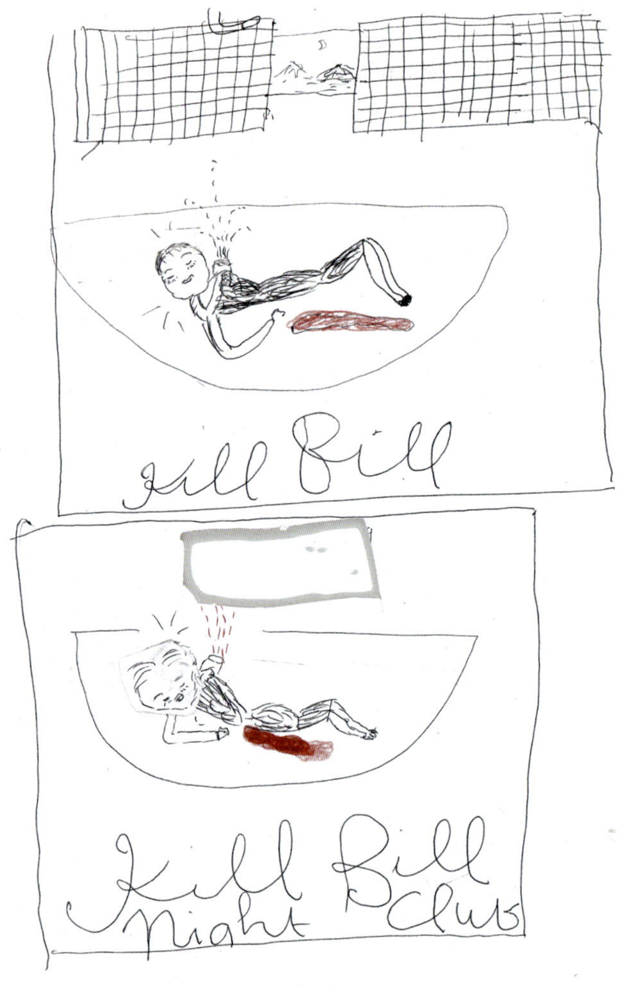

45

Doodlebug and Rosemount with Eyes, 1994
Marker, graphite, coloured pencil, marker and collage on paper, 30 × 27 cm
Courtesy the artist and David Zwirner

46

Kill Bill, 2006
Graphite, coloured pencil and collage on paper, 29.7 × 21 cm
Courtesy the artist and David Zwirner

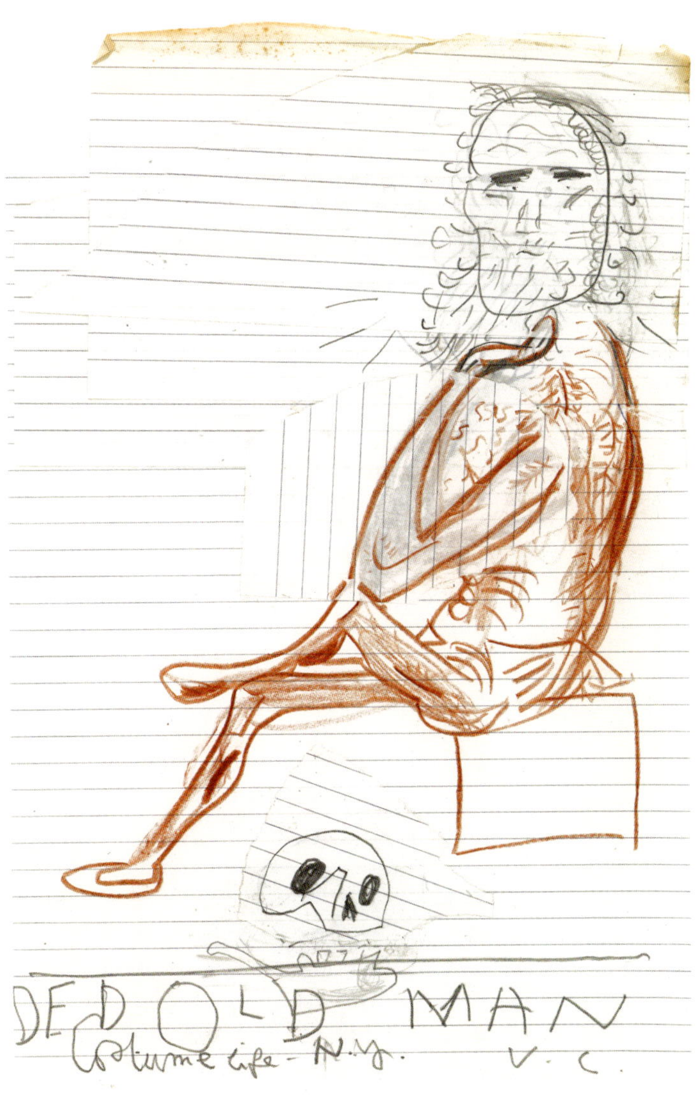

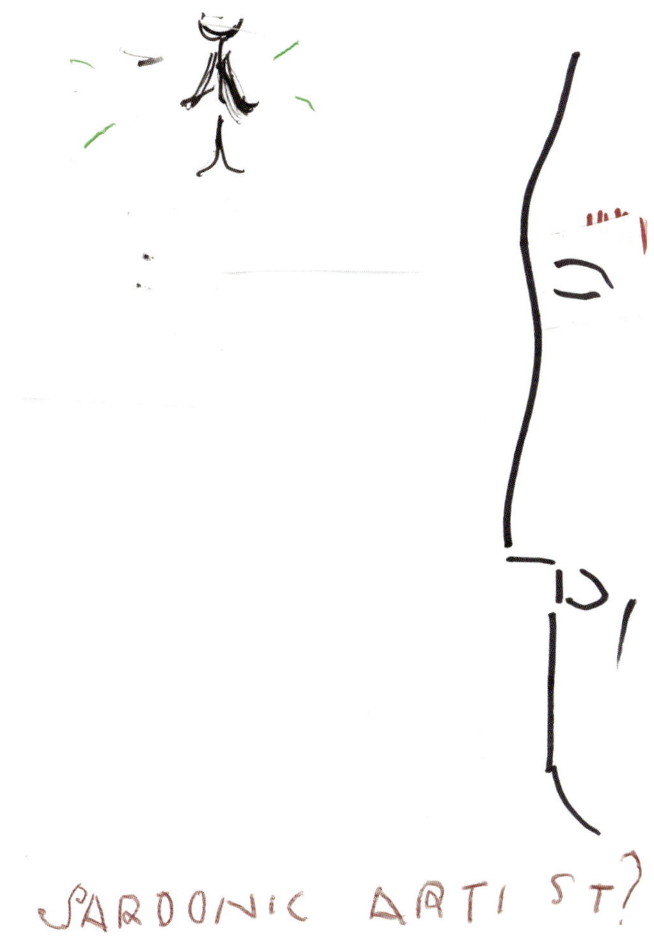

47

Old Man (Job Figure from Carpaccio), 1999
Graphite, coloured pencil and collage on lined paper, 32.3 × 21 cm
Courtesy the artist and David Zwirner

48

Sardonic Artist, 1991
Marker on paper, 29.7 × 21.2 cm
Courtesy the artist and David Zwirner

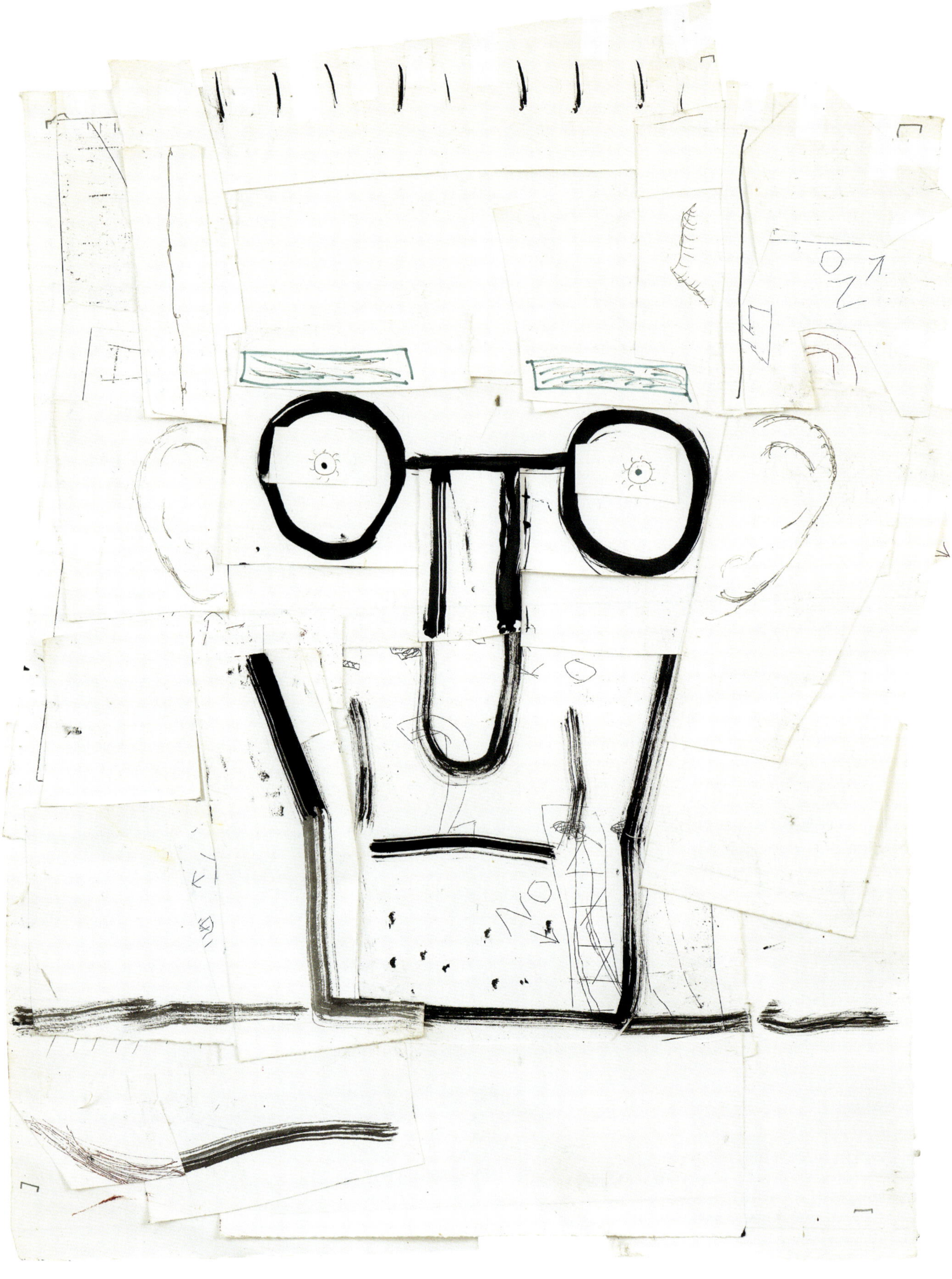

49

Roy Oxlade, 2014
Etching, ink and collage on paper, 82 × 64 cm
Courtesy the artist and David Zwirner

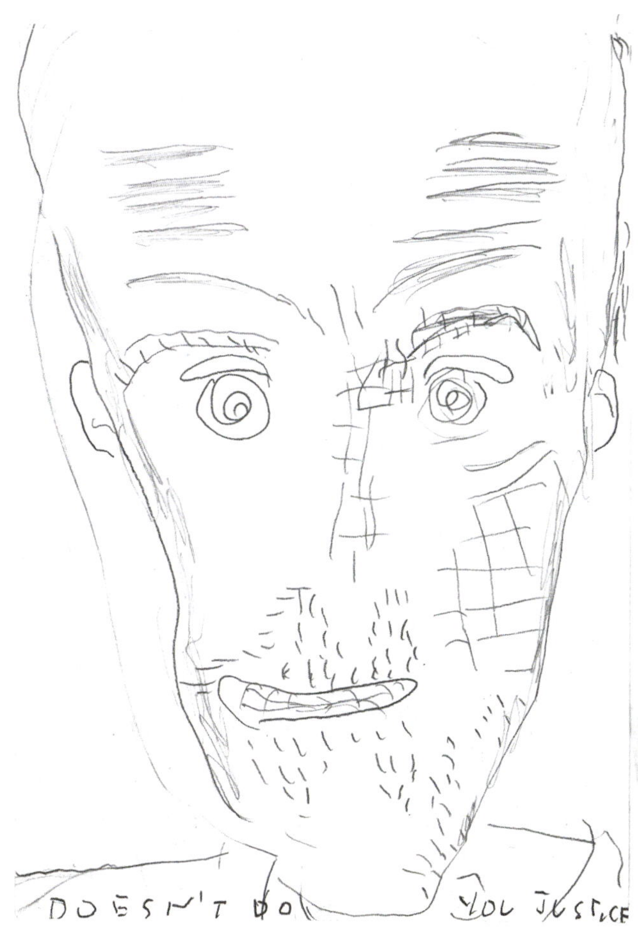

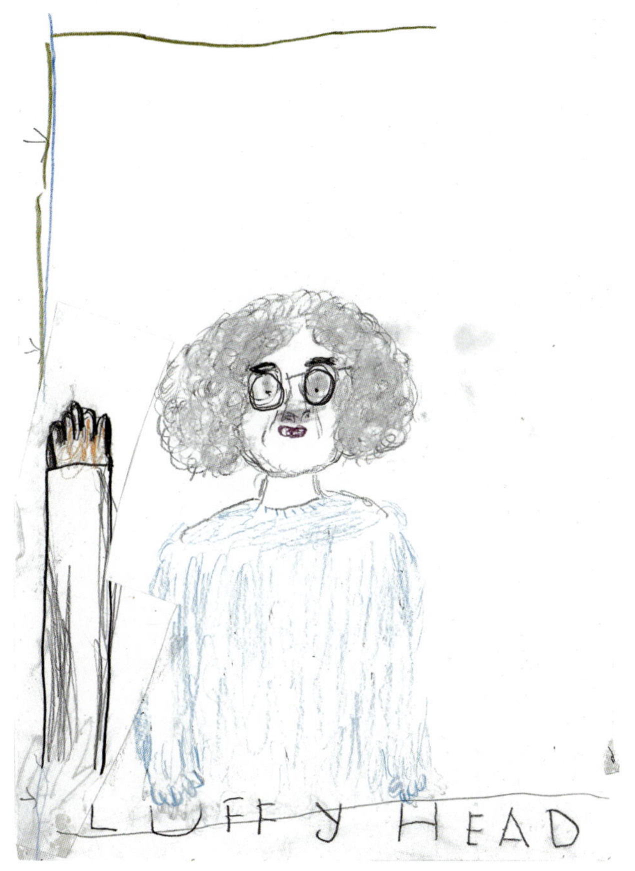

50

Doesn't Do You Justice, 2020
Graphite on paper, 30.3 × 21.5 cm
Courtesy the artist and David Zwirner

51

Fluffy Head with Extra Arm, 2020
Graphite, coloured pencil and collage on paper, 29.7 × 21 cm
Courtesy the artist and David Zwirner

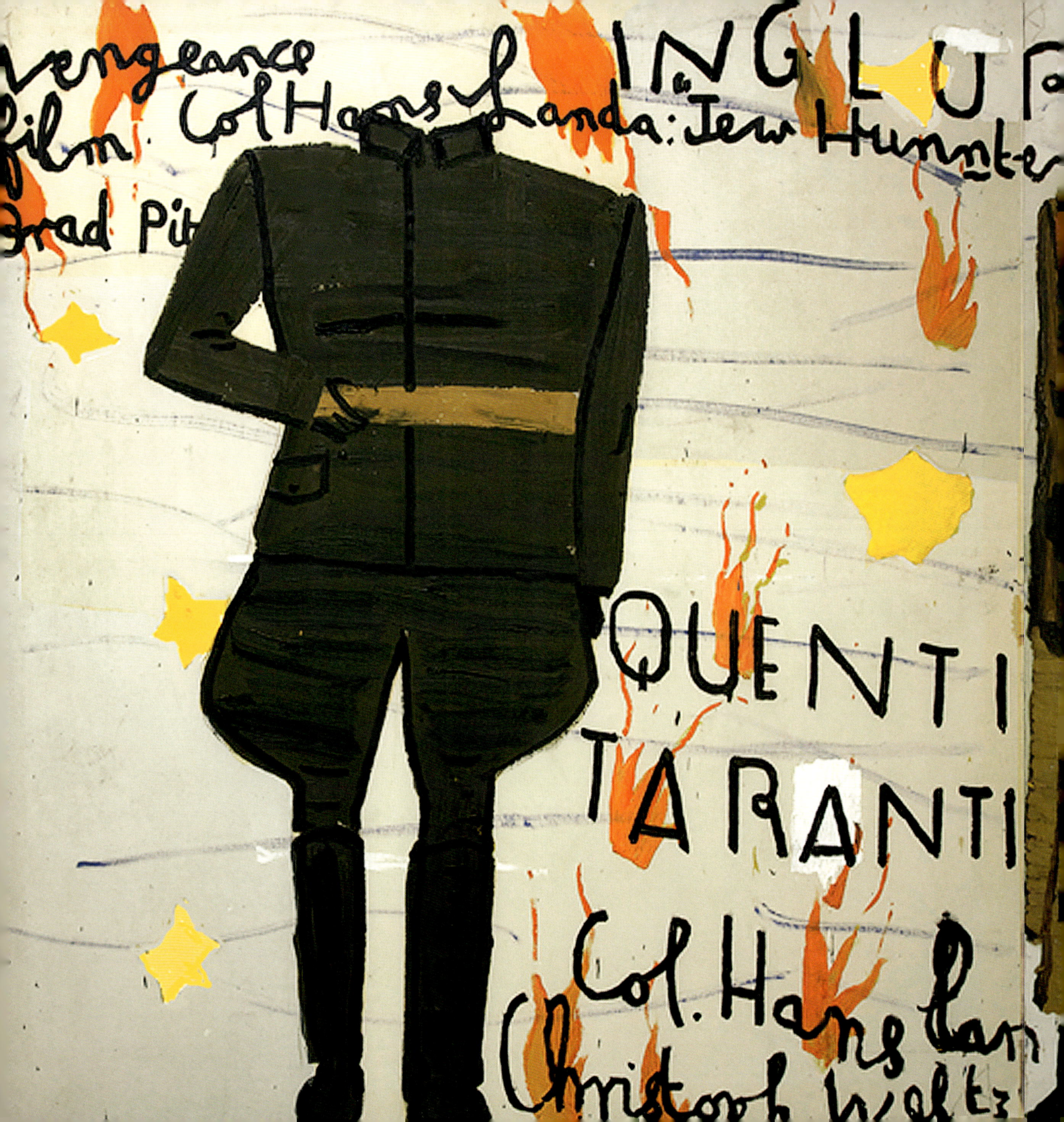

vengeance
film Col Hans Landa: Jew Hunnter
Brad Pit
INGLU
QUENTI
TARANTI
Col. Hans Lan
Christoph Waltz

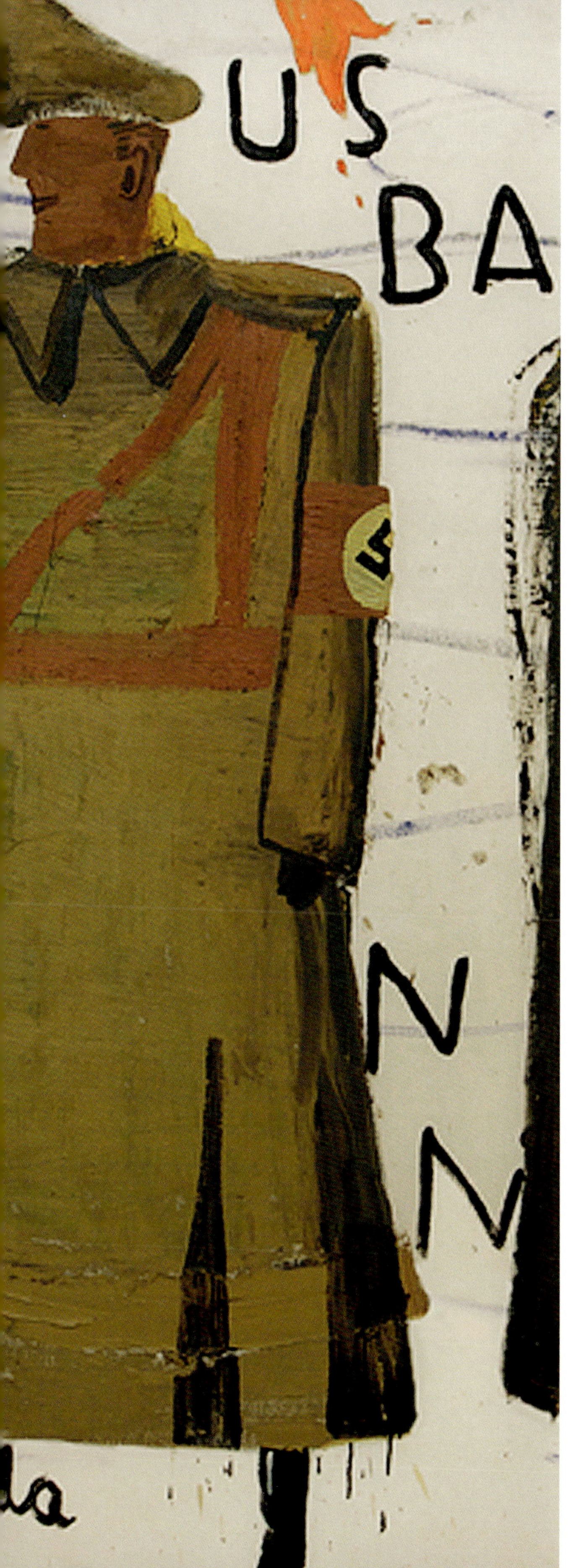

Film Notes

'The imagery is fantastic, I think, and I'm a sucker for close-ups, and cropping, and jumping around, it's totally flexible, as far as I can... It's a knockout, twenty-first-century art form. And I think it's close to painting in that way and photography, they're all linked together.'[4]

Rose Wylie loves the film lens, the way the camera can zoom in for a close-up or capture different perspectives and angles within the same scene. An avid film fan, she finds that certain shots become seared into her memory and materialise when painted to become one of her 'Film Notes'. Specific directors appeal to her appreciation of optical drama and contrast, such as Quentin Tarantino, as revealed by her paintings *Kill Bill (Film Notes)* (2007; cat. 59), which depicts the same frame from slightly different perspectives; *Inglourious Basterds (Film Notes)* (2010; cat. 57); and *Brunhilde (Film Notes)* (2024; cat. 52) after *Django Unchained* (2012). In other paintings, more incidental scenes are recreated in paint, such as Penélope Cruz sitting on a bench (cat. 53) in Pedro Almodóvar's *Volver* (2006), or Wylie's two versions of a surreal meeting in a desert at a table with a pink tablecloth, one with a panoramic long shot, the other a close-up from the 2005 film *Syriana*, directed by Stephen Gaghan (cats 55 and 56).

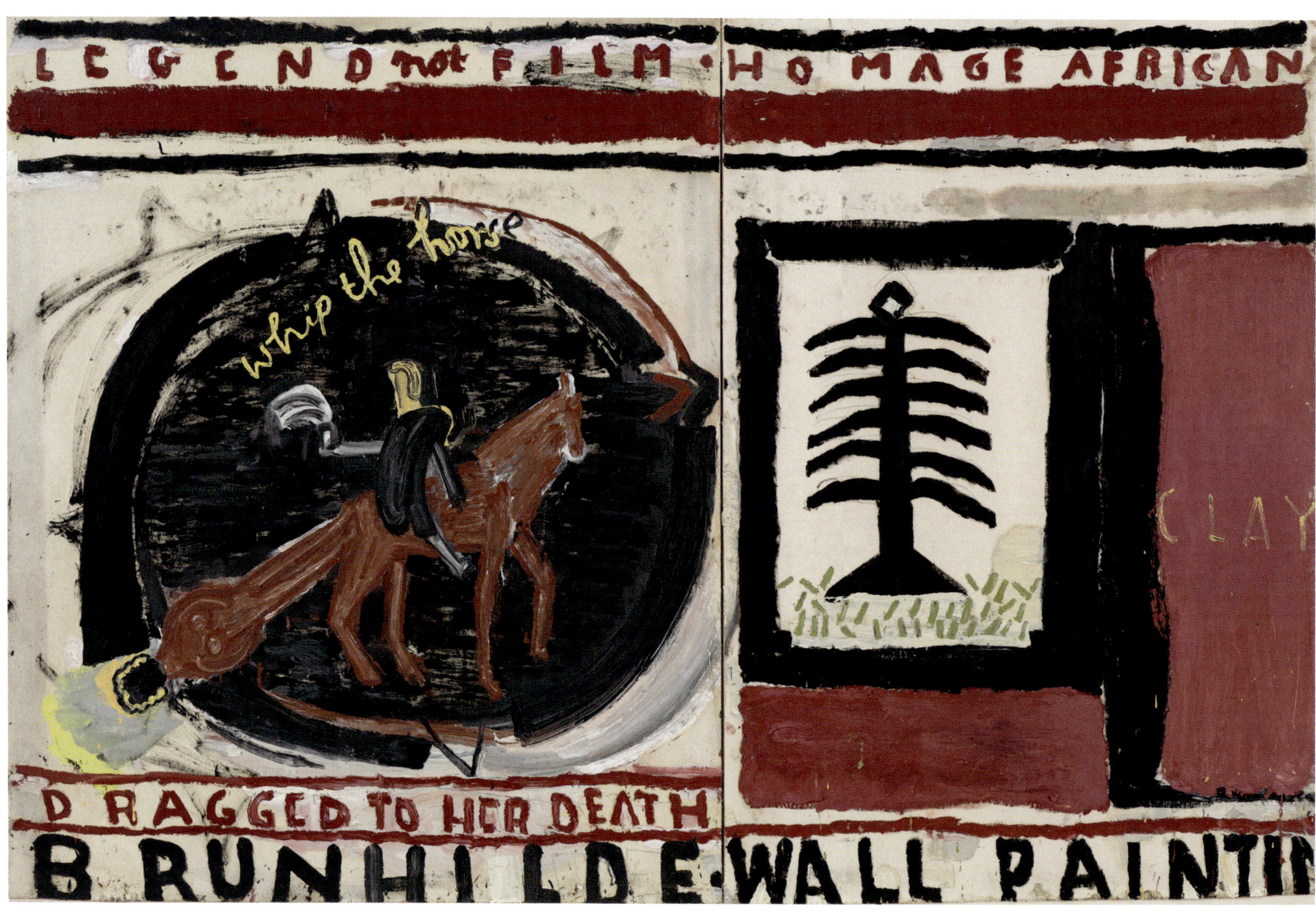

52

Brunhilde
(Film Notes), 2024
Oil on canvas,
184 × 278.5 cm (overall)
Courtesy the artist
and David Zwirner

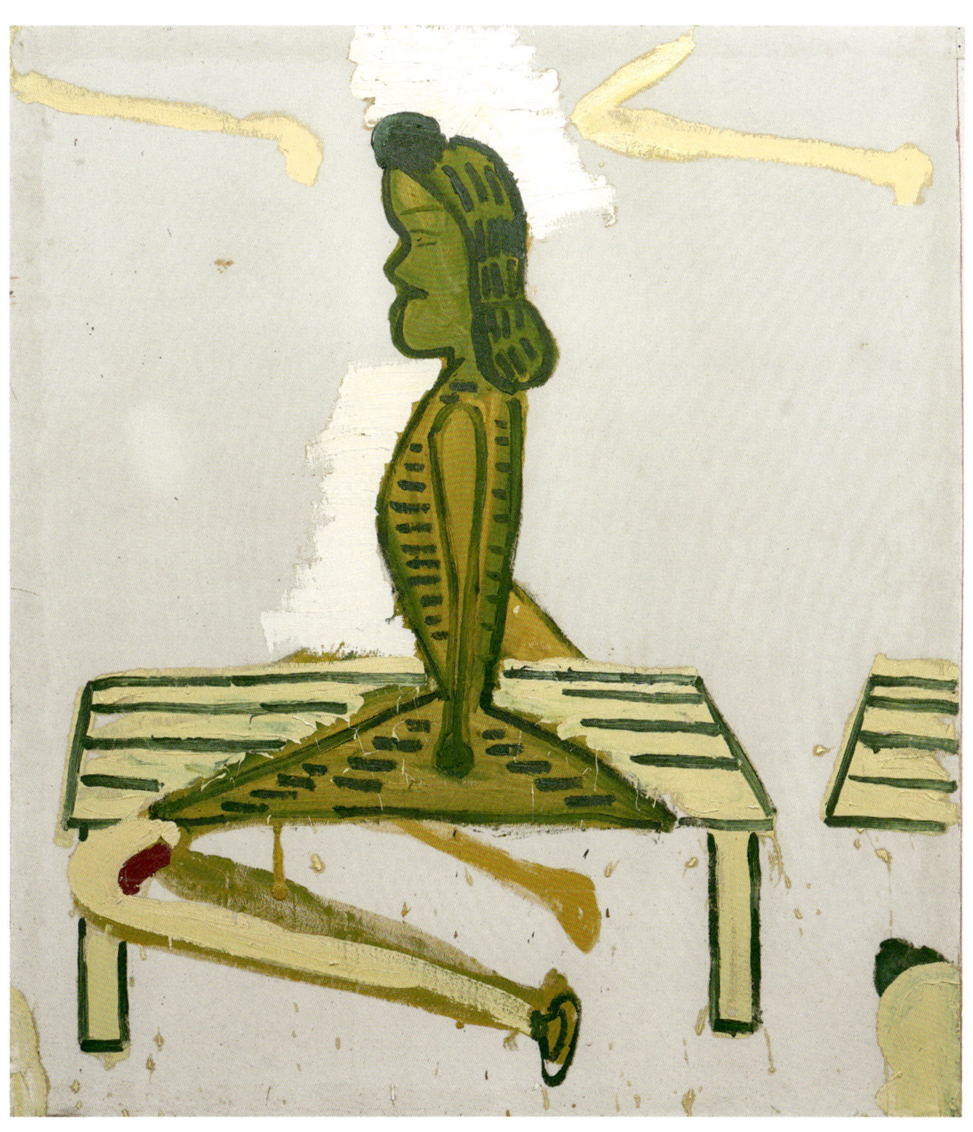

53

Sitting on Bench, Red Shadow, 2007
Oil on canvas,
184.5 × 169.5 cm
Courtesy the artist and David Zwirner

54 *(overleaf)*

Bagdad Café (Film Notes), 2015
Oil on canvas,
182 × 372 cm (overall)
British Council Collection

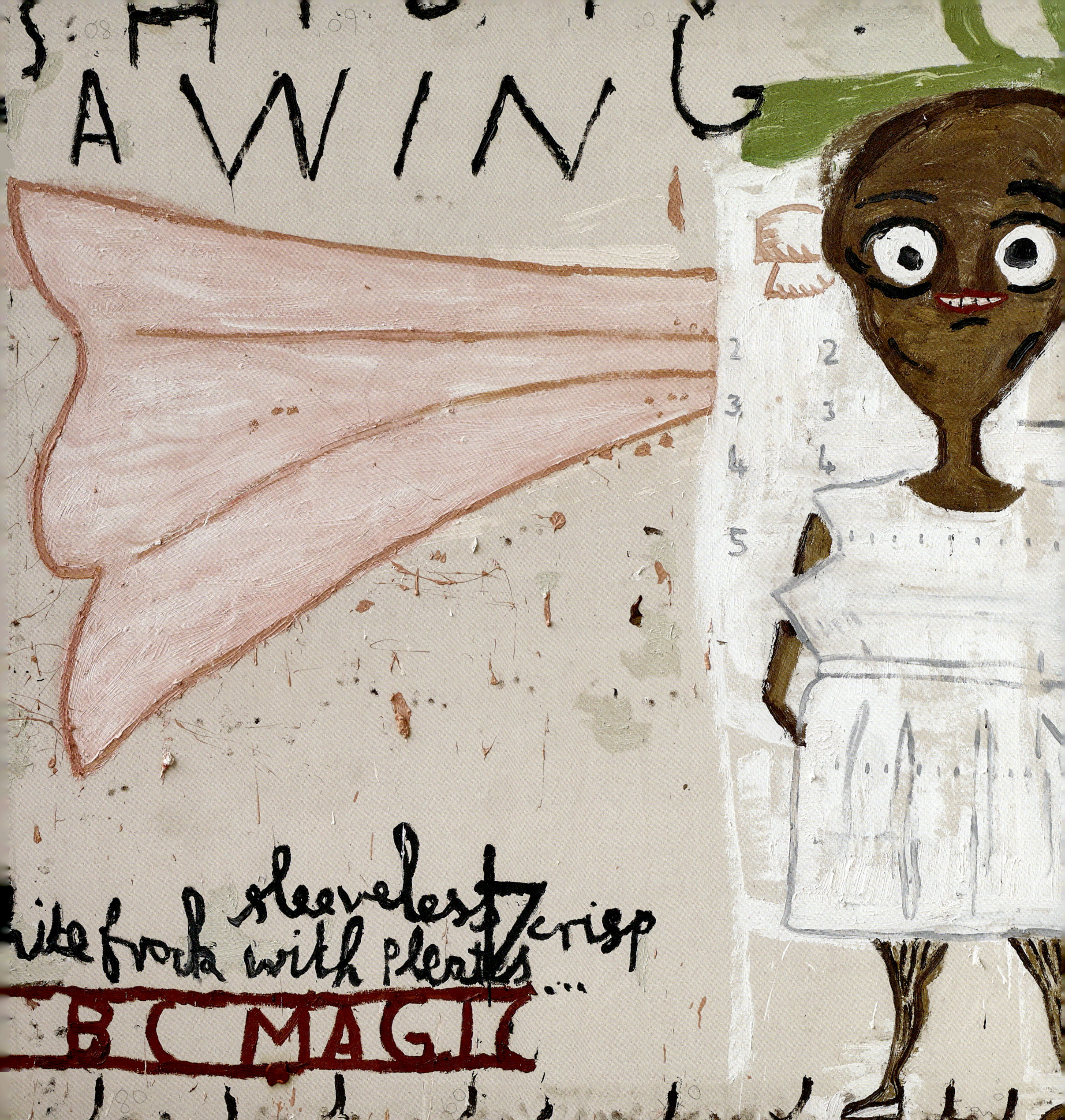

AWING
sleeveless crisp
ite frock with pleats...
B C MAGIC

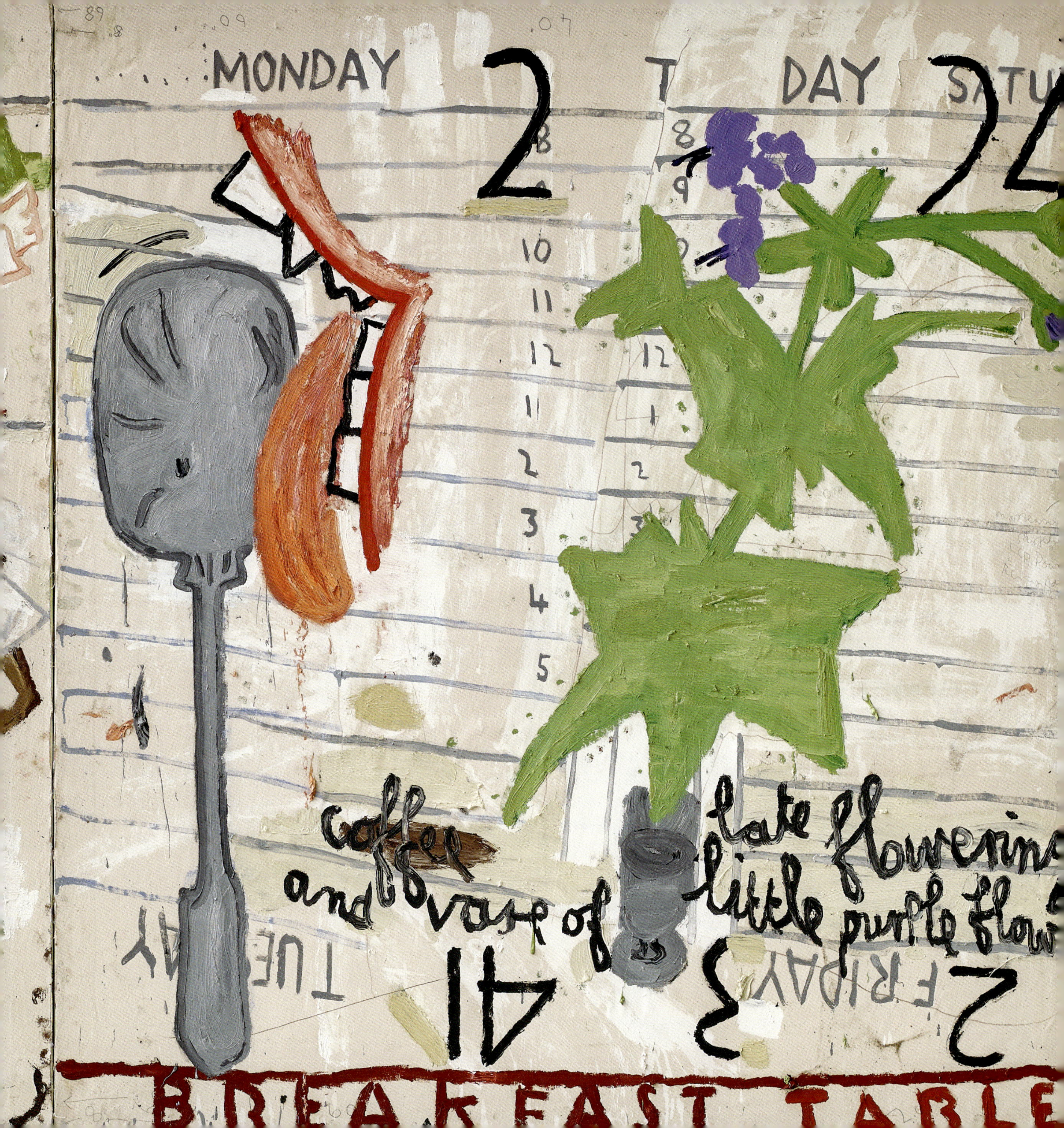

MONDAY 2 DAY SATU

coffee
and vase of late flowerin
little purple flow

BREAKFAST TABLE

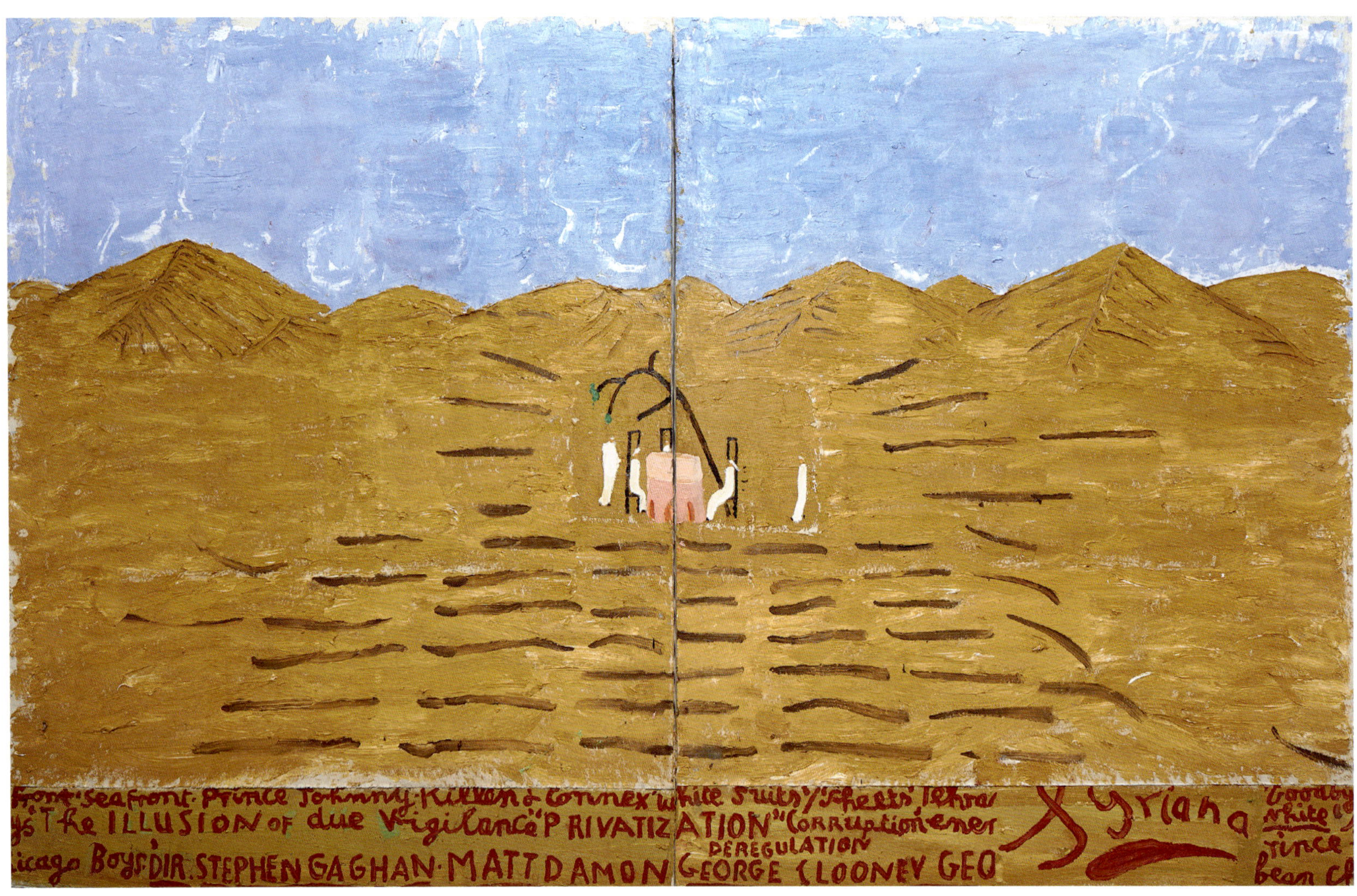

55

Pink Table Cloth (Film Notes), 2013
Oil on canvas,
208 × 330 cm (overall)
Courtesy the artist
and David Zwirner

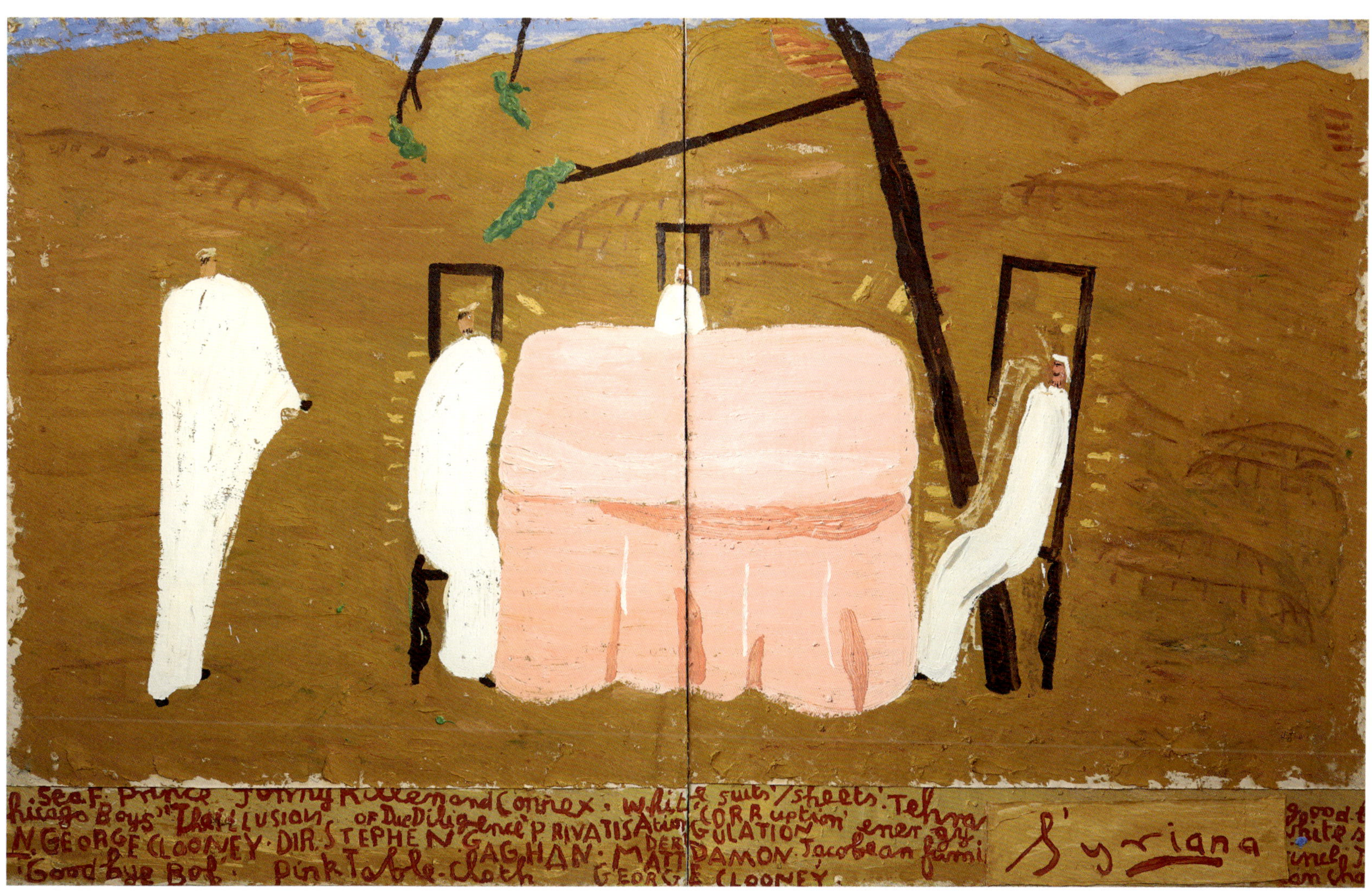

56

Pink Table Cloth, Short Shot (Film Notes), 2013
Oil on canvas,
207 × 303 cm (overall)
Courtesy Jeremy and Kathryn Levison

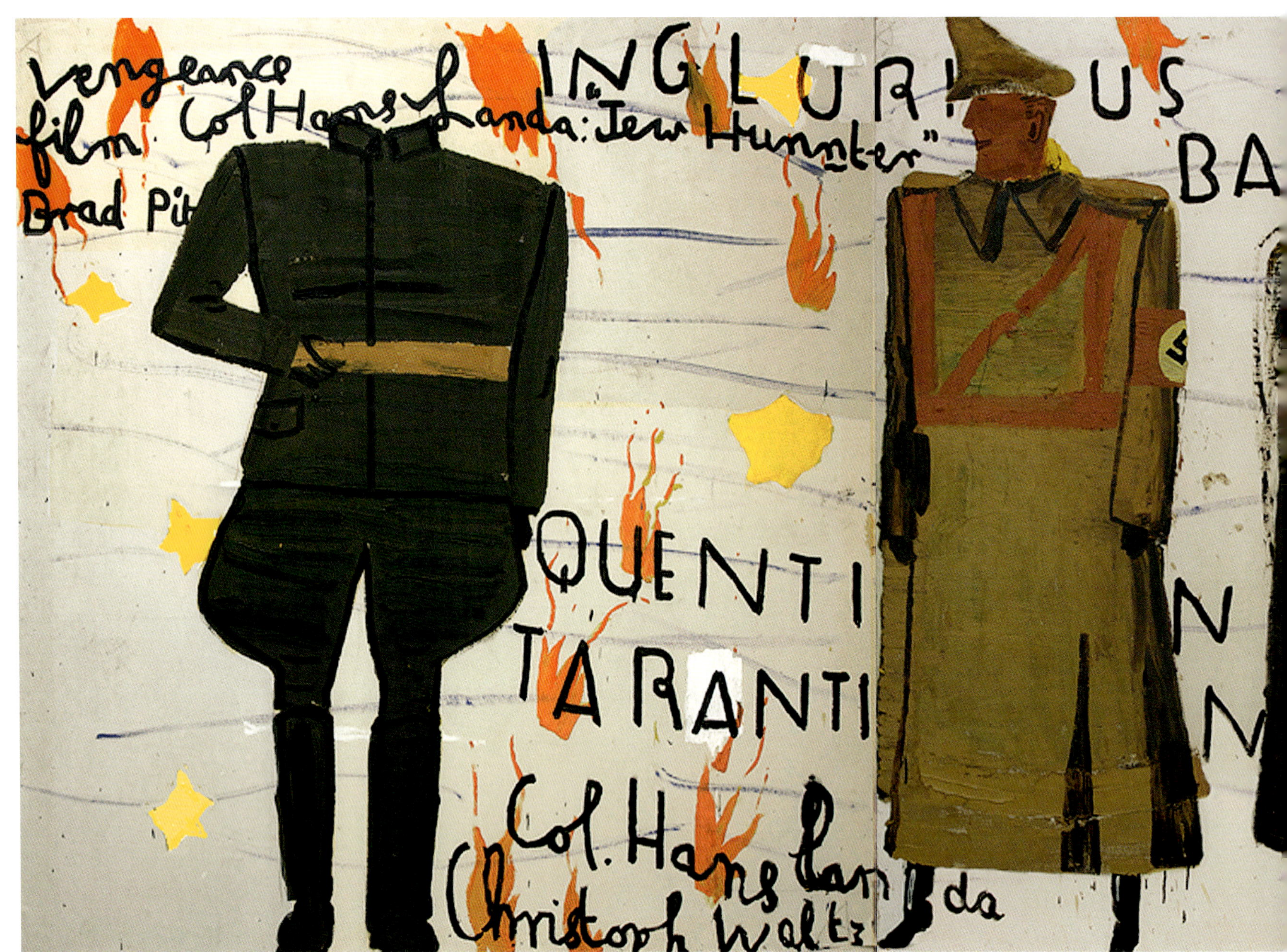

57

Inglourious Basterds (Film Notes), 2010
Oil on canvas,
181 × 338 cm (overall)
Courtesy private collection
and JARILAGER Gallery

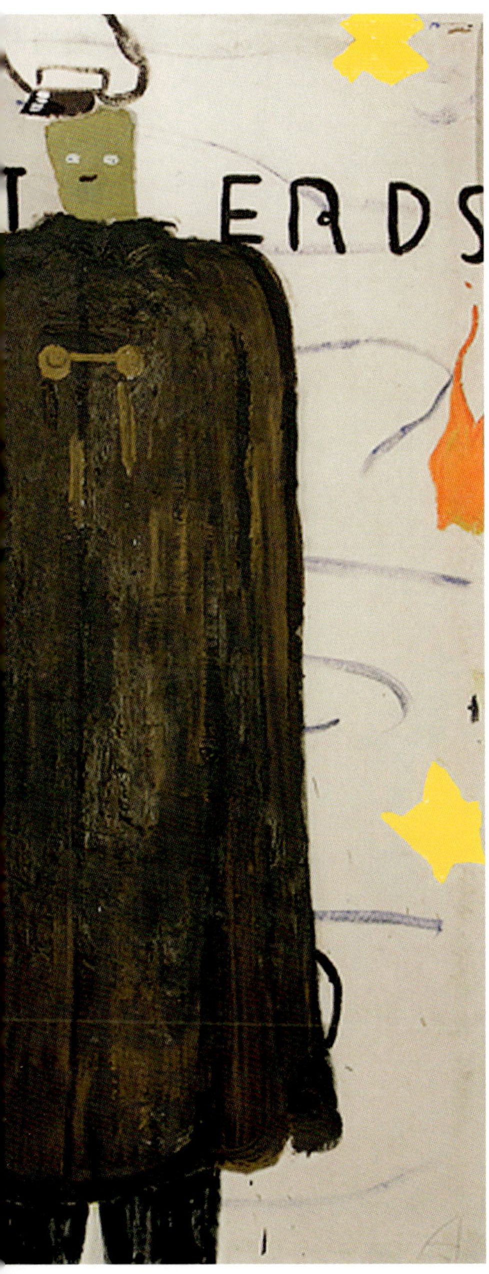

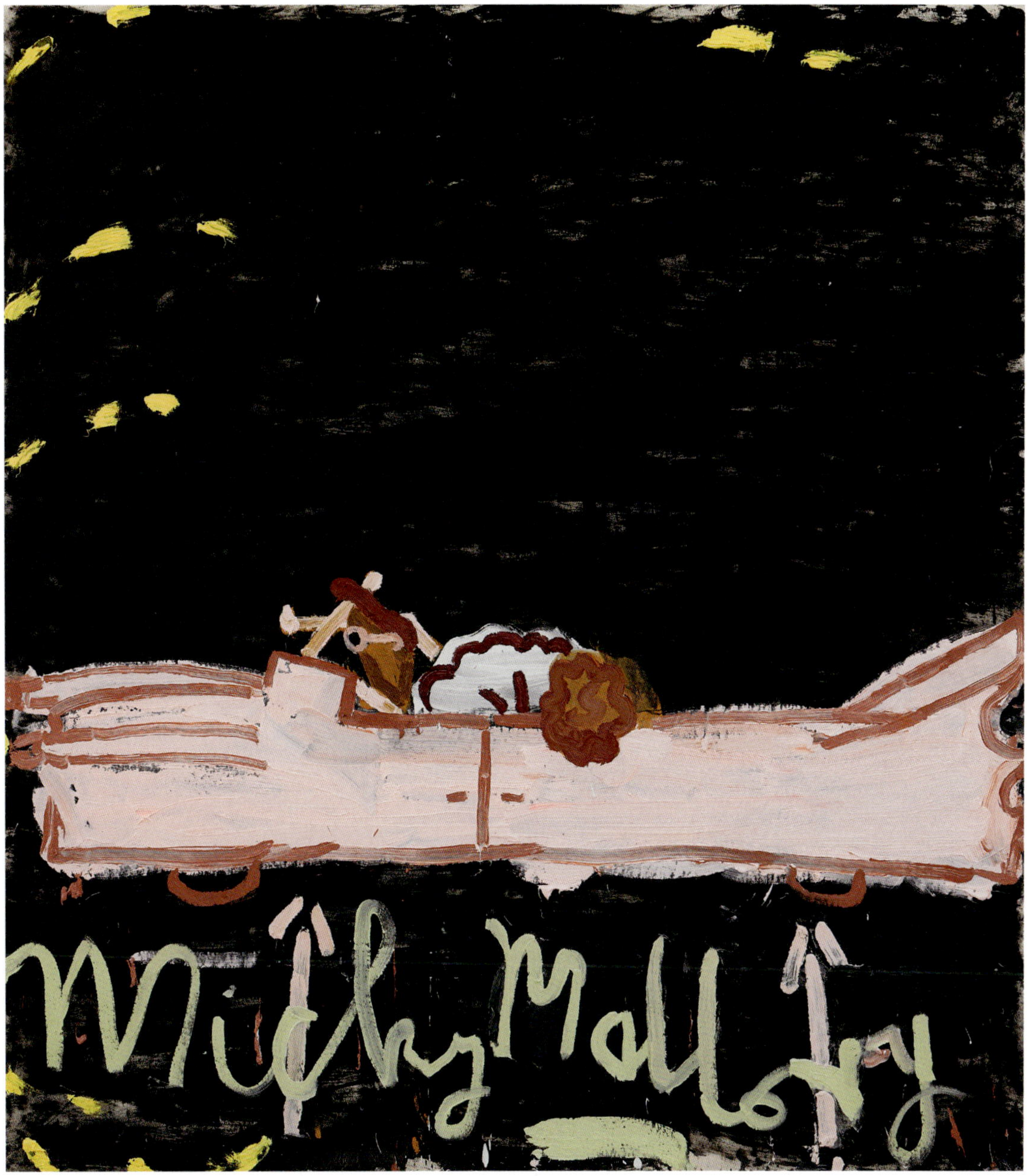

58

Natural Born Killers,
Long Shot (Film Notes),
2018
Oil on canvas,
183 × 165 cm
Courtesy the David and
Indré Roberts Collection

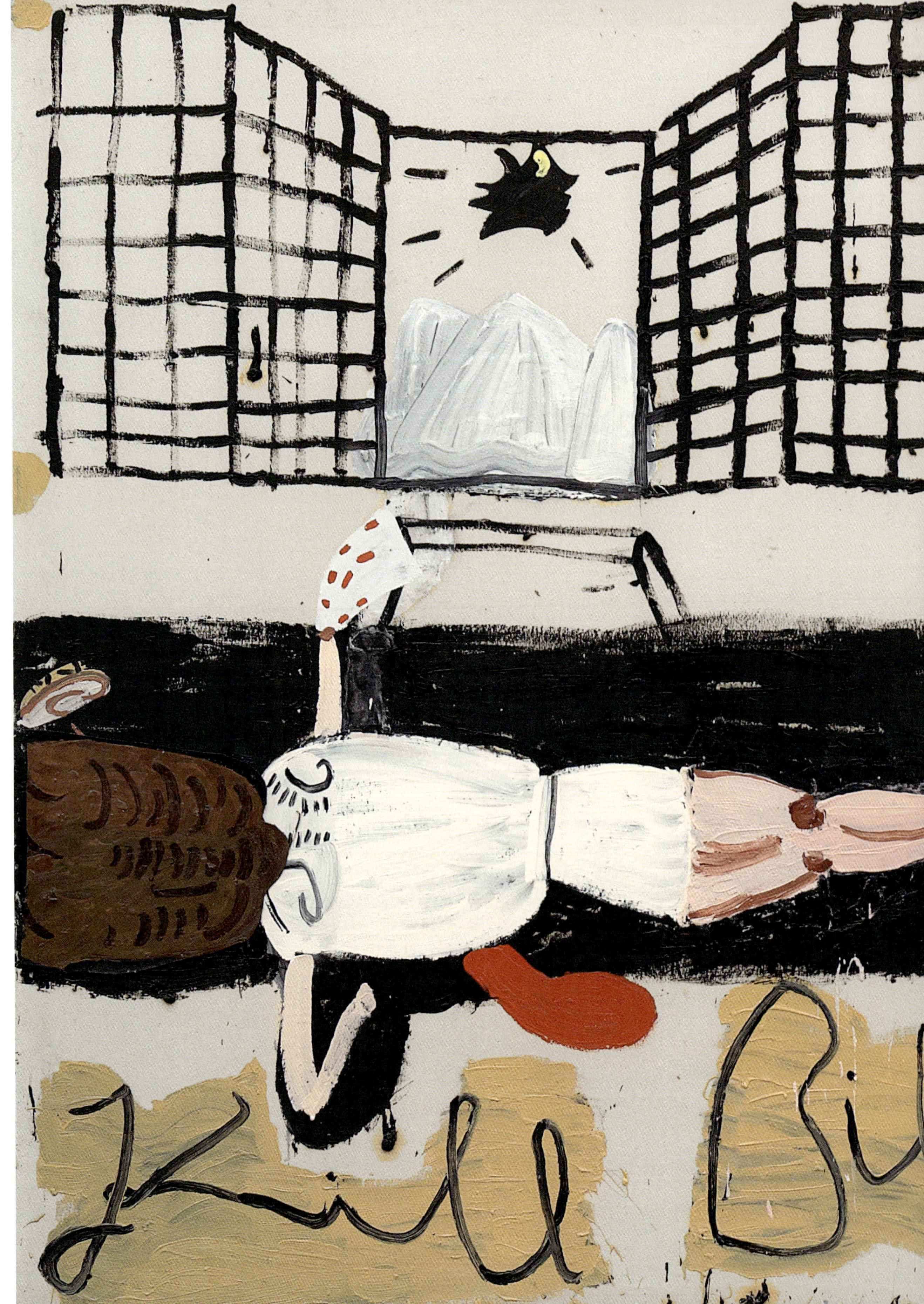

59

Kill Bill (Film Notes), 2007
Oil on canvas,
180 × 308 cm (overall)
Courtesy private collection
and JARILAGER Gallery

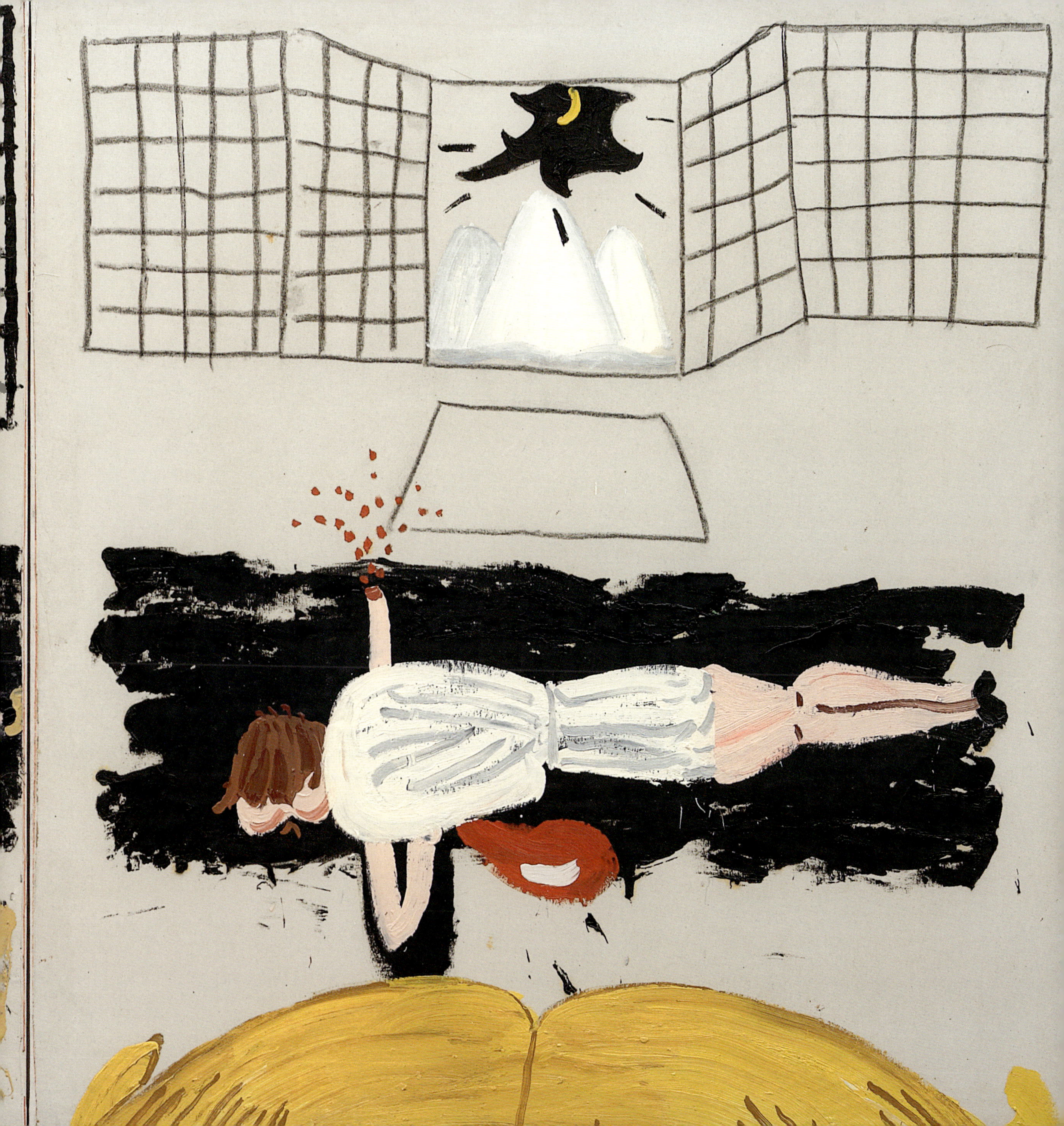

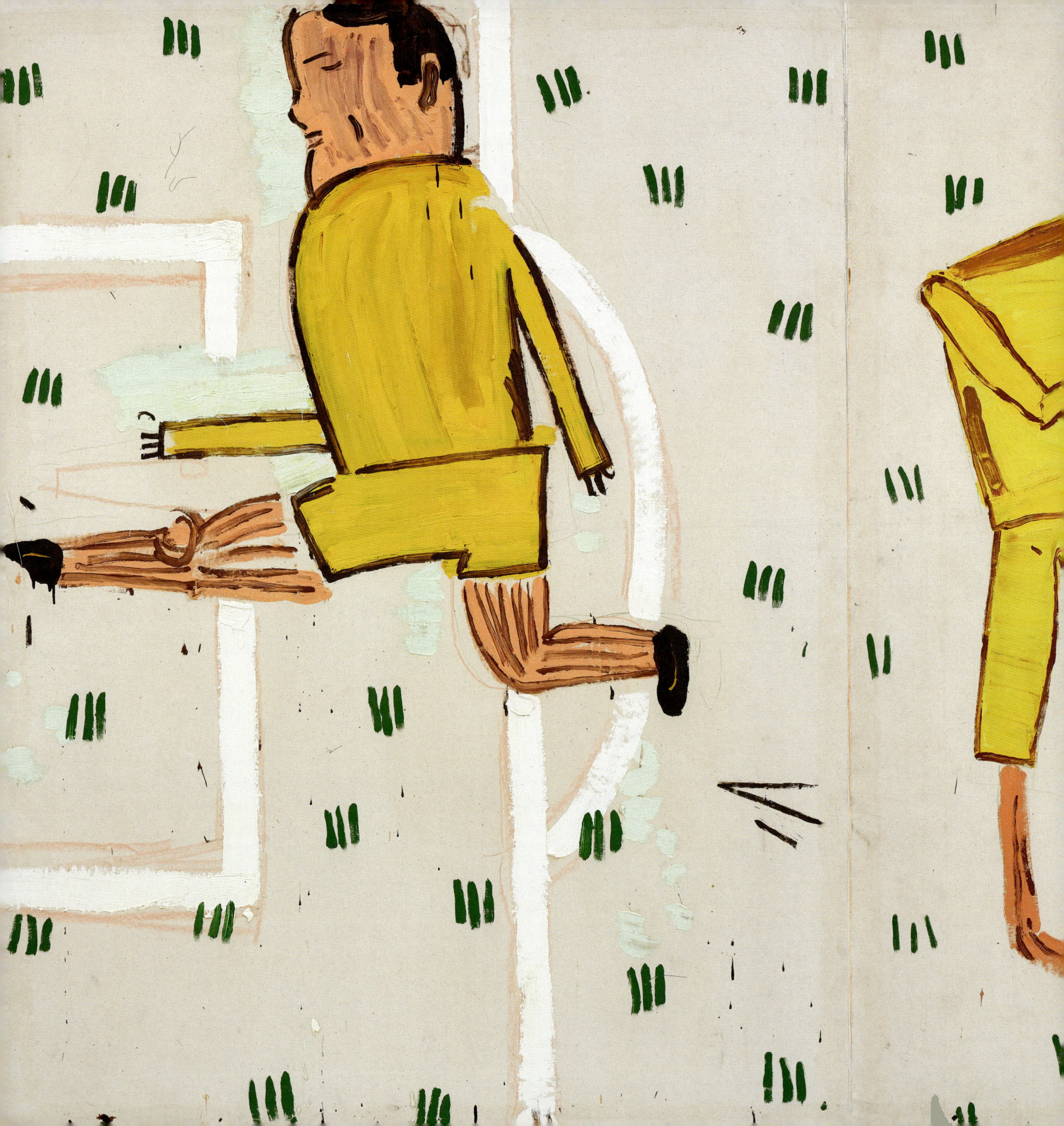

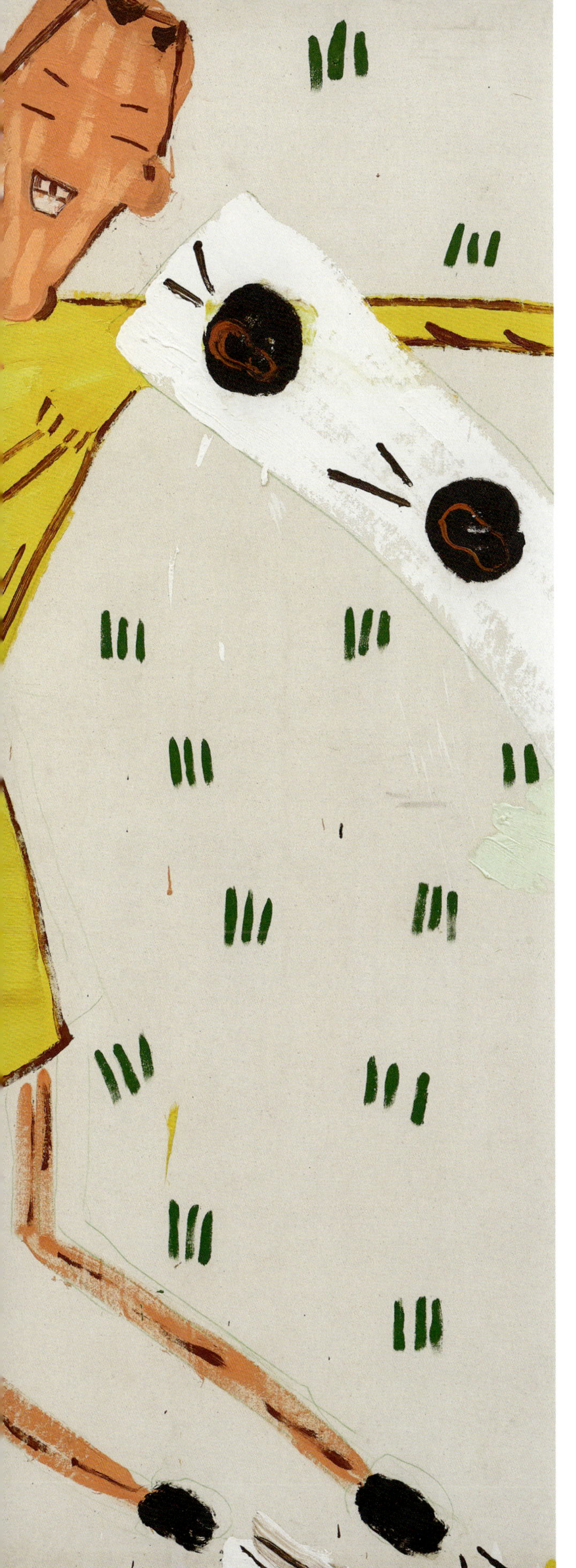

The Mediated Image

'Politics and other issues are often there, if you see it like that – some of my paintings have been called "mediated political". But that is not what they are about. I see a good photo in the paper (or television news) and use it for its visual/formal qualities, not the politics. The politics is why it's in the newspaper.'[5]

Rose Wylie's studio floor is covered with layers of newspaper. They arrive through her door daily and provide her with a source of photographs of individuals in the public eye, actors, politicians, sportsmen and women and reality TV celebrities – whoever is the current obsession of the world's press. Wylie also spends time on the computer, browsing through images that are sometimes sought and sometimes delivered to her; they might range from a Babylonian artefact to an actress on a red carpet. It is the visual impact of these reproduced images that merits Wylie's attention, not who they are, nor the story they tell. The fact that they are often recognisable is useful to Wylie, because it offers an accessible route into the work for the viewer, but ultimately, for the artist, they are just a starting point to be transformed into a drawing or a painting. As an ensemble, they reflect the twenty-first century's consumption of information through the mediated image.

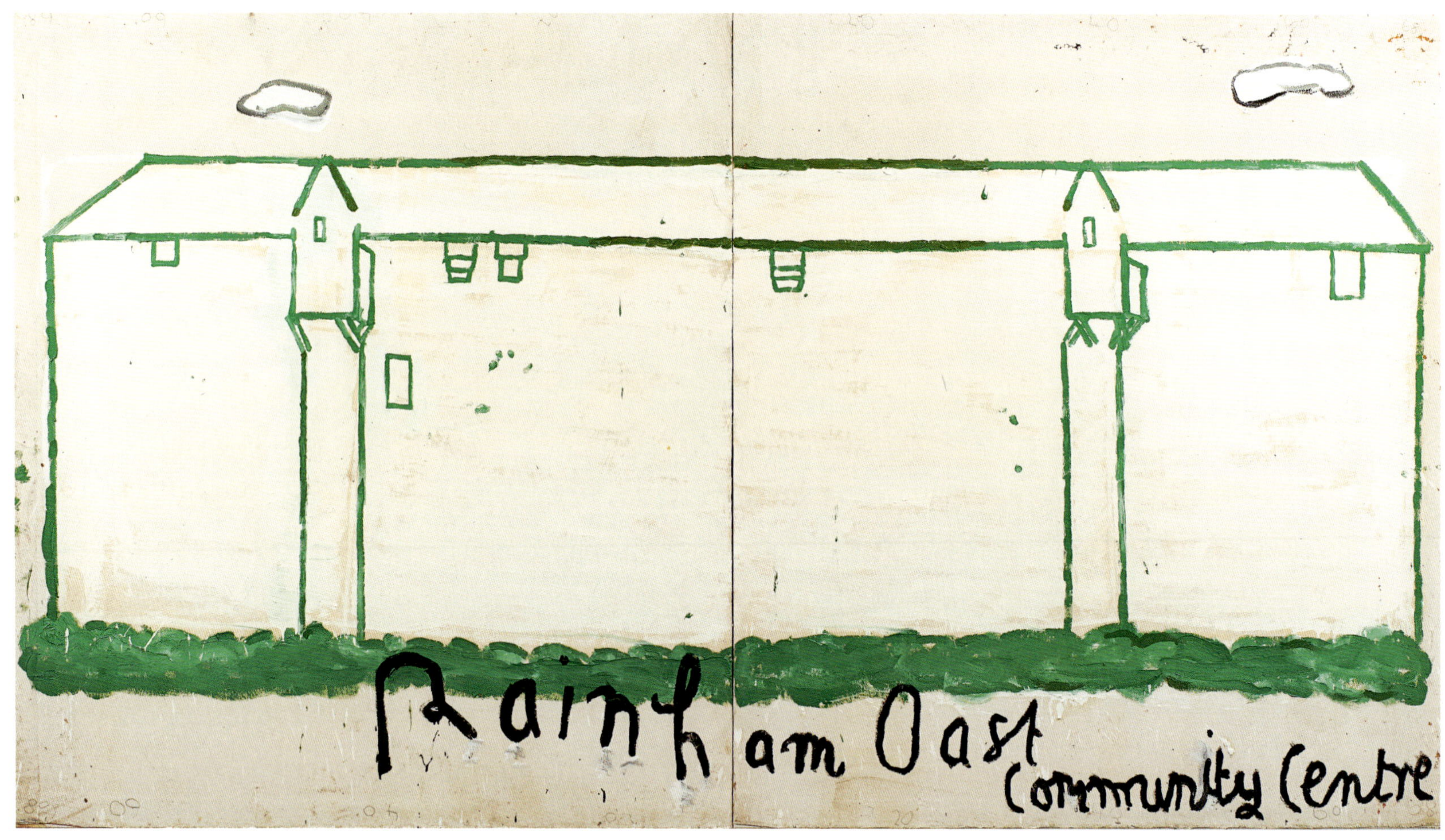

60

Rainham Oast, 2014
Oil on canvas,
184.5 × 332.7 cm (overall)
Courtesy the artist
and David Zwirner

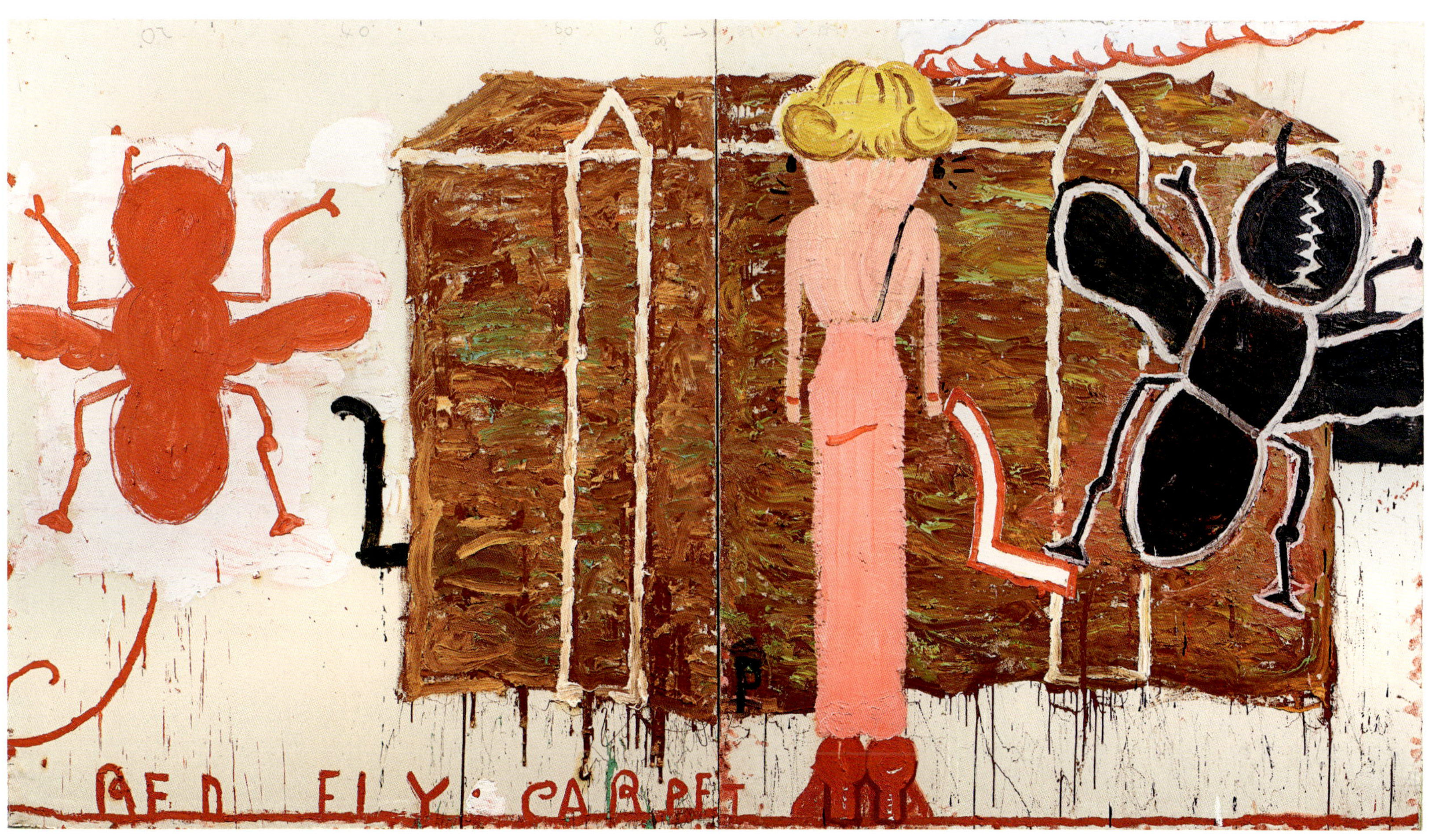

61

Black Strap (Red Fly), 2012
Oil, graphite, marker and
collage on canvas,
184.2 × 331.6 cm (overall)
Courtesy Charlotte and Philip Colbert

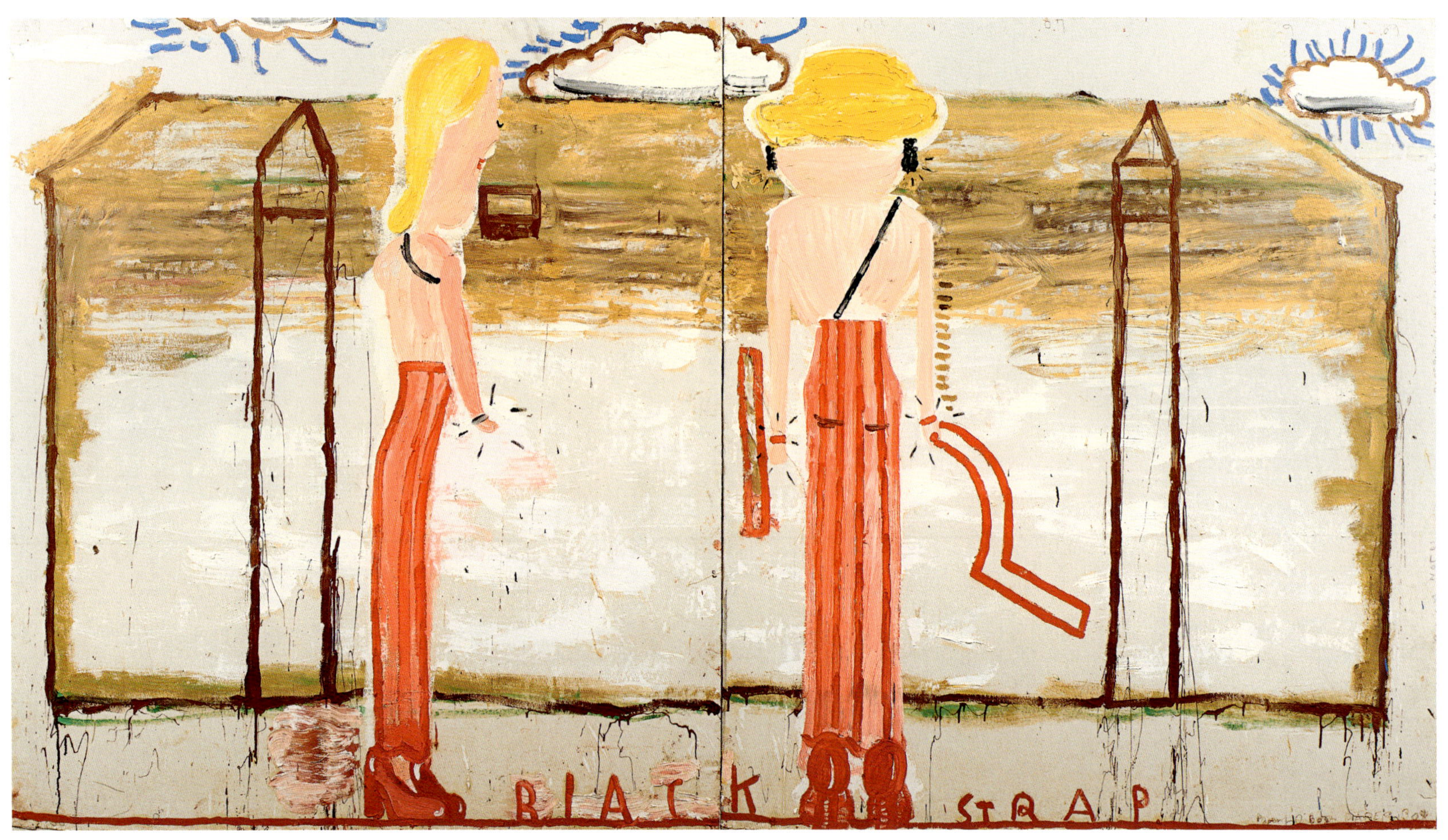

62

Black Strap (Eyelashes), 2014
Oil on canvas,
184.5 × 331 cm (overall)
Courtesy the artist
and David Zwirner

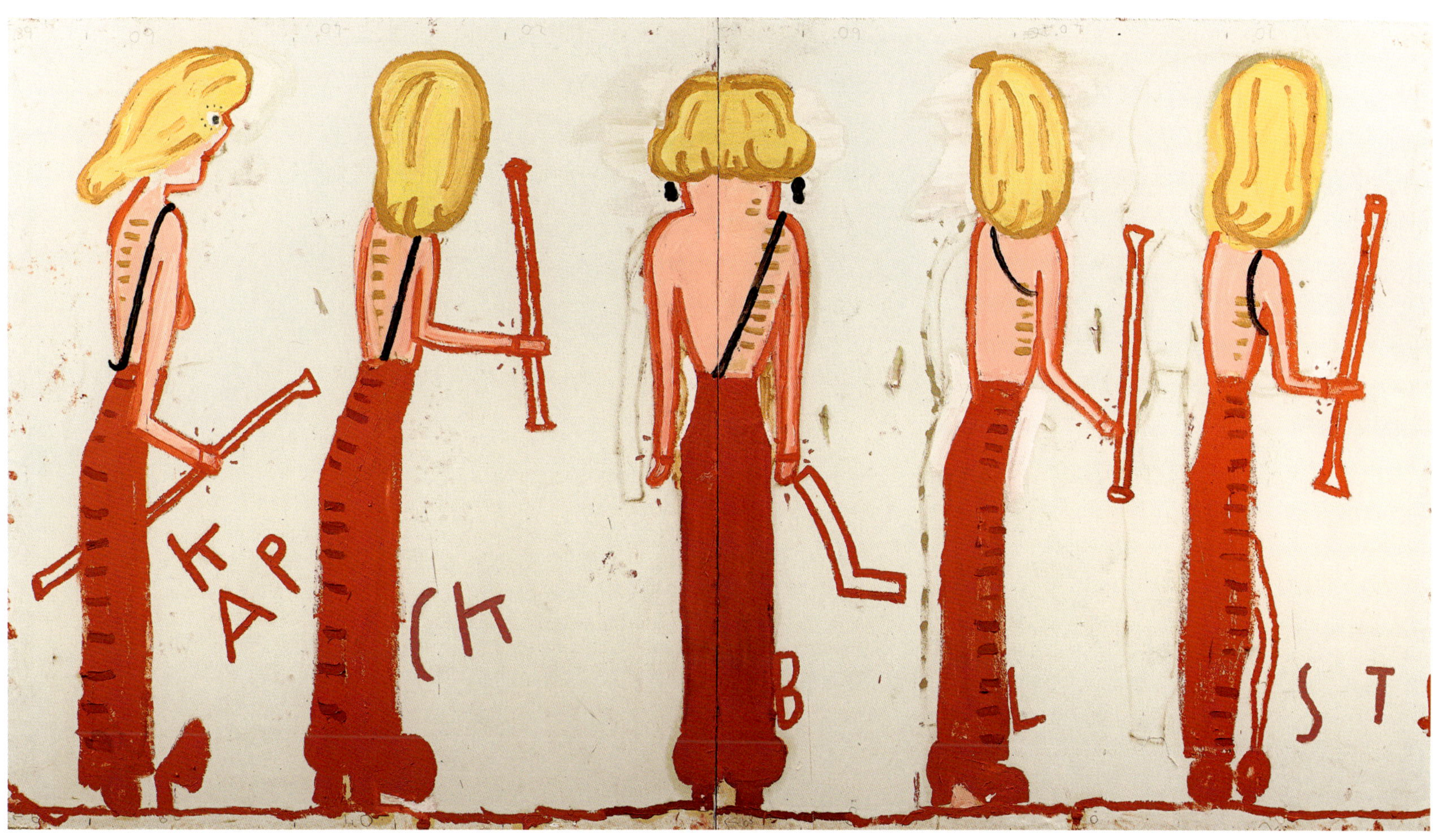

63

NK (Syracuse Line-up), 2014
Oil on canvas,
185 × 333 cm (overall)
Courtesy private collection,
CHOI&CHOI Gallery
and JARILAGER Gallery

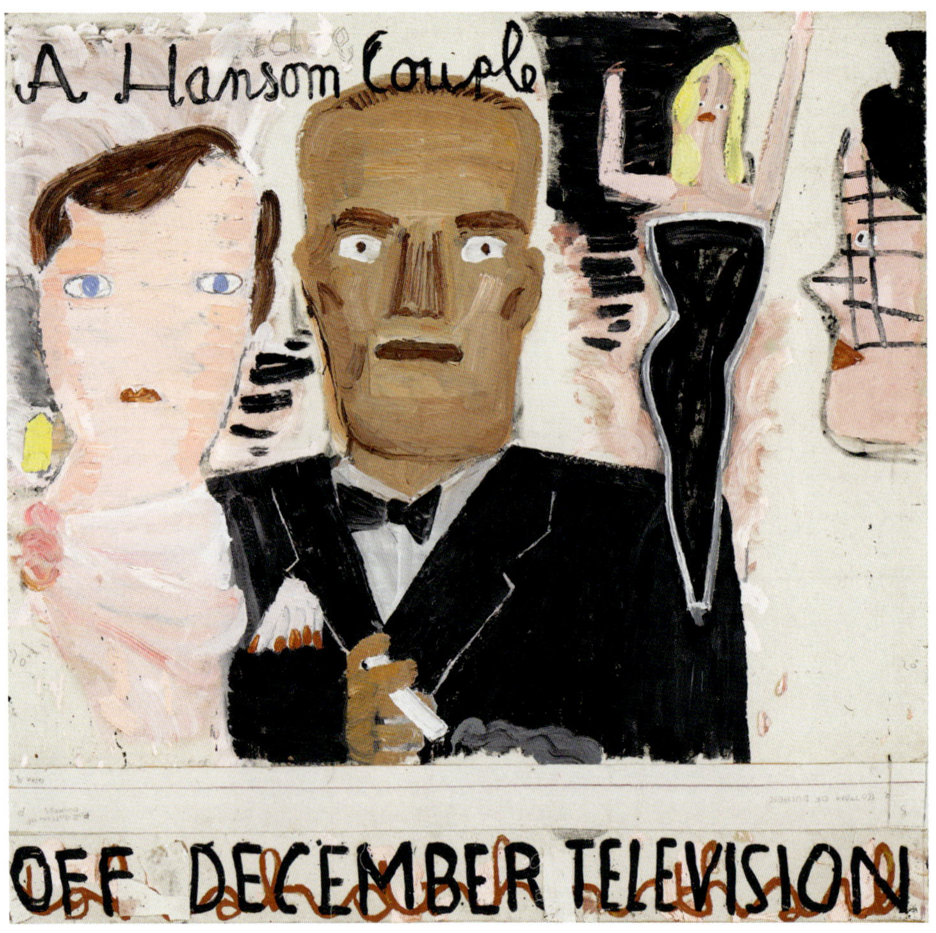

64

A Handsome Couple, 2022
Oil on canvas,
174.5 × 183.5 cm
Courtesy Edwin Oostmeijer

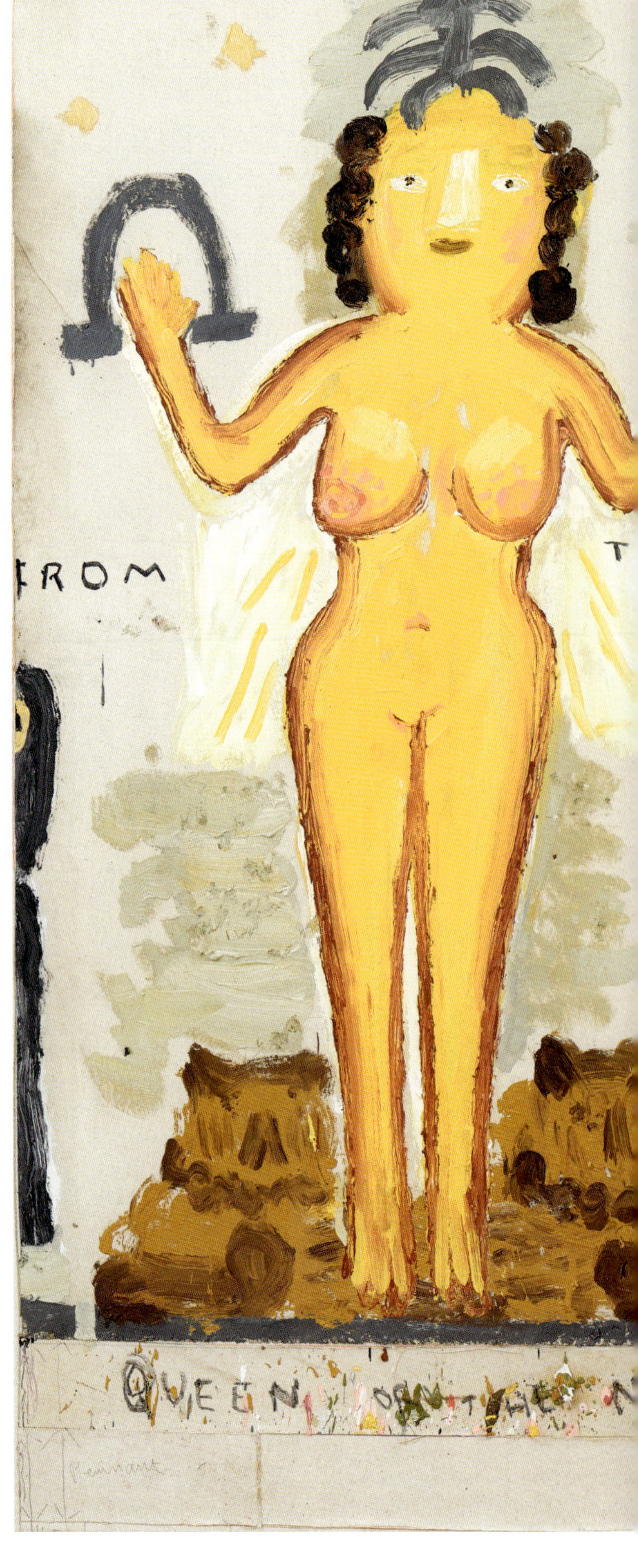

65

Lilith and Gucci Boy, 2024
Oil on canvas,
207 × 306 cm (overall)
Courtesy the artist and
David Zwirner

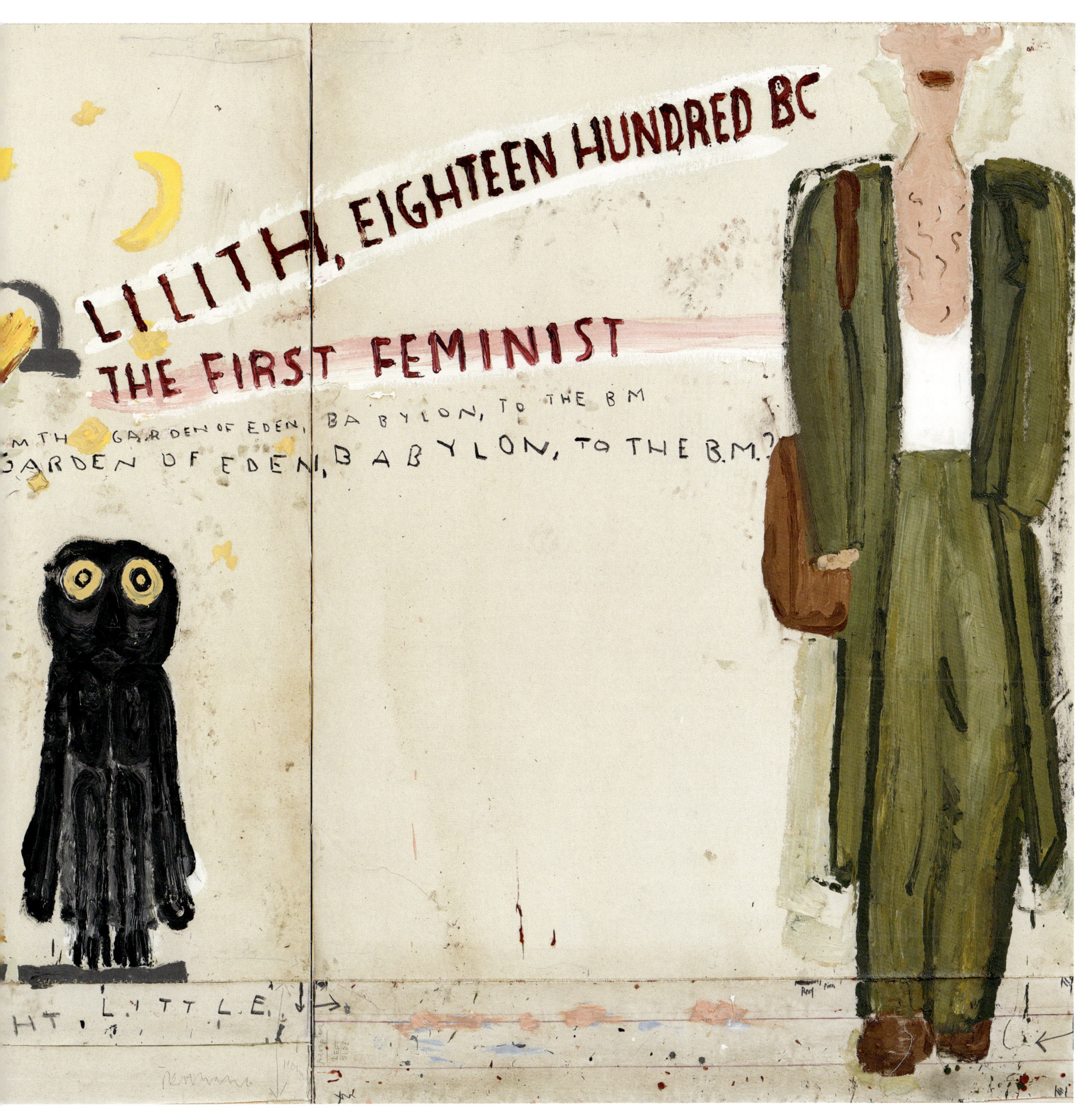
LILITH, EIGHTEEN HUNDRED BC
THE FIRST FEMINIST
GARDEN OF EDEN, BABYLON, TO THE BM
GARDEN OF EDEN, BABYLON, TO THE B.M.?
LITTLE

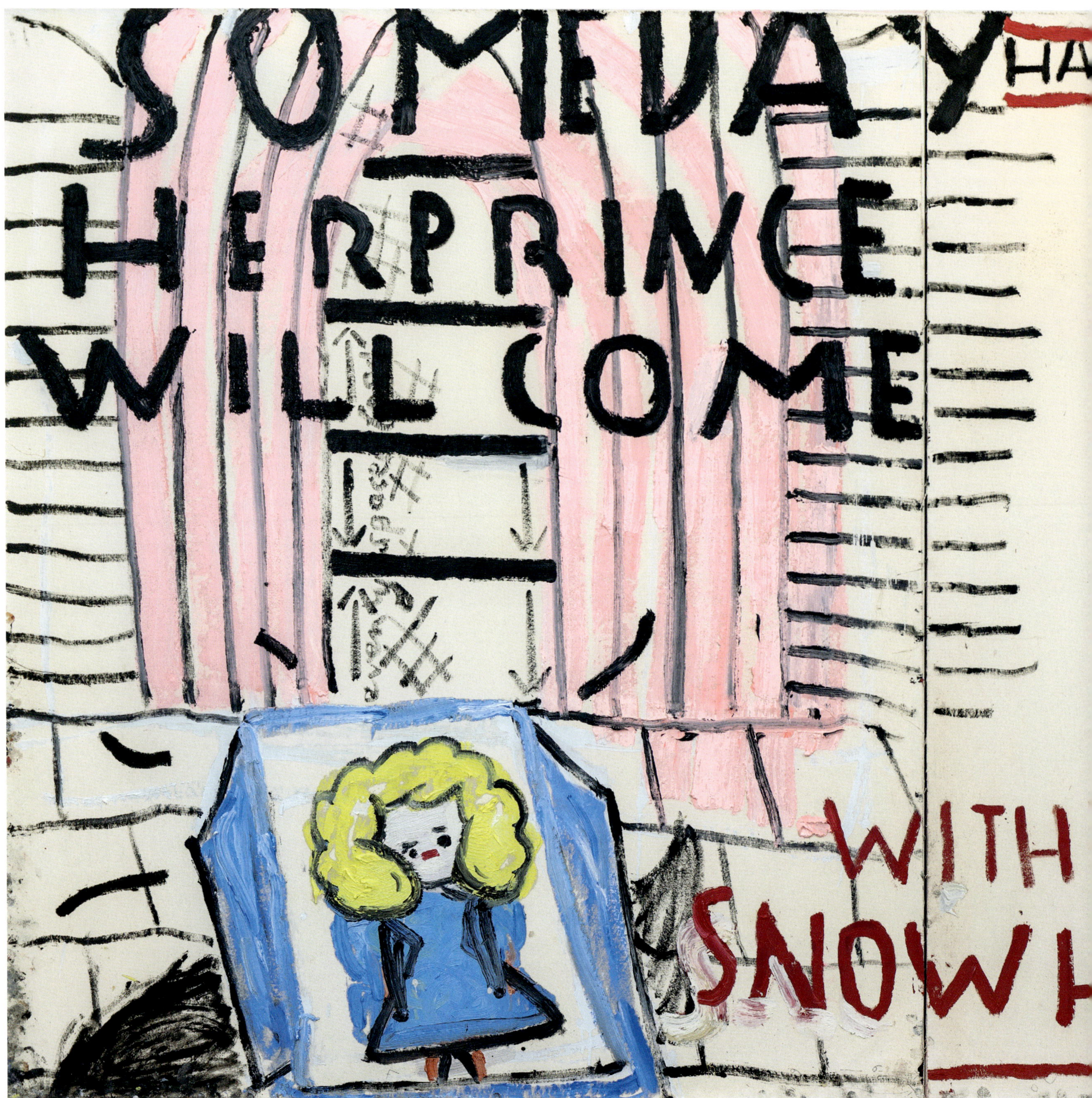
SOMEDAY
HERPRINCE
WILL COME
HA
WITH
SNOW

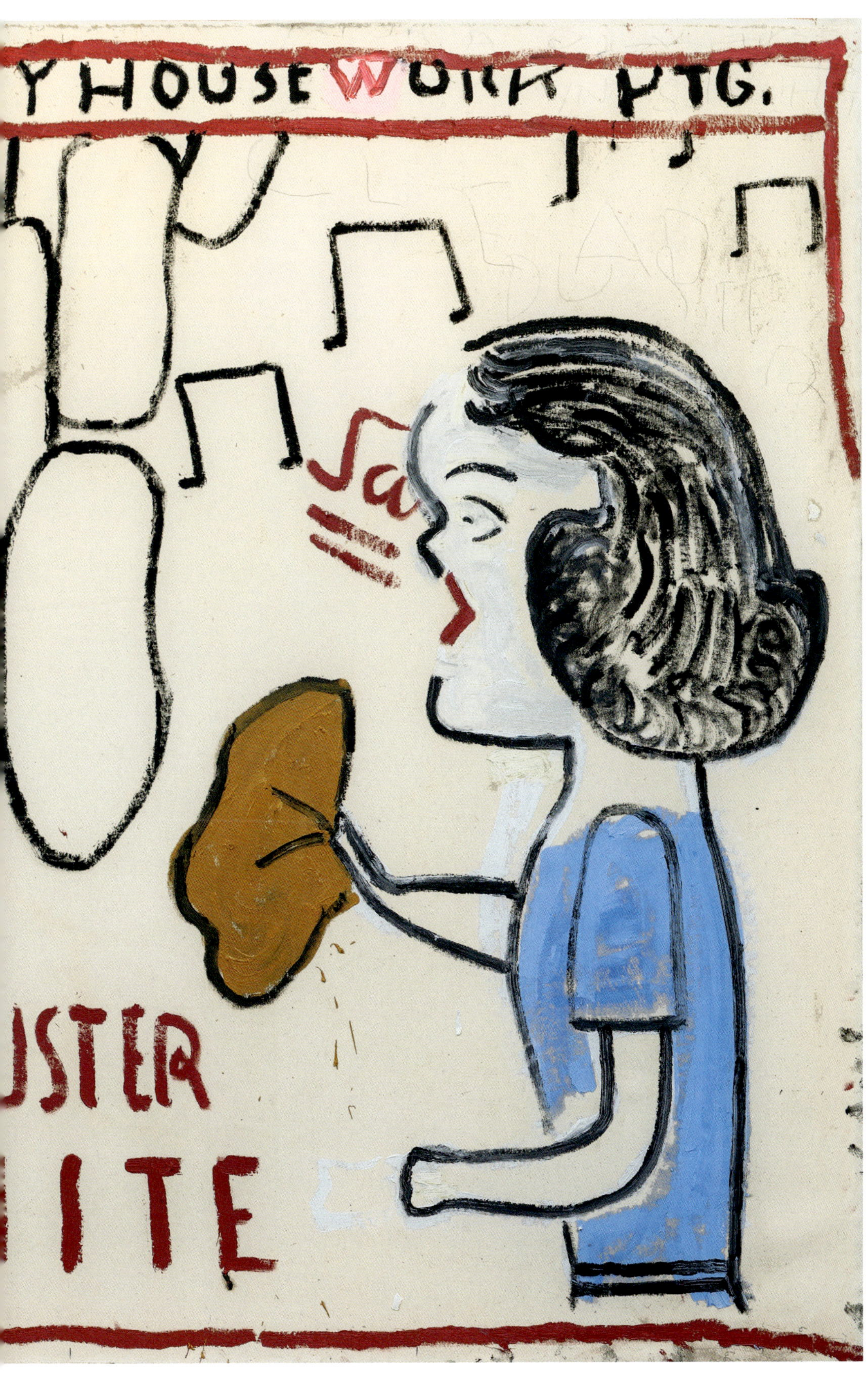

66

Snowwhite (3)
with Duster, 2018
Oil on canvas,
183.5 × 320 cm (overall)
Private collection

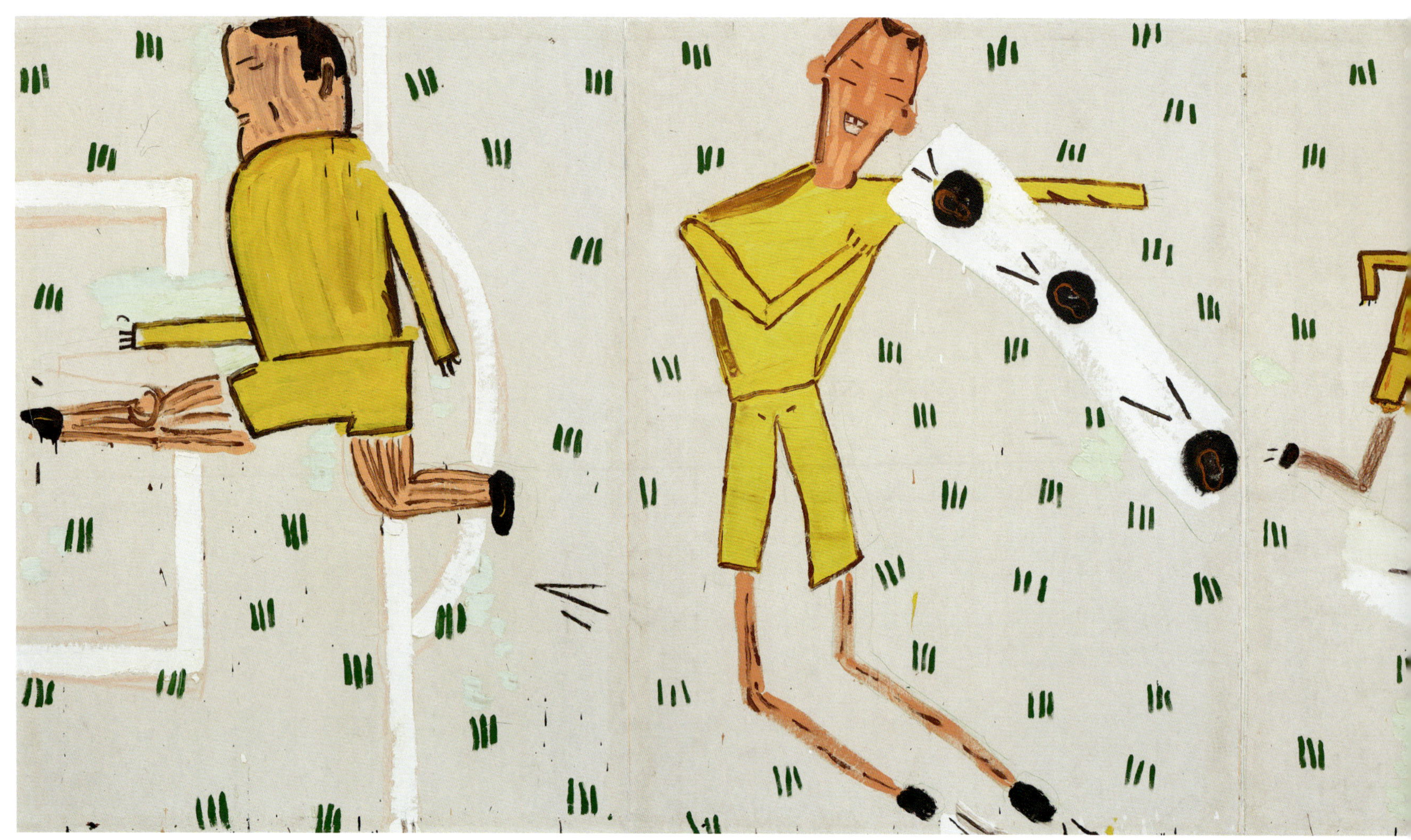

67

Yellow Strip, 2006
Oil on canvas,
186 × 670.7 cm (overall)
Courtesy the artist
and David Zwirner

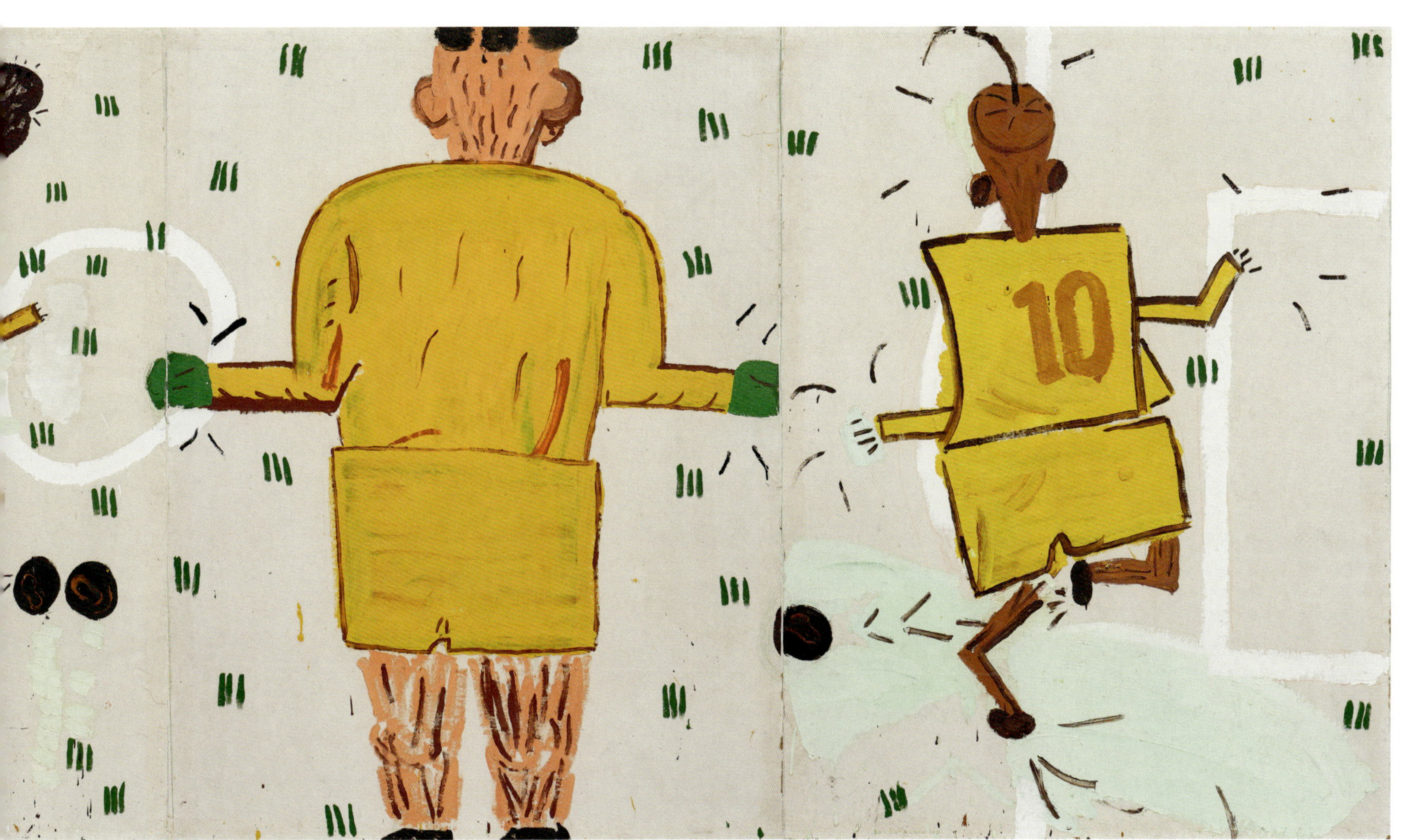
10

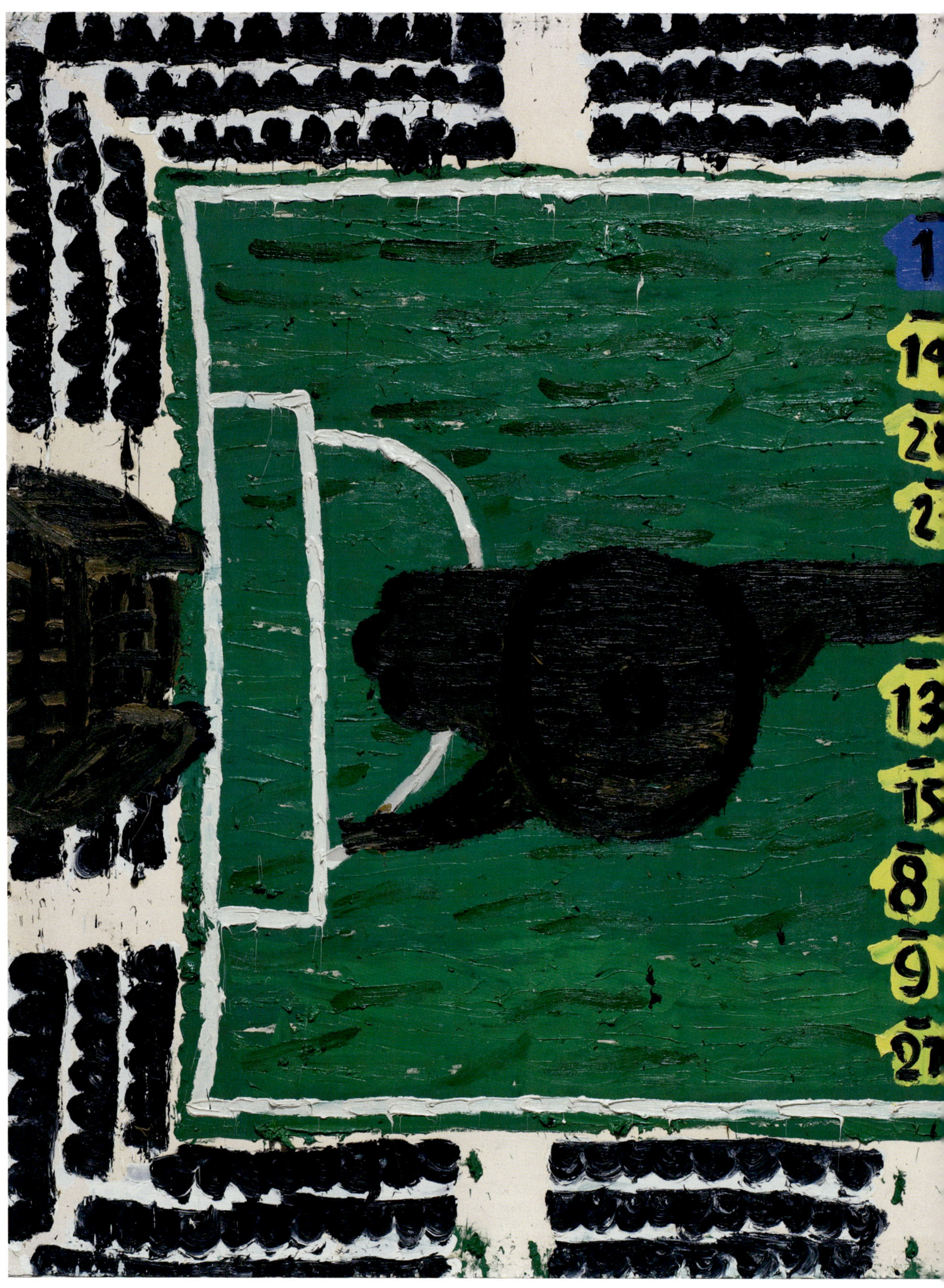

68

Arsenal & Spurs, 2006
Oil on canvas,
165 × 366 cm (overall)
Courtesy the artist
and David Zwirner

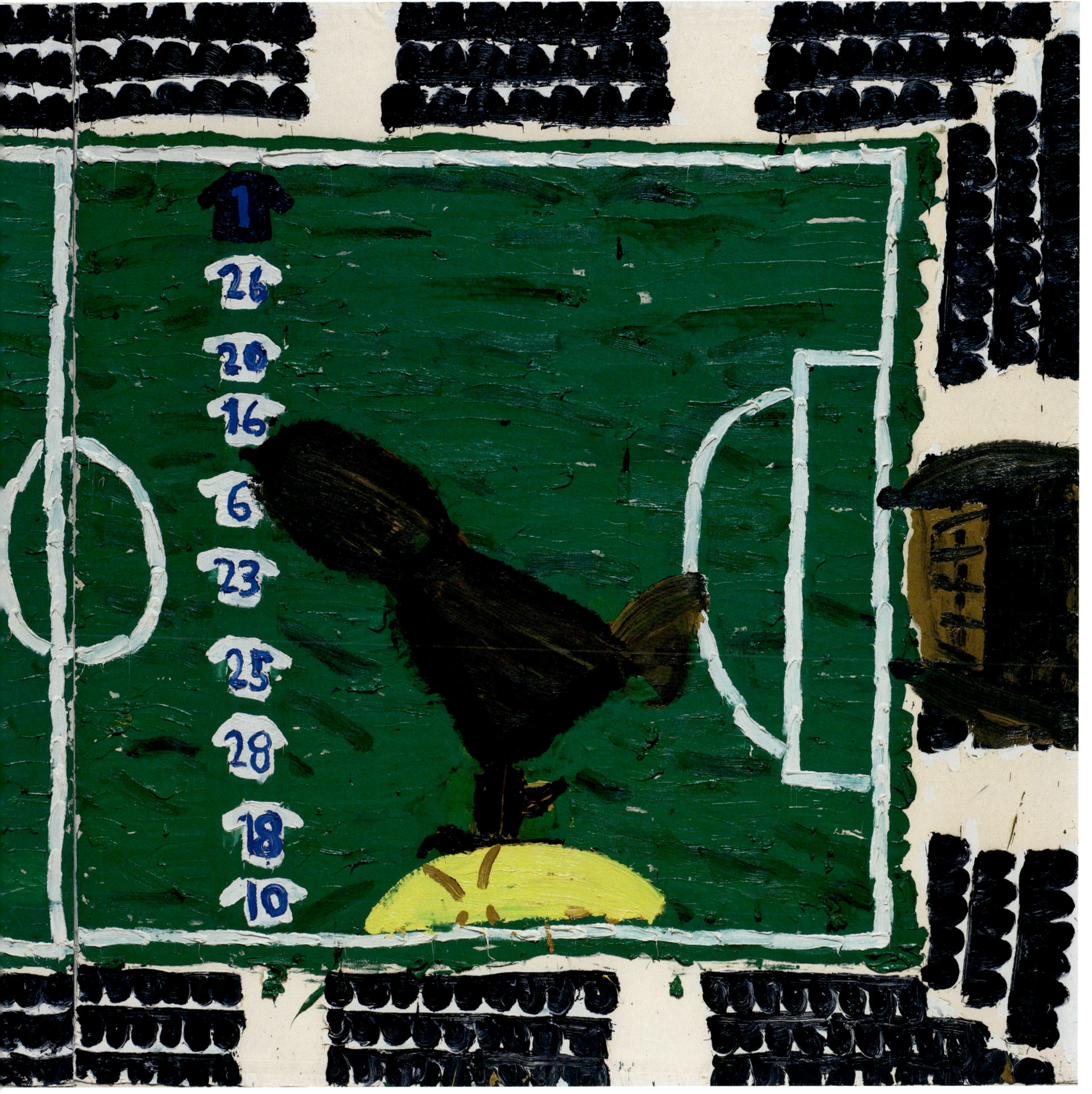

1
26
20
16
6
23
25
28
18
10

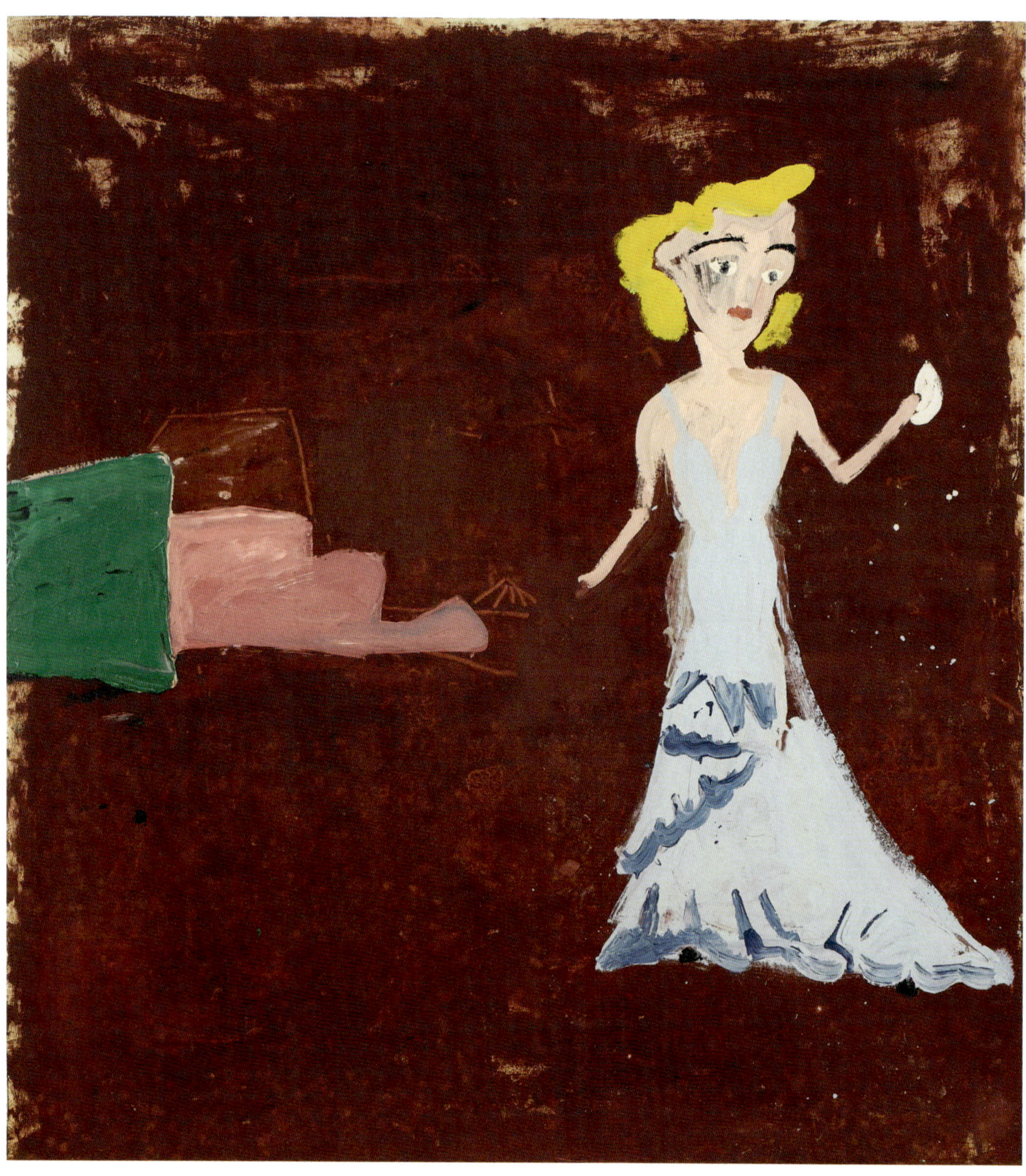

69

Girl on Liner, 1996
Oil on canvas,
183 × 163 cm
Arts Council Collection,
Southbank Centre, London

70

Pin-up and Porn Queen Jigsaw, 2005
Oil on canvas,
366 × 366 cm (overall)
Tate: Presented by
Tate Members 2013

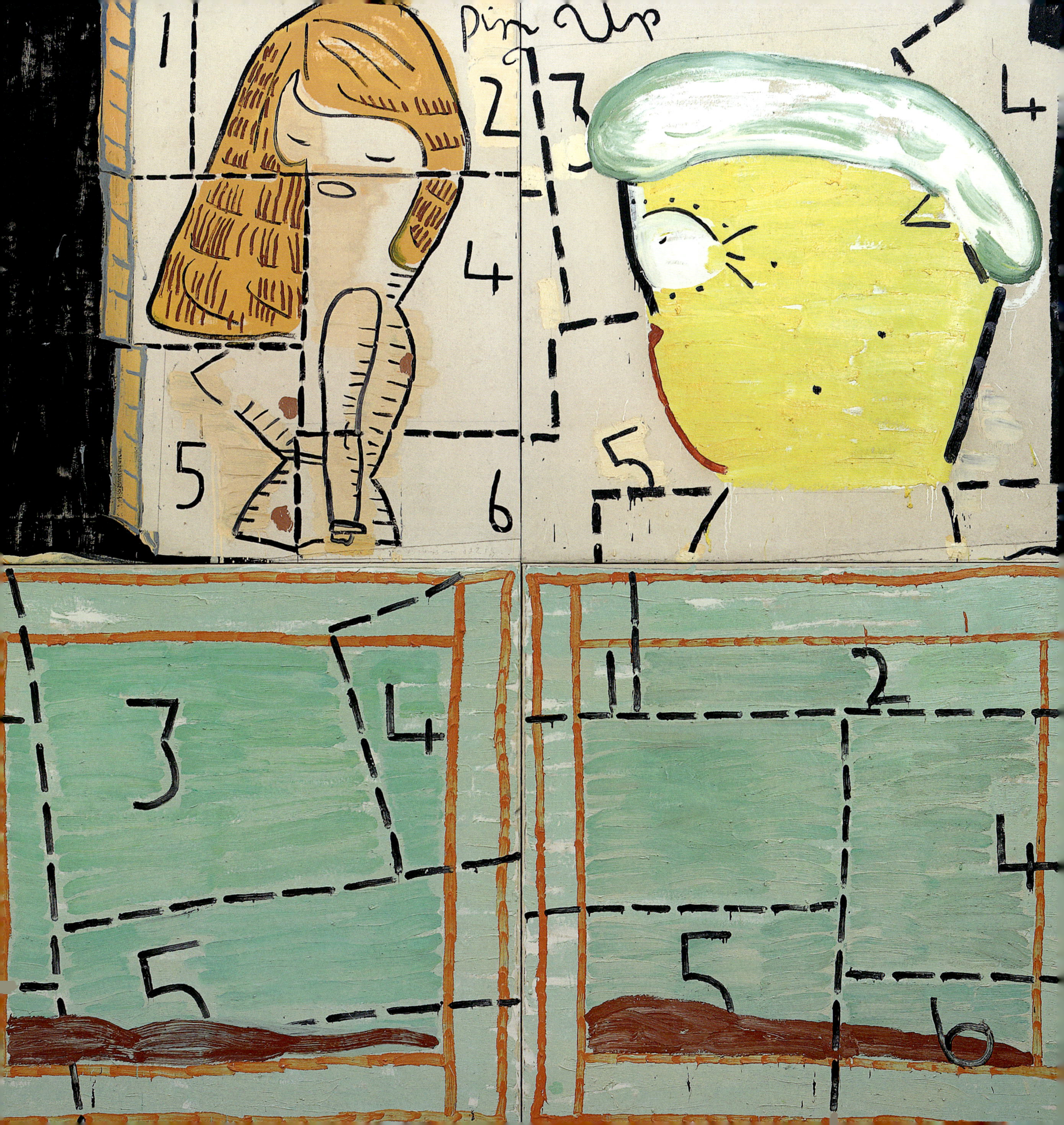
Pin Up

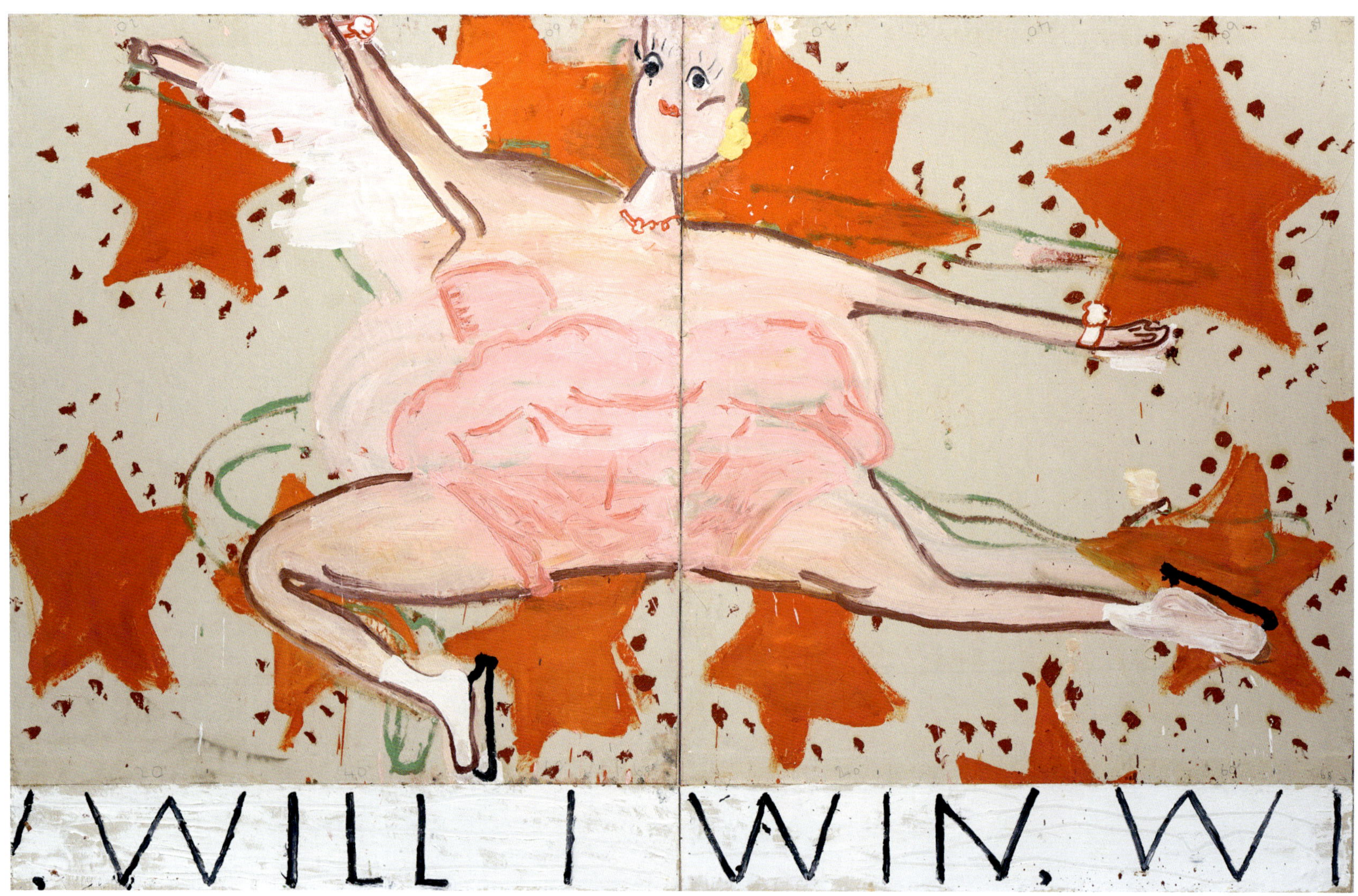

71

Pink Skater (Will I Win, Will I Win), 2015
Oil on canvas,
208 × 329 cm (overall)
Courtesy private collection
and JARILAGER Gallery

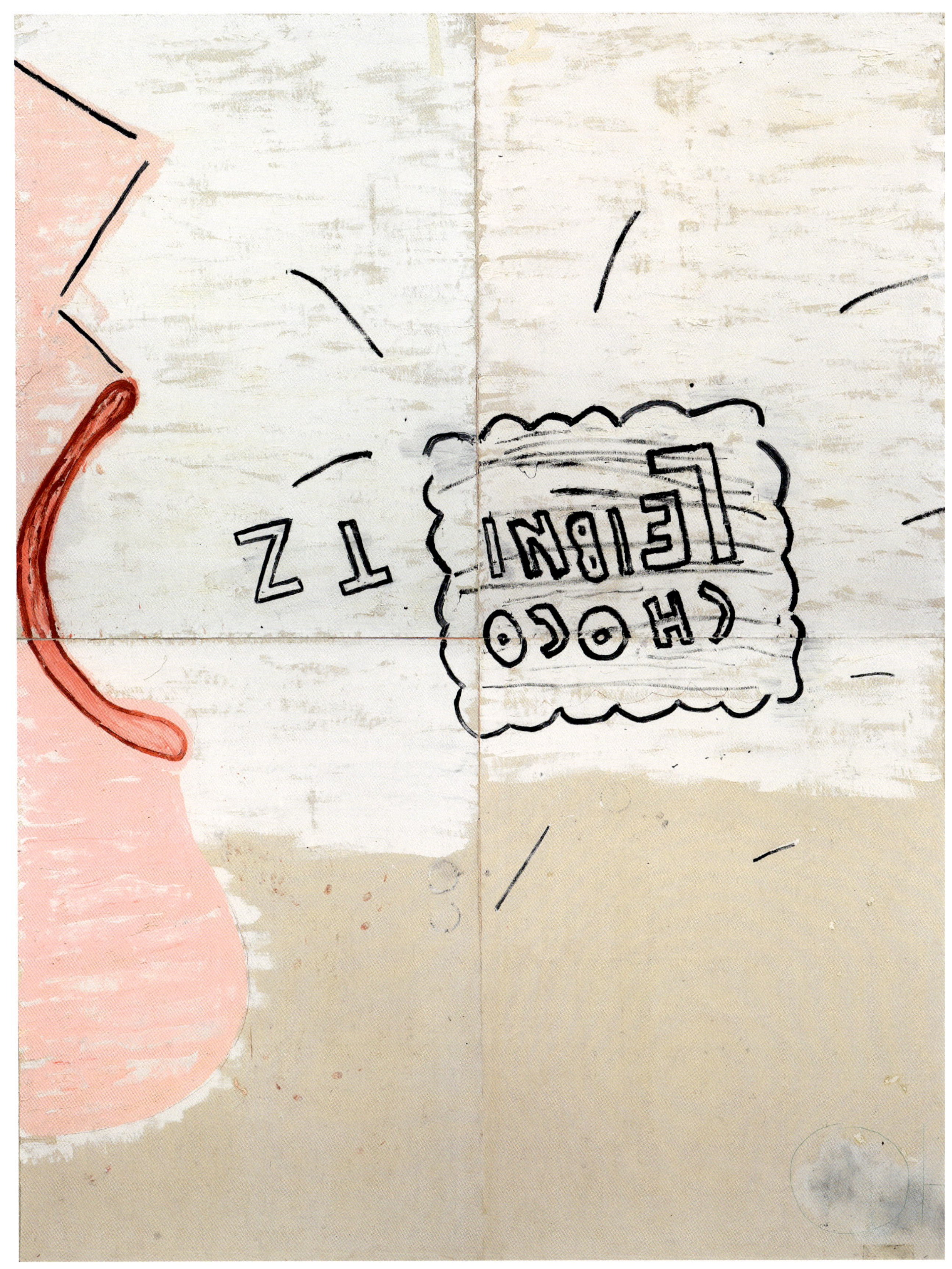

72

Choco Leibnitz, 2006
Oil on canvas,
366 × 285 cm (overall)
Tate: Lent from a private
collection 2023

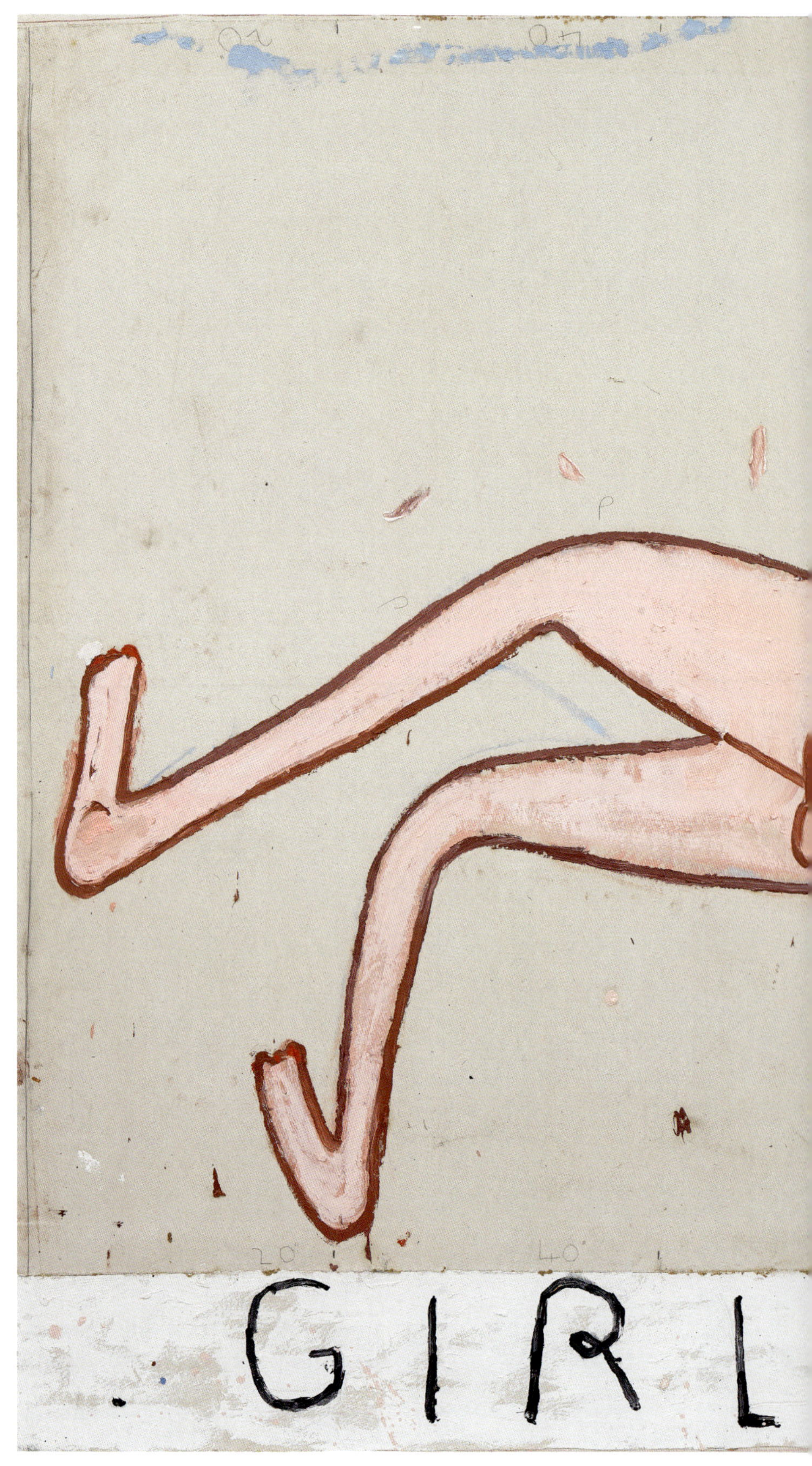

73

Girl in Lights, 2015
Oil on canvas,
209 × 328 cm (overall)
Courtesy private collection
and JARILAGER Gallery

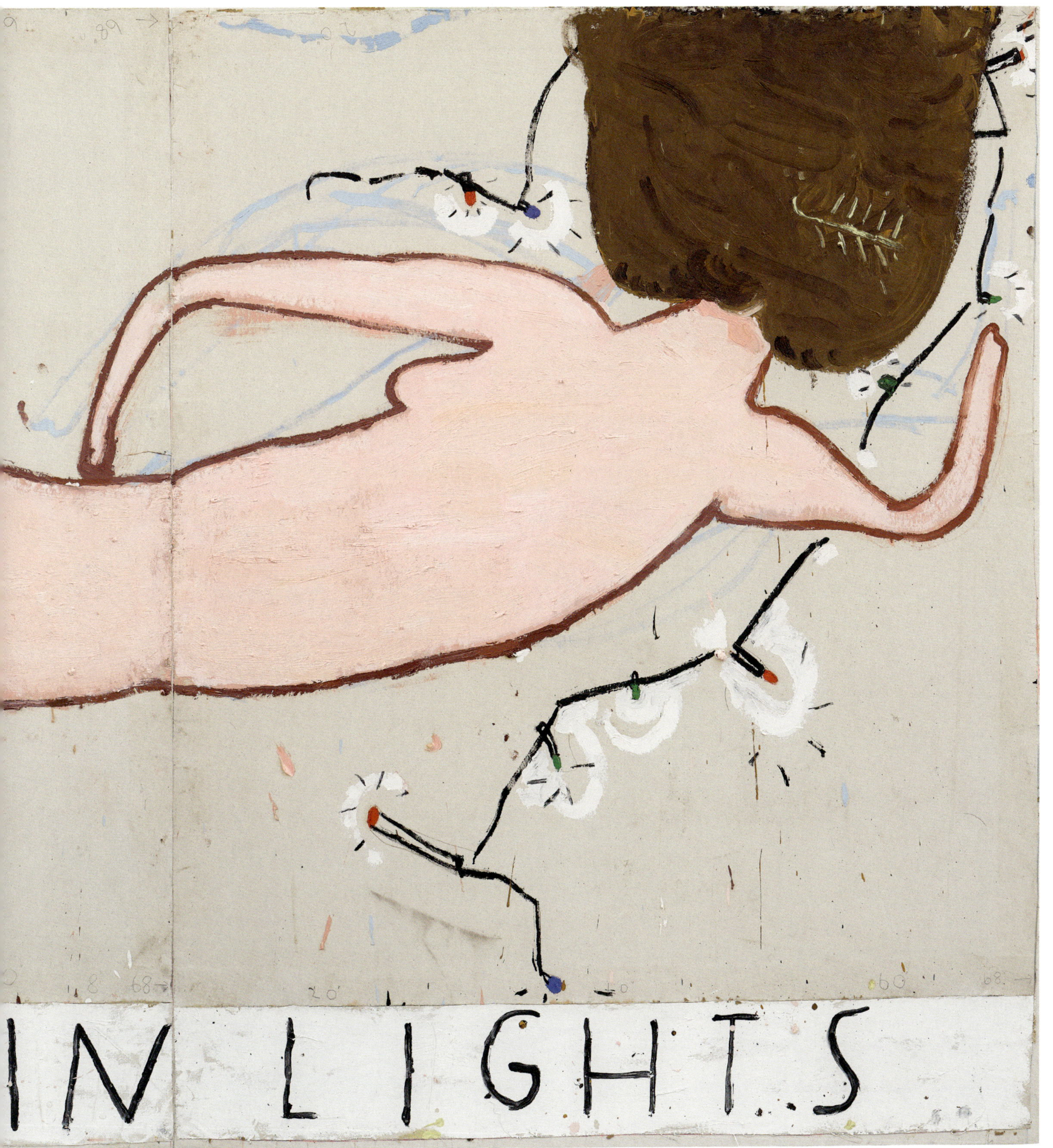
IN LIGHTS

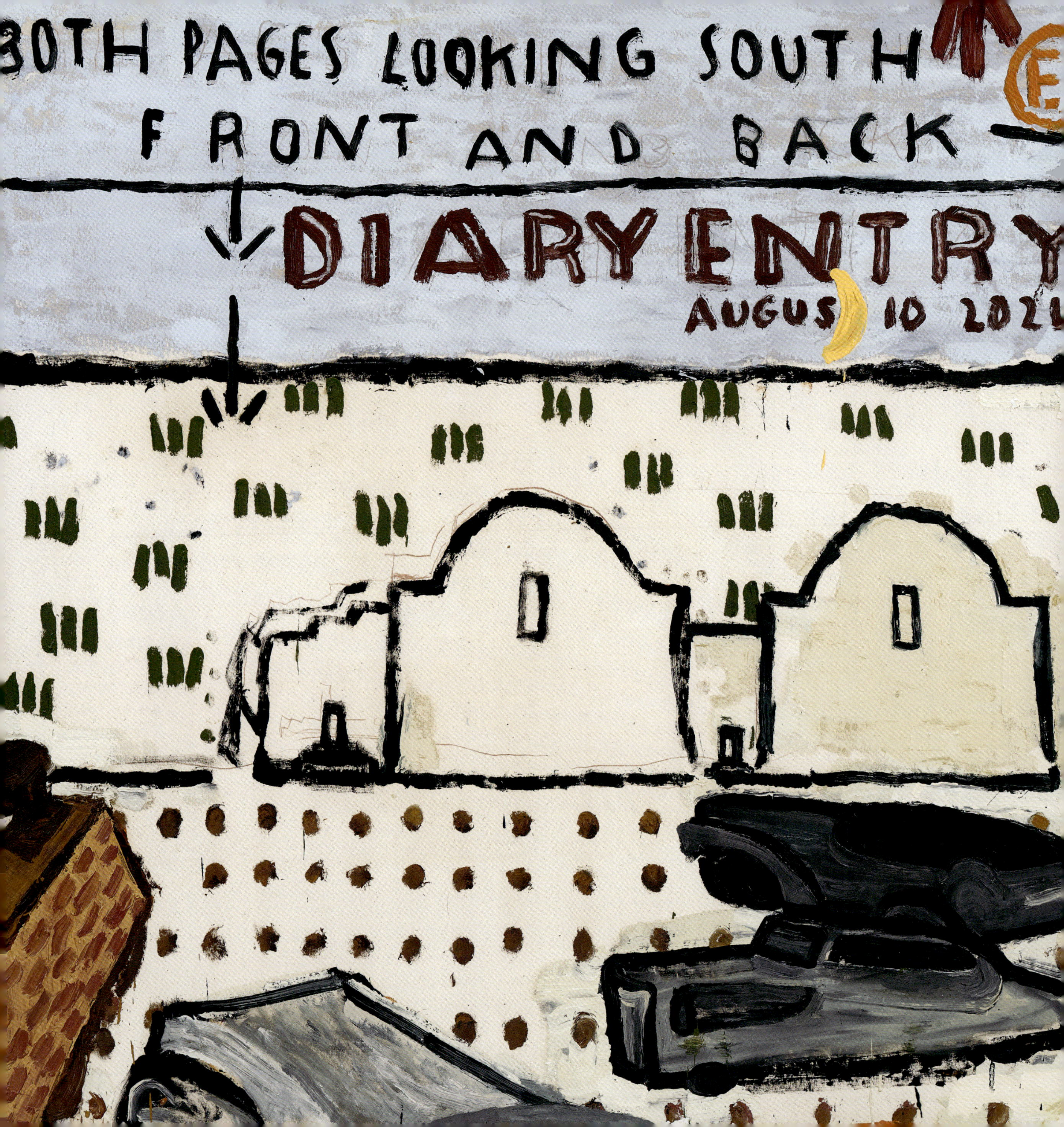

BOTH PAGES LOOKING SOUTH

FRONT AND BACK

E

DIARY ENTRY

AUGUS 10 2021

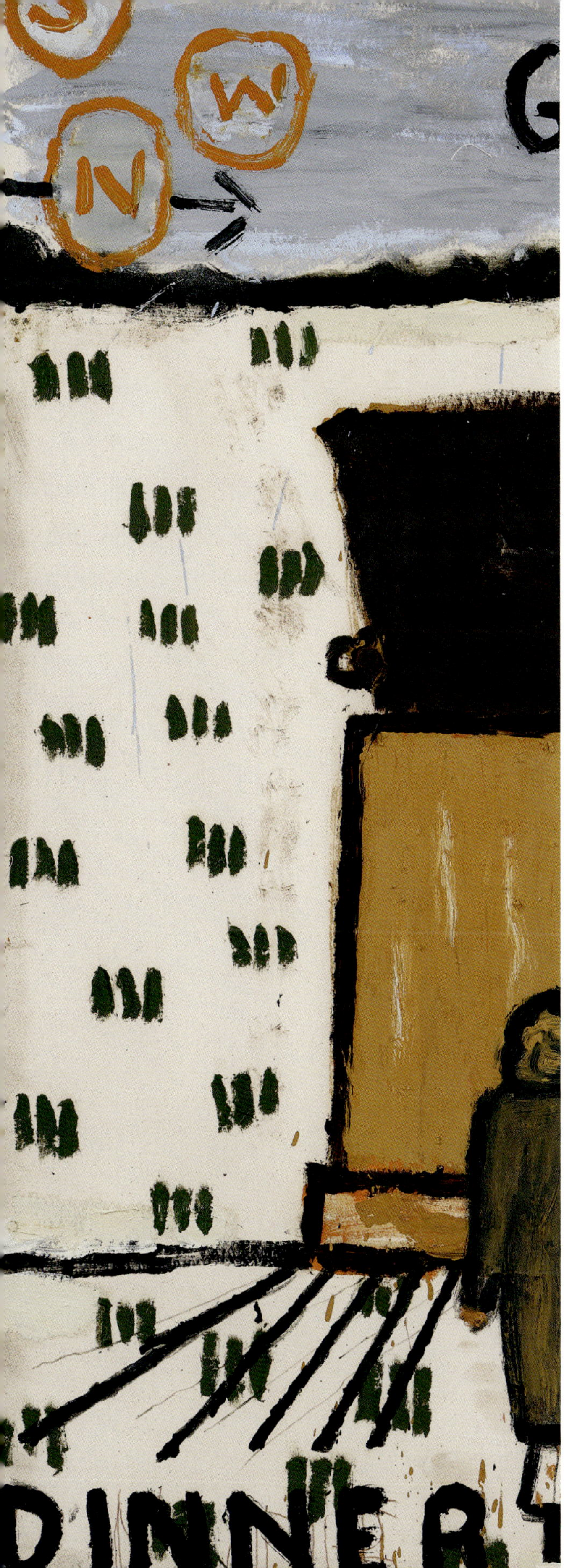

Diary as History Painting

'I do use a diary... as something to work with. I think for painting you've got to have something to work with and it's got to be real and it's better if it's not manufactured, and my life is real for me, so I delve into it... So I'm making diary paintings, which are also history paintings because the diary and the history merge.'[6]

Inspiration also comes from Wylie's immediate surroundings: her home filled with objects and items that accumulate meaning for her; her 'work-with-nature' garden, closely guarded by her cat, Pete; and the small community of neighbours and dwellings around her. For example, *A Dream* (2024; cat. 76) depicts a memorable dream in which the artist can never scrub her hall floor tiles clean enough. Daily life, whether the satisfaction of an enjoyable meal, or a stimulating evening dinner with friends, provides Wylie with endless source material for both drawings and paintings. As for us all, everyday life is peppered with public events, shared through the screen or radio, mixing personal occurrences and memories with historical ones.

74 *(overleaf)*

PV Windows and Floorboards, 2014
Oil on canvas,
185 × 339 cm (overall)
National Museums Liverpool, Walker Art Gallery
Purchased with financial assistance from the Art Fund, 2015

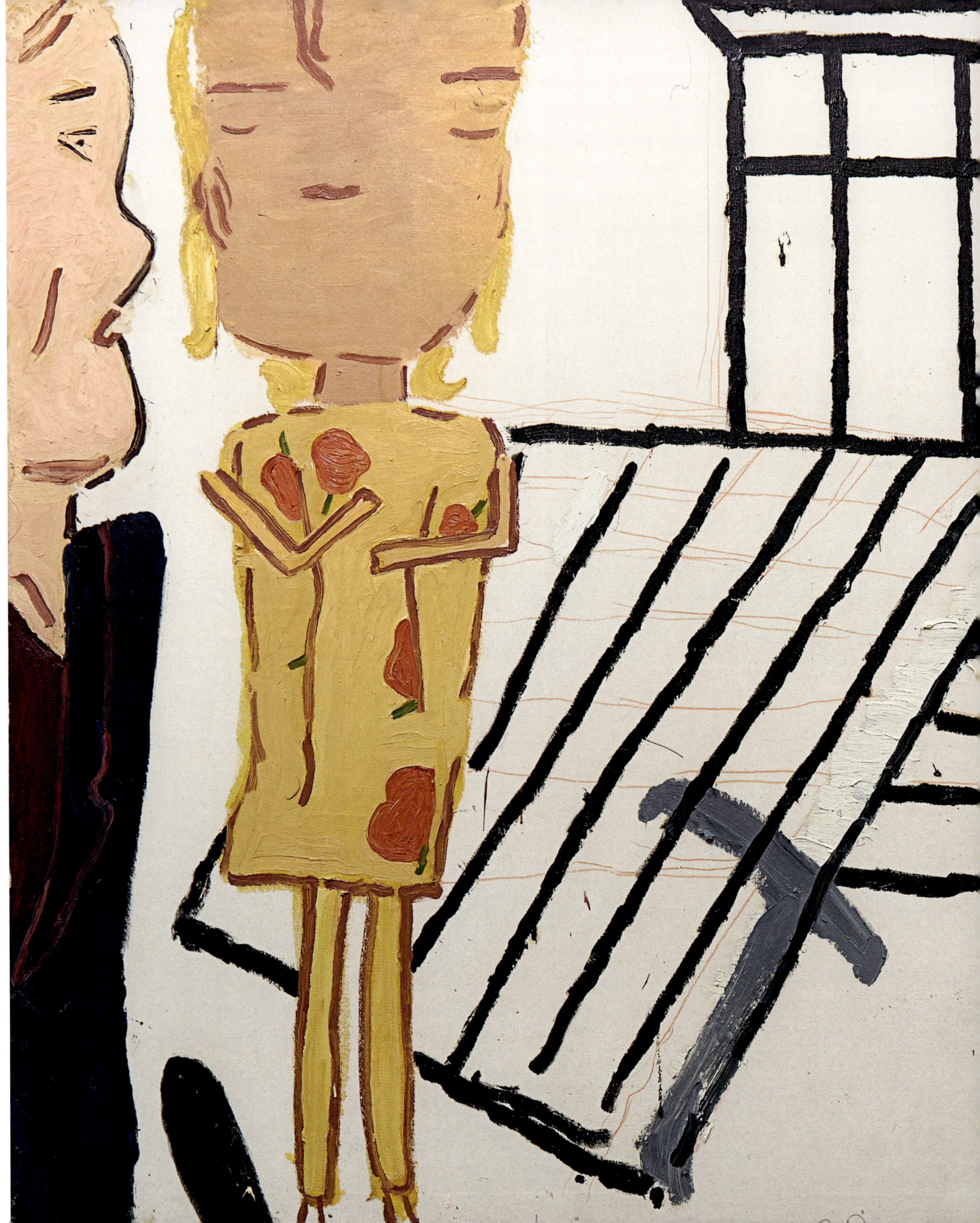

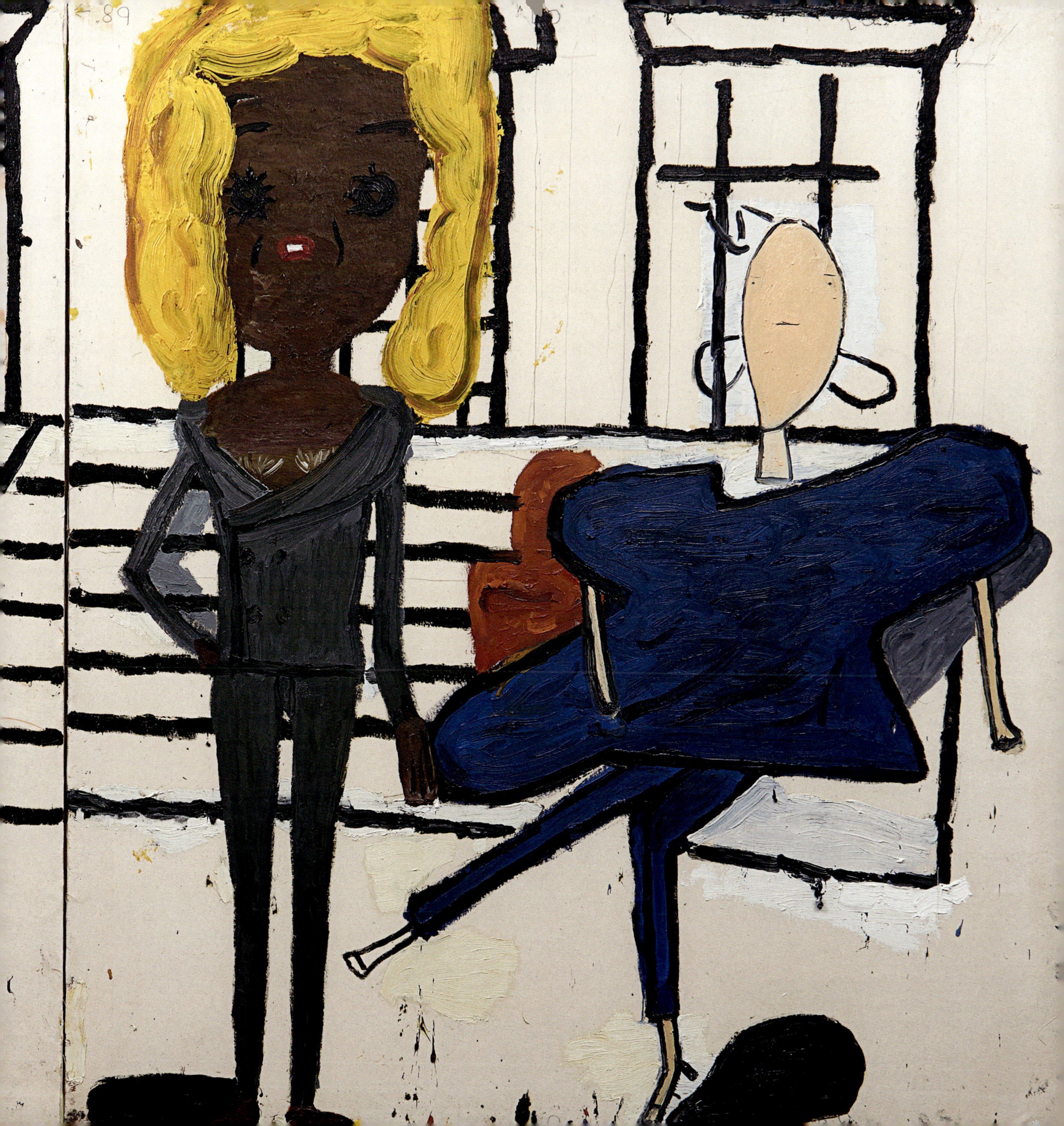

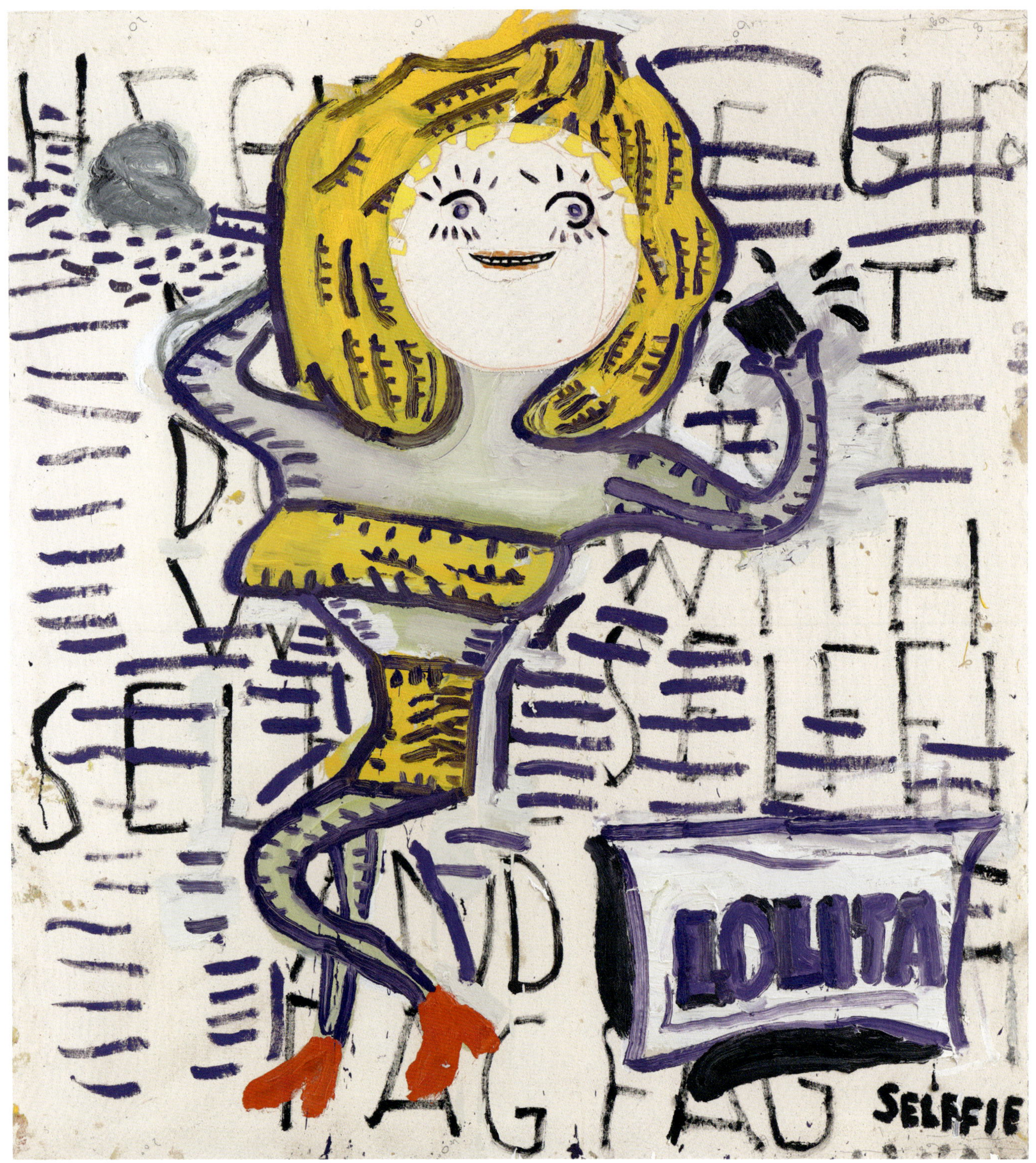

75

Lolita and Selffie, 2018
Oil on canvas,
182 × 166 cm
Private collection
courtesy David Zwirner

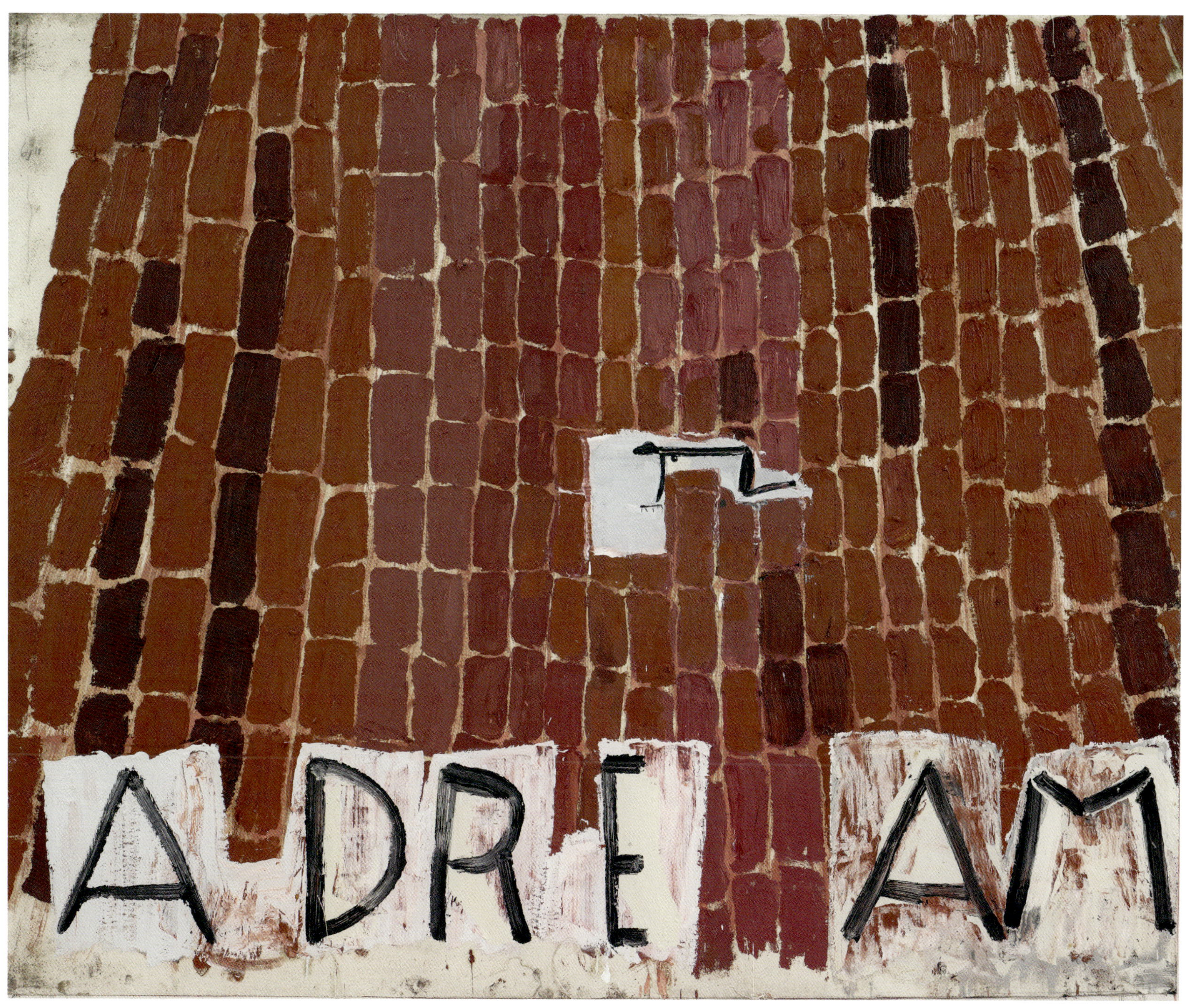

76

A Dream, 2024
Oil on canvas,
150 × 183 cm
Courtesy the artist
and David Zwirner

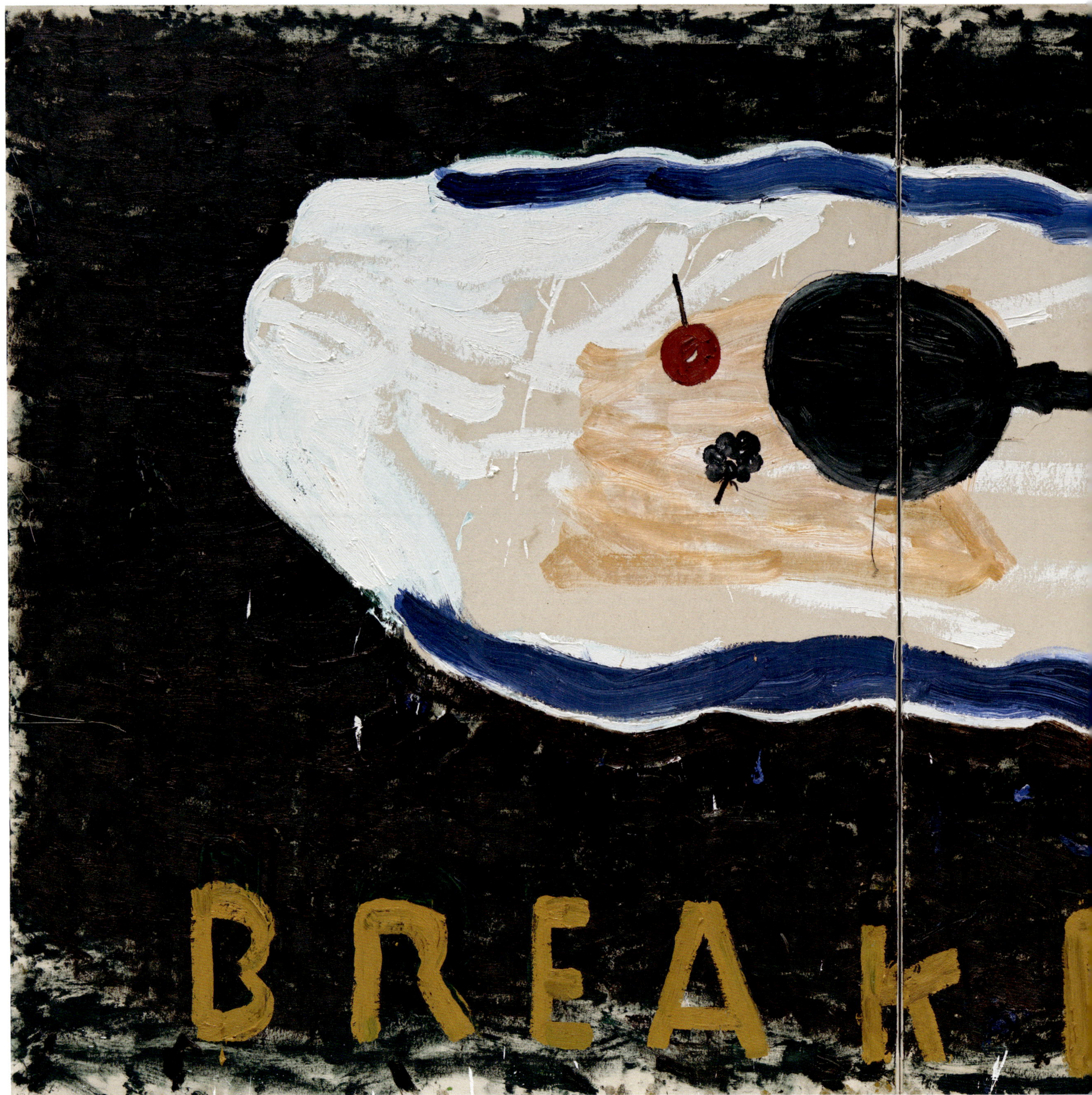
BREAK

77

Breakfast, 2020
Oil on canvas,
183 × 307 cm (overall)
Private collection

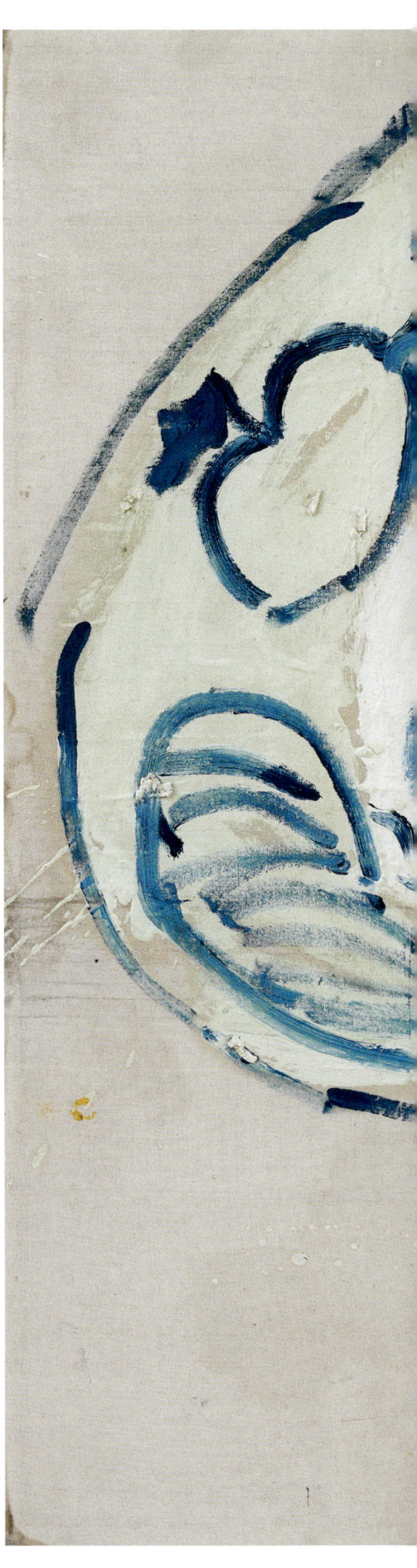

78

The Well-Cooked Omelette, 1989
Oil on canvas,
127.2 × 162.7 cm
Courtesy the artist and David Zwirner

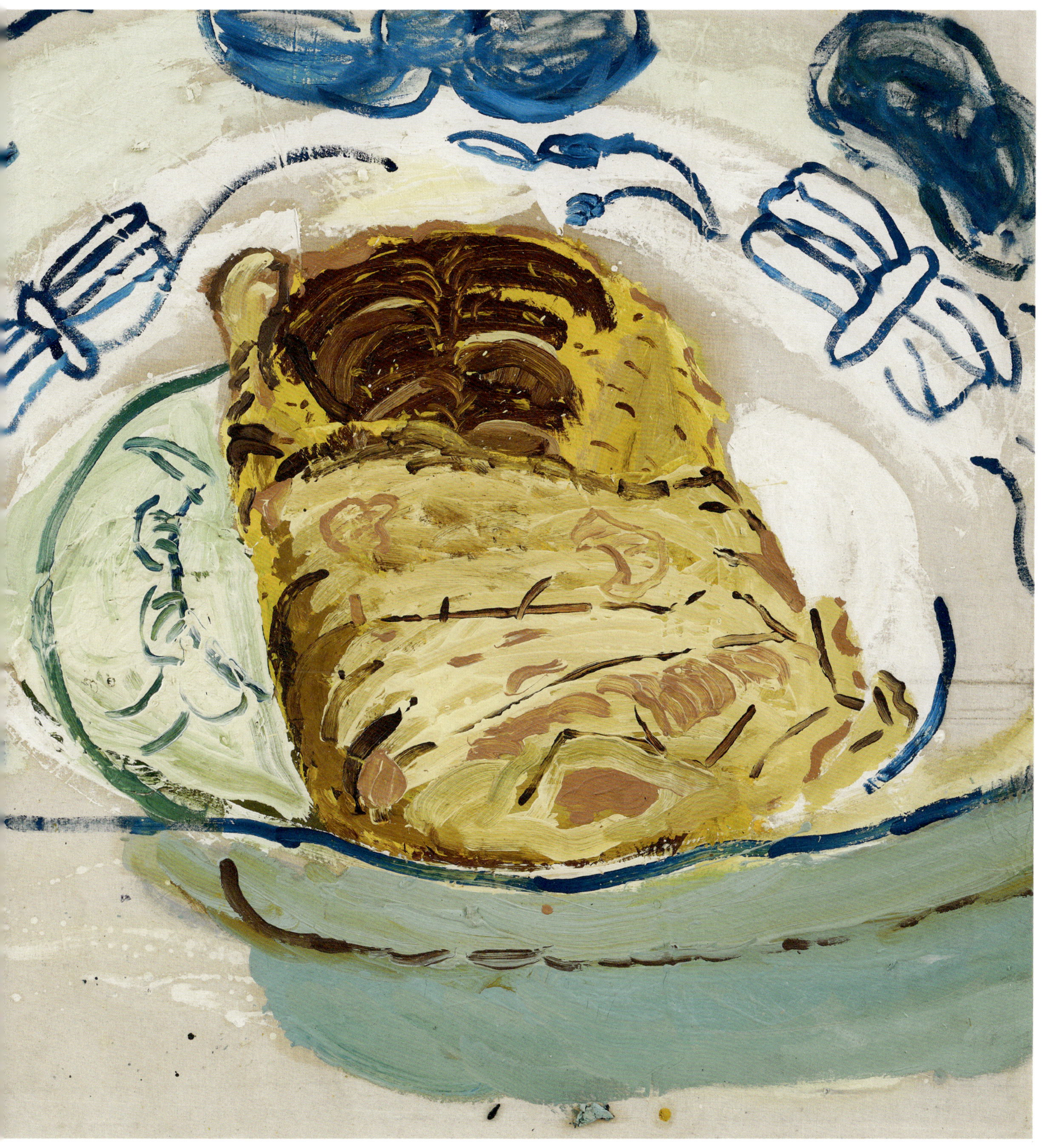

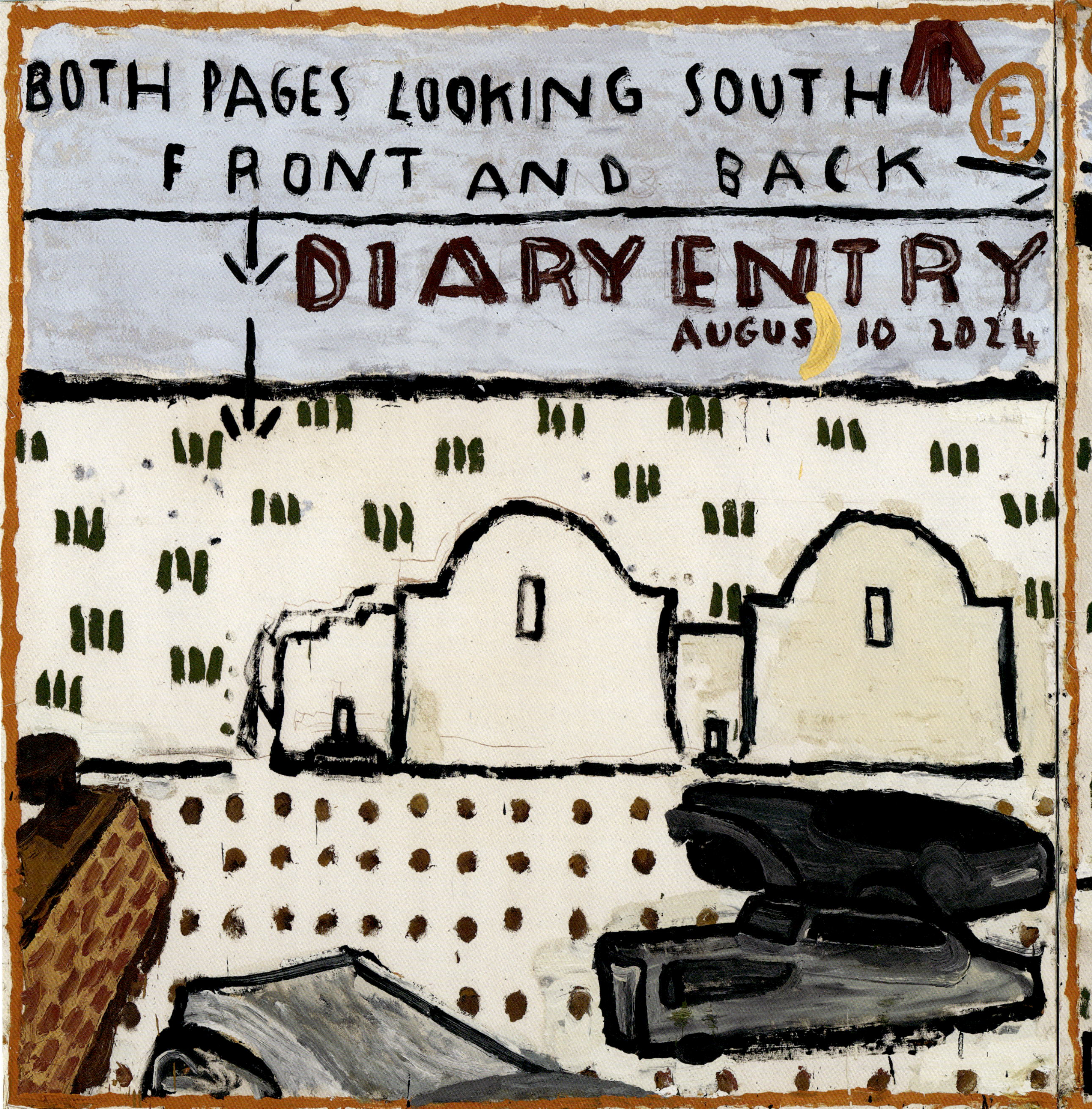

BOTH PAGES LOOKING SOUTH
FRONT AND BACK
E
DIARY ENTRY
AUGUS 10 2024

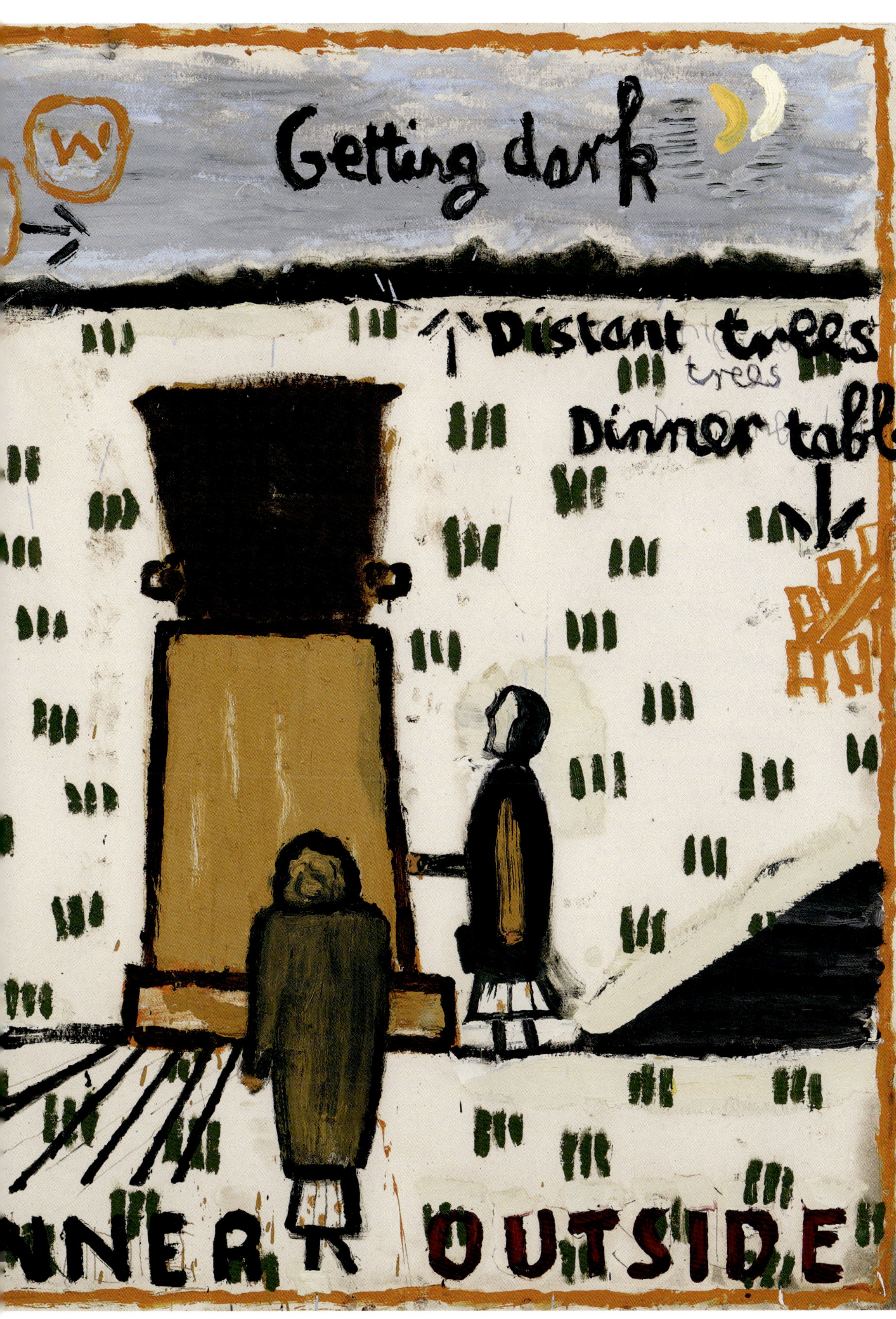

79

Dinner Outside, 2024
Oil on canvas,
183 × 328 cm (overall)
Courtesy the artist
and David Zwirner

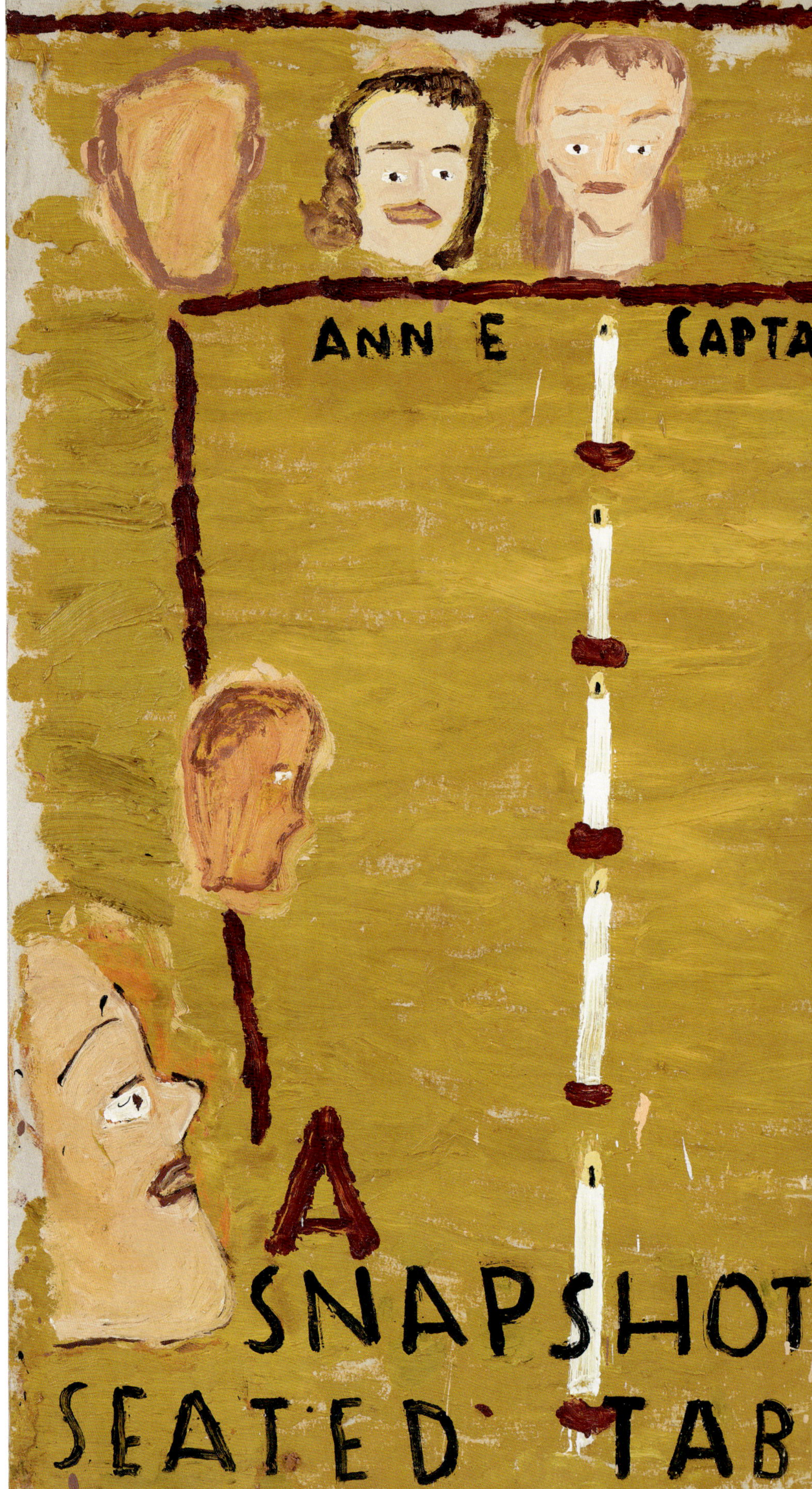

80

3 Seating Plans and Seated Table, 2025
Oil on canvas,
182 × 290 cm (overall)
Courtesy the artist and David Zwirner

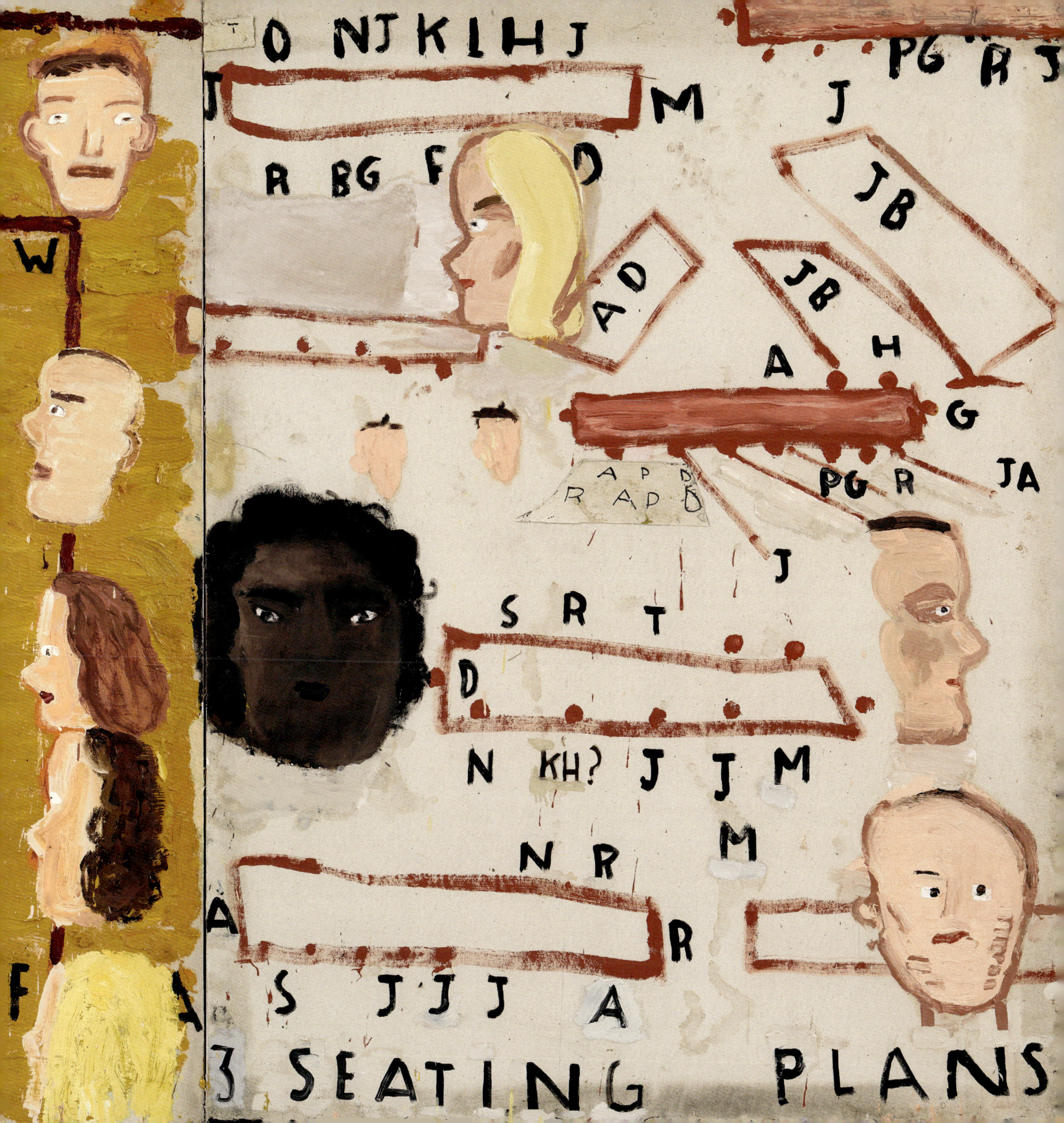

O NJKLHJ
J
M
PG R J
J
R BG F
D
JB
AD
JB
W
A
H
G
A P D
R A P D
PG R
JA
J
S R T
D
N KH? J J M
N R
M
A
R
F
A
S J J J A
3 SEATING PLANS

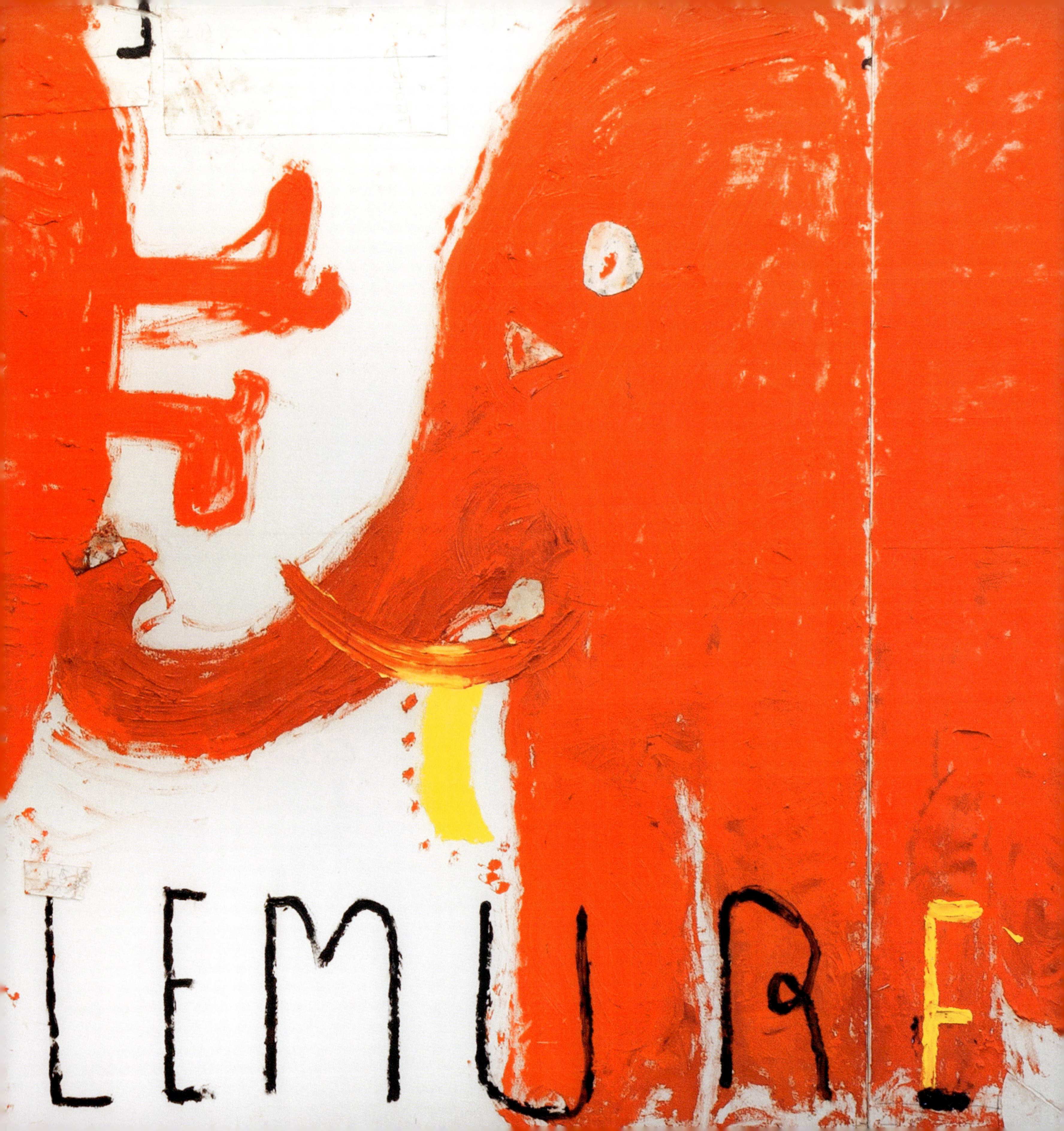
LEMURE

The Process Makes the Image

'The strength that her figurative paintings can carry is not simply reduced to the physicality of gestural expression – they are metaphysically powerful too.'[7]

When making this series of four monochromatic paintings of animals in ginger, black, blue and red, Wylie abandoned the paint brush and painted directly with her hands, letting the process of manipulating her medium determine the image. Looming large at five metres wide each, the forms are reduced to the simplest means possible while still allowing the shapes to be recognisably a spider, a horse or an elephant. Unconcerned with representing the physical reality of a living animal, these paintings hover on the edge of figuration and abstraction, with the painted words just tipping each image into an identifiable picture. The thickly applied and occasionally smudged paint imbues these monumental works with a visceral, tactile presence that reflects the energy and enjoyment of their making.

Frick (2025; cat. 85) was inspired by a drawing Wylie made of a light-blue chinoiserie ceiling at the Frick Collection in New York: the wash of luminescent paint evokes a gush of water, or of looking down on legs gently parted. She then painted a second version (the left-hand canvas), adding details from the ceiling. As with the earlier series, the process of painting had determined the image.

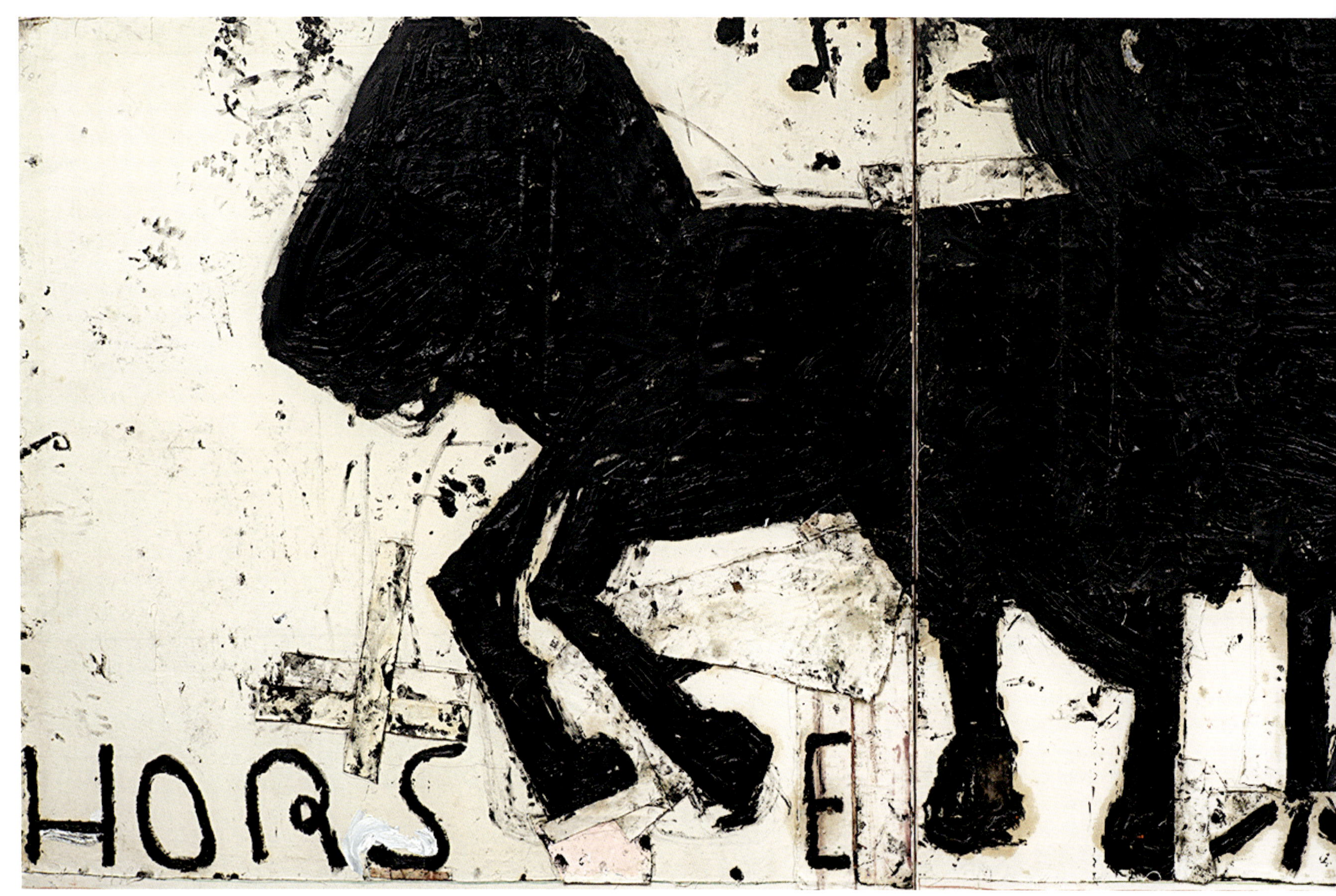

81

Horse, Bird and Cat, 2016
Oil on canvas,
173 × 546 cm (overall)
Courtesy private collection
and JARILAGER Gallery

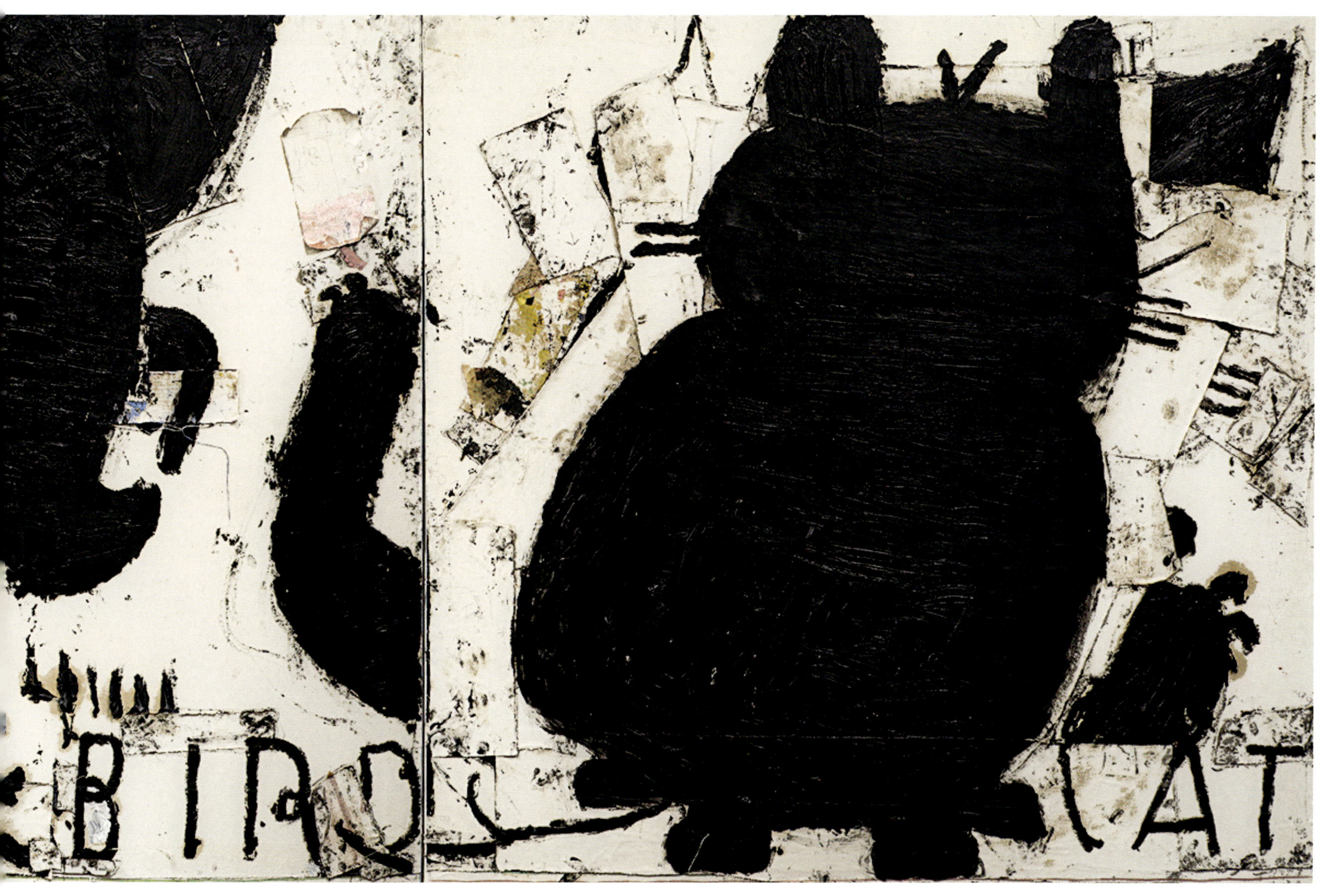
BIRD
CAT

82

Bird, Lemur and Elephant, 2016
Oil on canvas,
183 × 499 cm (overall)
Courtesy private collection
and JARILAGER Gallery

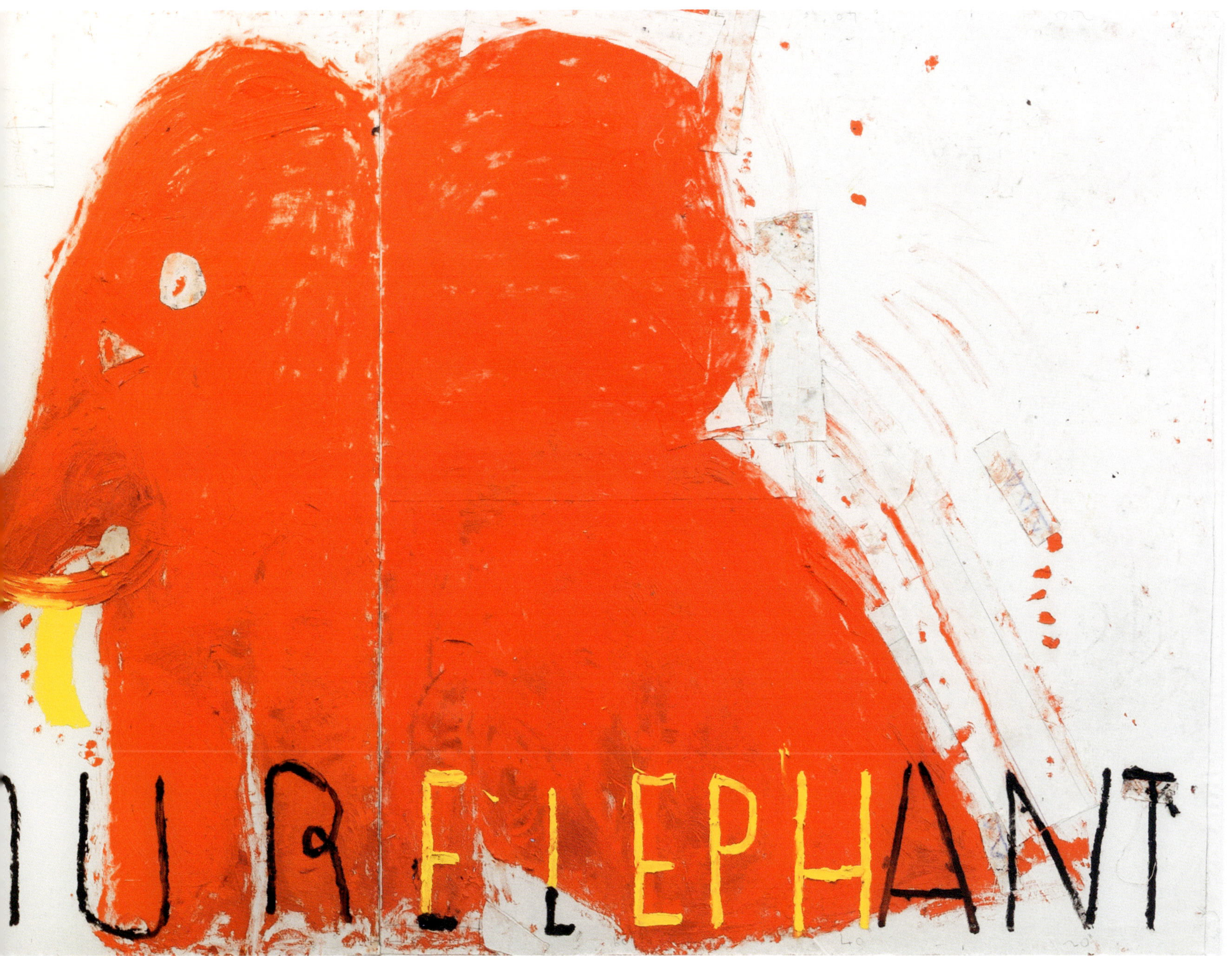
UR ELEPHANT

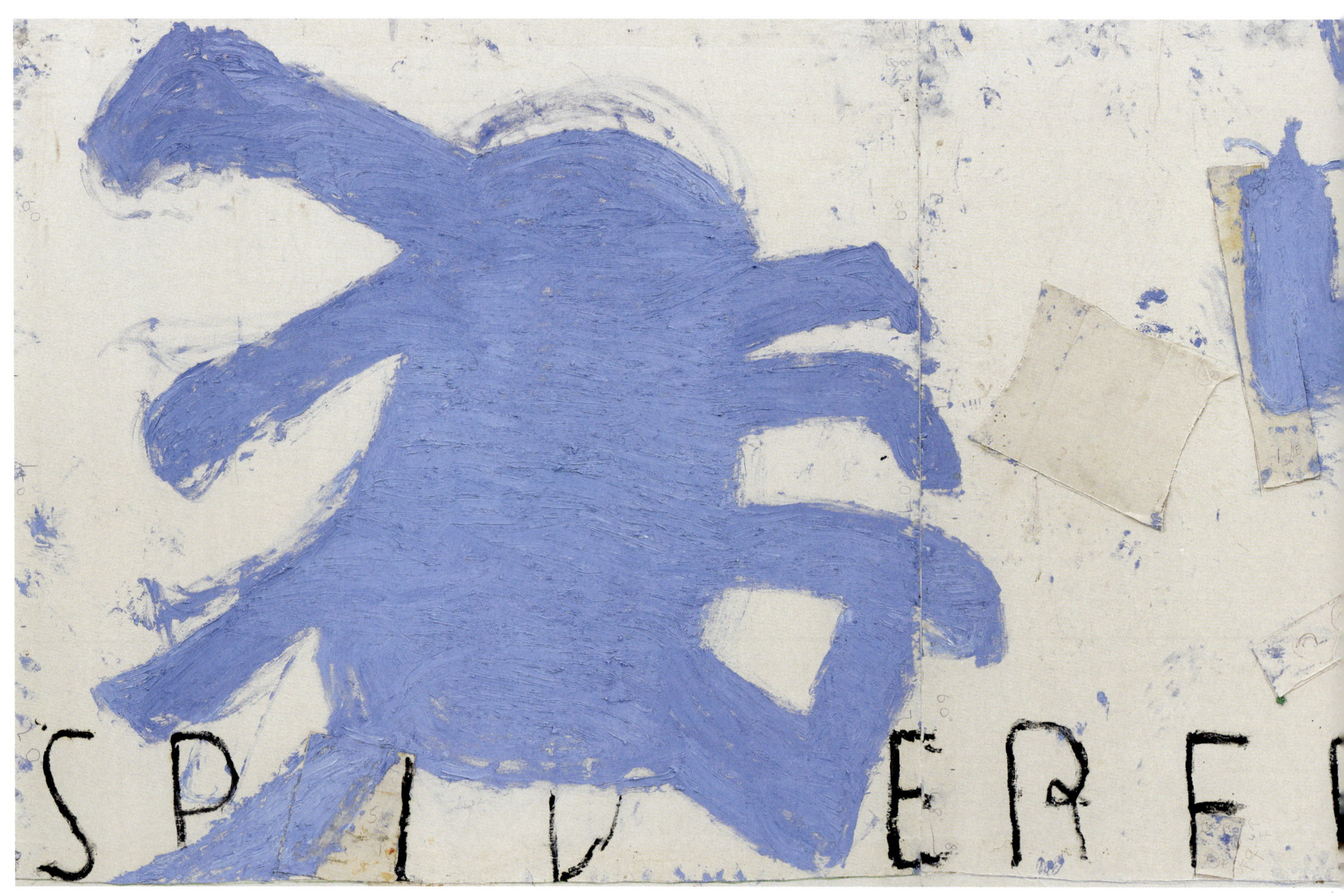

83

Spider, Frog and Bird, 2015
Oil on canvas,
170 × 549 cm (overall)
Courtesy private collection
and JARILAGER Gallery

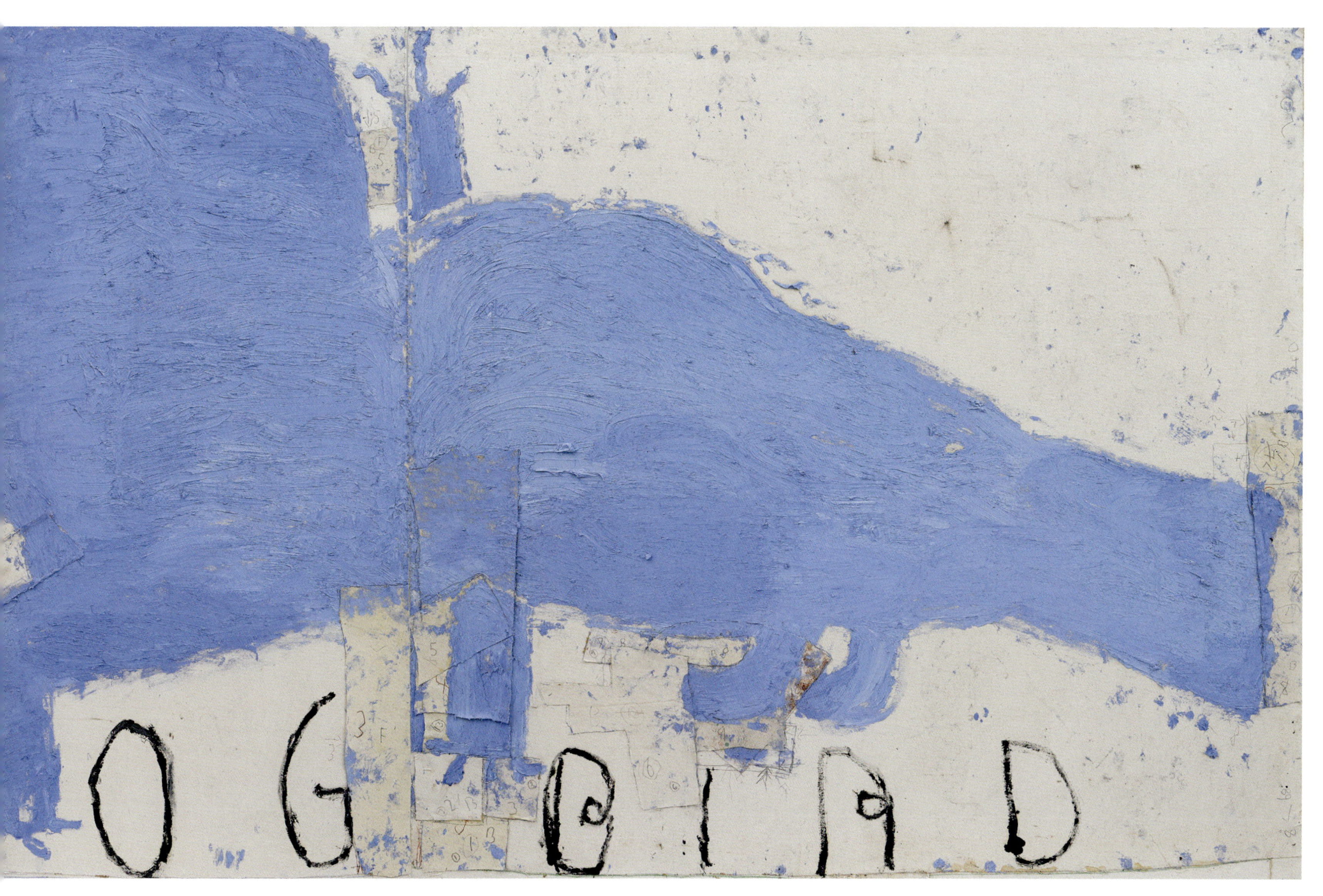

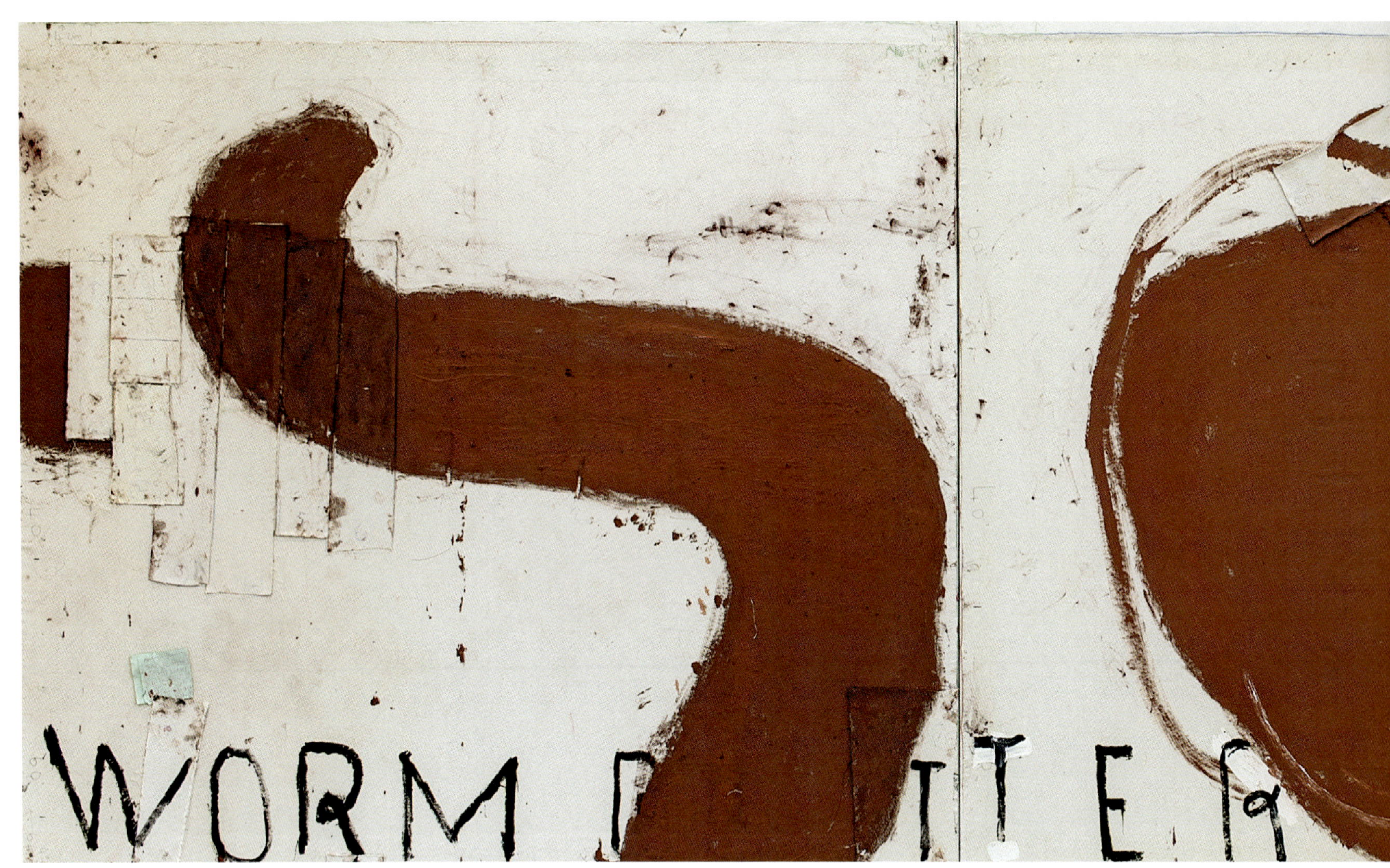

84

Bird, Butterfly and Worm,
2015
Oil on canvas,
159 × 548 cm (overall)
Courtesy Michael
Werner Gallery

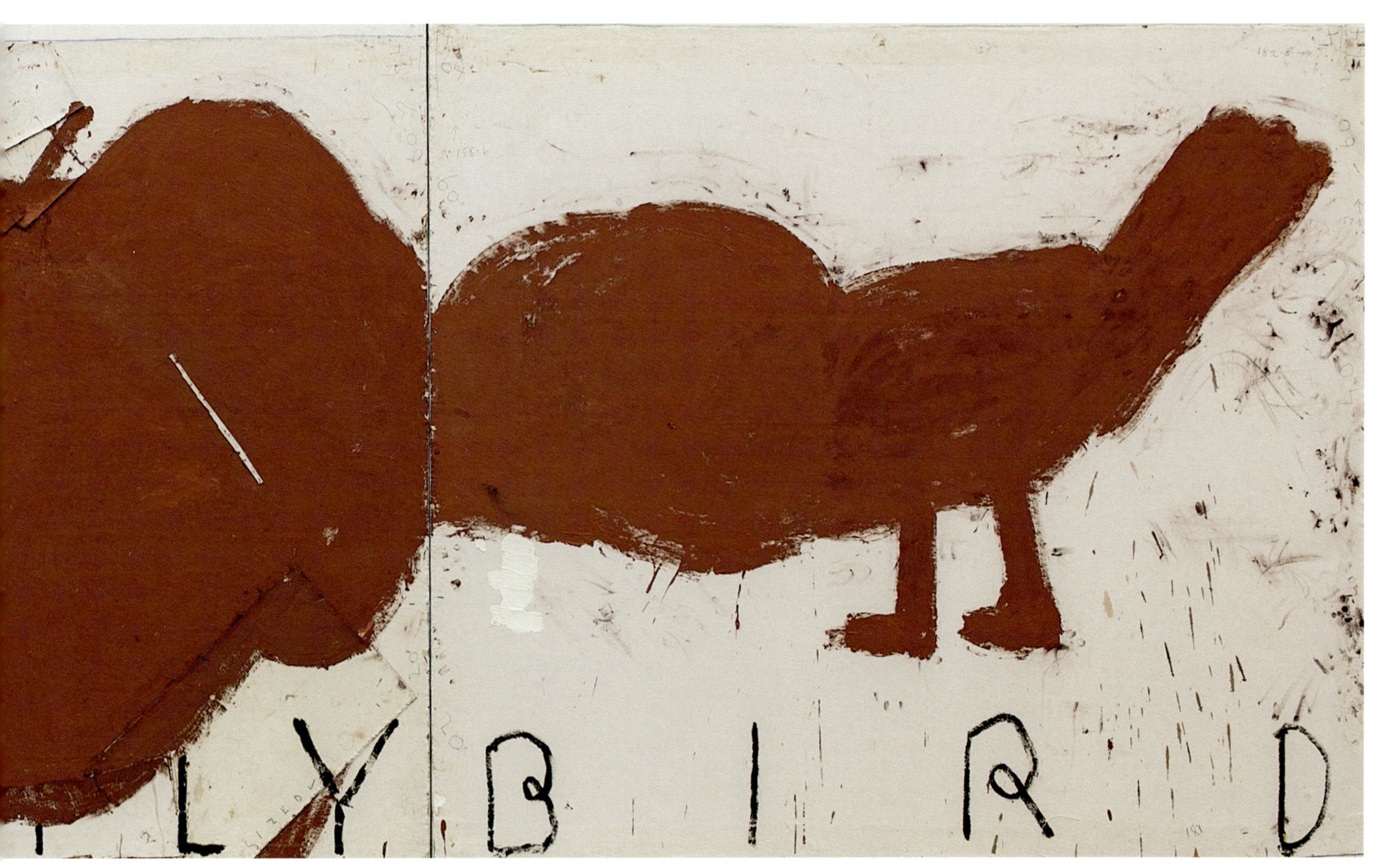
LYBIRD

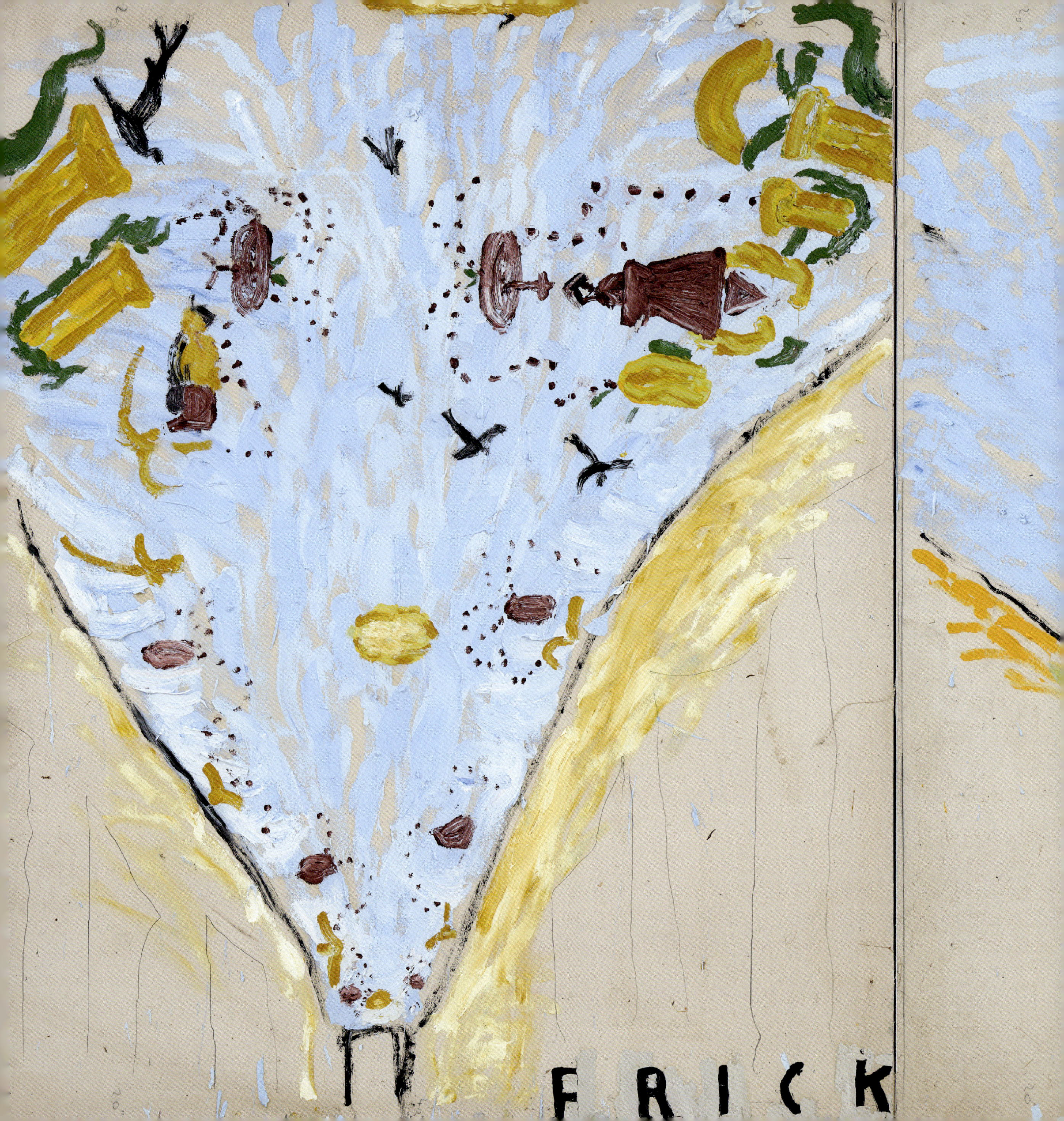
FRICK

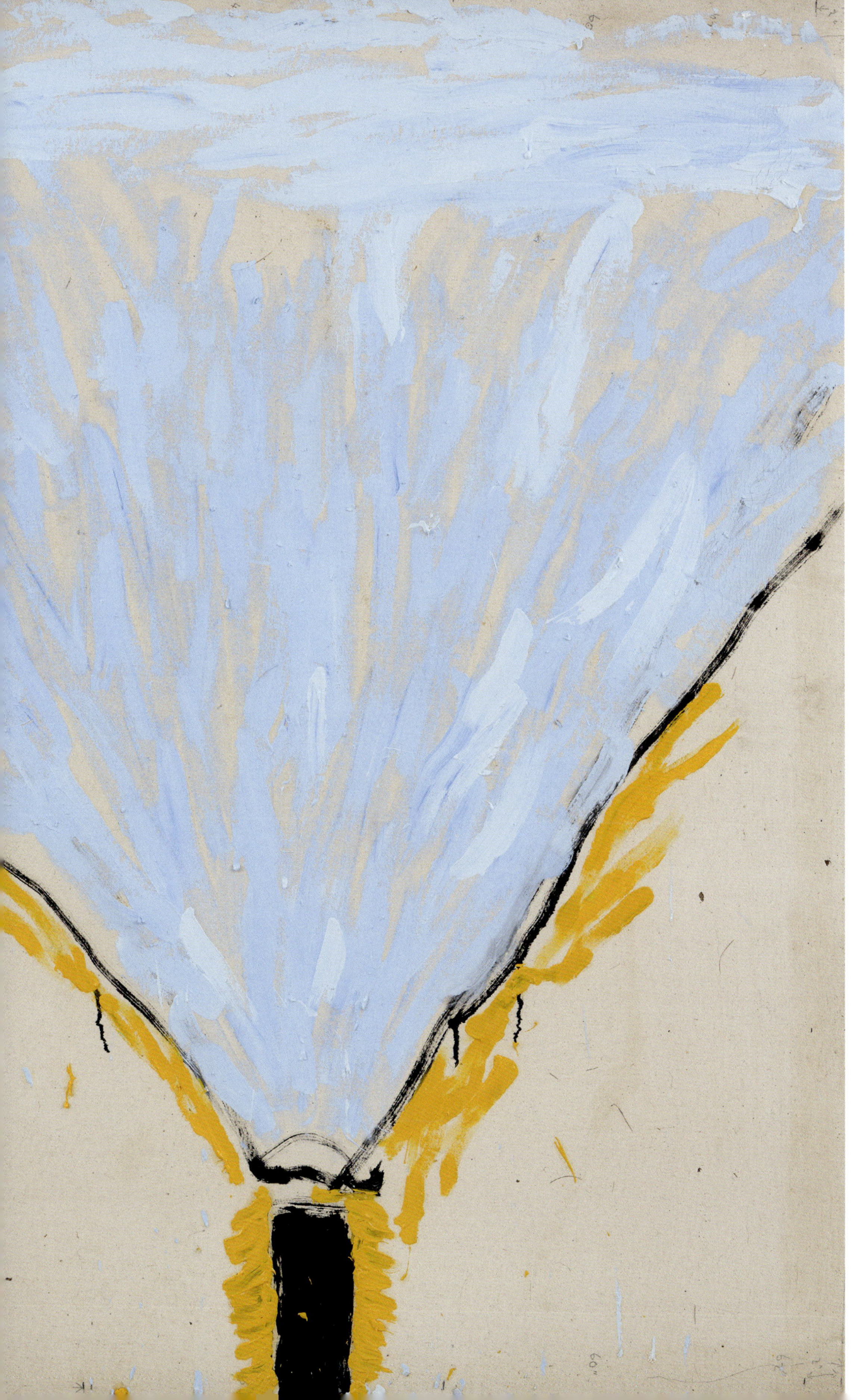

85

Frick, 2025
Oil on canvas,
182 × 302.5 cm (overall)
Courtesy the artist
and David Zwirner

Endnotes

The Picture Comes First

KATHARINE STOUT

1 Charles Baudelaire, *Le Peintre de la vie moderne*, 1860. First published in three instalments in *Le Figaro*, November–December 1863, https://www.writing.upenn.edu/library/Baudelaire_Painter-of-Modern-Life_1863.pdf [accessed 16 July 2025].
2 Hans Ulrich Obrist, in Anne Wehr (ed.), *Rose Wylie: Which One*, London, 2023, p. 11.
3 Rose Wylie in conversation with Russell Tovey, *Dialogues: The David Zwirner Podcast*, 2018, https://www.youtube.com/watch?v=6vgMVFMLvMg.
4 Conversation with Harold Rosenberg, in Philip Guston, *I Paint What I Want to See*, London and New York, 2022, p. 221.
5 Conversation with Clark Coolidge, in Guston, *I Paint*, p. 115.
6 Interview with David Sylvester, in Guston, *I Paint*, p. 18.
7 Rose Wylie, 'A for Abstraction', in Fabienne Eggelhöfer (ed.), *Rose Wylie: Flick and Float*, exh. cat., Zentrum Paul Klee, Bern, 2025.
8 Samuel Taylor Coleridge, *On Poesy or Art*, 1818, https://viscomi.sites.oasis.unc.edu/viscomi/coursepack/coleridge/Coleridge-On_Poesy_or_Art.pdf, p. 4 [accessed 3 August 2025].
9 Ibid. p. 3.
10 Clarrie Wallis, *Rose Wylie*, London, 2018, p. 40.
11 Rose Wylie in conversation with Suzanne Hudson, *Brooklyn Rail*, October 2023, https://brooklynrail.org/2023/10/art/Rose-Wylie-with-Suzanne-Hudson/ [accessed 5 May 2025].
12 Jennifer Higgie, '8 Painters on Painting', *Frieze*, issue 160, 11 Jan 2013, https://www.frieze.com/article/8-painters-painting [accessed 23 July 2025].
13 Jaś Elsner, 'From Empirical Evidence to the Big Picture: Some Reflections on Riegl's Concept of *Kunstwollen*', *Critical Inquiry* (University of Chicago Press), 32, 4, Summer 2006, pp. 741–66.
14 The closest translation for this German word is 'artistic will' or 'intention'. See Henri Zerner, 'Alois Riegl: Art, Value and Historicism', *Daedalus* (MIT Press/American Academy of Arts & Sciences), 105, 1, Winter 1976, 'In Praise of Books', pp. 177–88.
15 Correspondence between Rose Wylie and the author, 8 August 2025.
16 *David Zwirner Podcast*, 2018.
17 Emily Stokes, 'Reading Upside Down: A Conversation with Rose Wylie', *Paris Review*, 7 December 2021, https://www.theparisreview.org/blog/2021/12/07/reading-upside-down-a-conversation-with-rose-wylie/ [accessed 2 August 2025].
18 Obrist, in Wehr (ed.), *Rose Wylie*, p. 205.
19 Rose Wylie, guest blog, National Museums Liverpool, https://www.liverpoolmuseums.org.uk/whatson/walker-art-gallery/exhibition/john-moores-painting-prize-2014#section–the-exhibition [accessed 16 May 2025].
20 Wallis, *Rose Wylie*, p. 90.
21 Myra Barrs, *Vygotsky the Teacher: A Companion to His Psychology for Teachers and Other Practitioners*, Abingdon, 2022, p. 102.
22 *David Zwirner Podcast*, 2018.
23 Obrist, in Wehr (ed.), *Rose Wylie*, p. 206.
24 Higgie, '8 Painters on Painting' [updated by the artist, August 2025].
25 Susan Sontag, 'Against Interpretation' (1964), in Susan Sontag, *Against Interpretation and Other Essays*, New York, 1966, p. 8.
26 Ibid., p. 12.
27 Rose Wylie in conversation with Rosalind Nashashibi, in Tanja Boon (ed.), *Rose Wylie, picky people notice...*, exh. cat., S.M.A.K., Ghent, 2022, p. 67.
28 Wallis, *Rose Wylie*, p. 35.
29 David Salle, 'Going on Her Nerve', *New York Review of Books*, 12 May 2022, https://www.nybooks.com/articles/2022/05/12/going-on-her-nerve-rose-wylie-david-salle/ [accessed 16 May 2025].
30 Henri Matisse, 'Notes of a Painter', first published in *La Grande Revue*, Paris, 25 December 1908. Reproduced in Charles Harrison and Paul Wood (eds), *Art in Theory 1900–1990: An Anthology of Changing Ideas*, 3rd edn, Oxford and Cambridge, MA, 1993, p. 73.
31 *David Zwirner Podcast*, 2018.
32 Harrison and Wood, *Art in Theory*, p. 75.
33 Gertrude Stein, 'Pictures', from 'Lectures in America' (1934), in *The Complete Works of Gertrude Stein (Illustrated)*, (e-book) Kyiv, 2023, p. 4630.

Various Instances: Rose Wylie's Relationship with Time

JENNIFER HIGGIE

1 W. H. Auden, 'Musée des Beaux Arts', in W. H. Auden, *Collected Poems*, London, 1991, p. 179.
2 Rose Wylie in the film *Studio Visit with Rose Wylie*, Zentrum Paul Klee, Bern, 2025, https://www.youtube.com/watch?v=CHA-D02eAAk, 00:42–00:45.
3 Rose Wylie quoted on David Zwirner's website, https://www.davidzwirner.com/exhibitions/2025/rose-wylie-selected-museum-works.
4 Rose Wylie in conversation with Suzanne Hudson, *Brooklyn Rail*, October 2023, https://brooklynrail.org/2023/10/art/Rose-Wylie-with-Suzanne-Hudson/.
5 Rose Wylie interviewed in her studio by the author, 26 February 2025.
6 Ibid.
7 Rose Wylie, *Brooklyn Rail*.
8 Email from Rose Wylie, 8 September 2025.
9 Rose Wylie, *Brooklyn Rail*.
10 Clarrie Wallis quoting an email to her from Rose Wylie, 30 January 2013, in 'Paint It Like It Looks', *Rose Wylie*, London, 2018, p. 99.
11 Rose Wylie, *Studio Visit*, 07:45.
12 Ibid., 08:08.
13 Ibid., 13:11.
14 Rose Wylie, *Brooklyn Rail*.
15 Ibid.
16 Unless otherwise mentioned, all quotations come from my discussion with the artist in her studio on 22 July 2025.
17 Clarrie Wallis quoting Rose Wylie in conversation with Hans Ulrich Obrist at the Goethe-Institut, London, on 12 December 2017; reproduced in Wallis, *Rose Wylie*, p. 13.
18 Rose Wylie in her studio, 22 July 2025.

Further Reading

Catalogue Plates

WITH SECTION INTRODUCTIONS BY KATHARINE STOUT

1 Hans Ulrich Obrist, in Anne Wehr (ed.), *Rose Wylie: Which One*, London, 2023, p. 211.
2 Melissa Blanchflower (ed.), *Rose Wylie: Quack Quack*, exh. cat., Serpentine Gallery, London, 2017, p. 28.
3 Rose Wylie in conversation with Rosalind Nashashibi, in Tanja Boon (ed.), *Rose Wylie, picky people notice...*, exh. cat., S.M.A.K., Ghent, 2022, p.64.
4 Rose Wylie in conversation with Russell Tovey, *Dialogues: The David Zwirner Podcast*, 2018, https://www.youtube.com/watch?v=6vgMVFMLvMg.
5 Jennifer Higgie, '8 Painters on Painting', *Frieze*, issue 160, 11 Jan 2013, https://www.frieze.com/article/8-painters-painting [accessed 23 July 2025].
6 Rose Wylie in conversation with Frances Morris, Royal Academy of Arts, 2019, https://soundcloud.com/royalacademy/rose-wylie-ra-in-conversation-with-frances-morris [accessed 23 July 2025].
7 Alvaro Barrington, in Blanchflower (ed.), *Rose Wylie*, p.38.

Publications

Fabienne Eggelhöfer (ed.), *Rose Wylie: Flick and Float*, exh. cat., Zentrum Paul Klee, Bern, 2025

Anne Wehr (ed.), *Rose Wylie: Which One*, London, 2023

Tanja Boon (ed.), *Rose Wylie, picky people notice...*, exh. cat., S.M.A.K., Ghent, 2022

Clarrie Wallis, *Rose Wylie*, London, 2018

Rose Wylie: Hullo Hullo..., exh. cat., Centro de Arte Contemporáneo de Málaga, 2018

Melissa Blanchflower (ed.), *Rose Wylie: Quack Quack*, exh. cat., Serpentine Gallery, London, 2017

Articles

Rose Wylie in conversation with Suzanne Hudson, *Brooklyn Rail*, October 2023, https://brooklynrail.org/2023/10/art/Rose-Wylie-with-Suzanne-Hudson/

David Salle, 'Going on Her Nerve', *New York Review of Books*, 12 May 2022, https://www.nybooks.com/articles/2022/05/12/going-on-her-nerve-rose-wylie-david-salle/

Emily Stokes, 'Reading Upside Down: A Conversation with Rose Wylie', *Paris Review*, 7 December 2021, https://www.theparisreview.org/blog/2021/12/07/reading-upside-down-a-conversation-with-rose-wylie/

Harriet Baker, 'When you're an artist, you don't have to do what you're told to do' – an interview with Rose Wylie, *Apollo Magazine*, 2020, https://apollo-magazine.com/interview-rose-wylie/

Rose Wylie, guest blog, National Museums Liverpool, https://www.liverpoolmuseums.org.uk/whatson/walker-art-gallery/exhibition/john-moores-painting-prize-2014#section–the-exhibition

Jennifer Higgie, '8 Painters on Painting', *Frieze*, issue 160, 11 Jan 2013, https://www.frieze.com/article/8-painters-painting

Podcasts and Video Interviews

Katy Hessel, *The Great Women Artists Podcast: Rose Wylie*, March 2025, https://podcasts.apple.com/gb/podcast/rose-wylie/id1480259187?i=1000701803200

Rose Wylie in the film *Studio Visit with Rose Wylie*, Zentrum Paul Klee, Bern, 2025, https://www.youtube.com/watch?v=CHA-D02eAAk

Rose Wylie in conversation with Frances Morris, Royal Academy of Arts, 2019, https://soundcloud.com/royalacademy/rose-wylie-ra-in-conversation-with-frances-morris

Rose Wylie in conversation with Russell Tovey, *Dialogues: The David Zwirner Podcast*, 2018, https://www.youtube.com/watch?v=6vgMVFMLvMg

Lenders to the Exhibition

Arts Council Collection, Southbank Centre, London
British Council Collection
CHOI&CHOI Gallery
Charlotte and Philip Colbert
Brett and Julia Frankle
Brian Garish
JARILAGER Gallery
Jeremy and Kathryn Levison
Michael Werner Gallery
National Museums Liverpool, Walker Art Gallery
Edwin Oostmeijer
Vladimir Ovcharenko
Luke and Louisa Oxlade
Sven Petersen and Holly Frean
The David and Indrė Roberts Collection
Stedelijk Museum voor Actuele Kunst, Ghent
Tate
Rose Wylie
York Museums Trust (York Art Gallery)
David Zwirner

and others who wish
to remain anonymous

Photographic Acknowledgements

All works of art are reproduced by kind permission of the owners. Every attempt has been made to trace the copyright holders of works reproduced. Specific acknowledgements are as follows:

Photographic Credits

Florence, © Art Resource/Scala, Florence: fig. 3 (Image copyright The Metropolitan Museum of Art); fig. 17 (Photo Smithsonian American Art Museum). Photo: Genevieve Hanson: fig. 2. Photograph courtesy Jari Lager: figs 6, 12, 15; cats 8–11, 14, 15, 17, 53–7, 59–63, 68, 70, 71, 74, 82 (Photo: Soon-Hak Kwon); cat. 43 (Photo: Jo Moon Price). London, © Arts Council Collection, Southbank Centre: cat. 69. London, © Bridgeman Images: fig. 7; fig. 11 (Christie's Images). London, © The Trustees of the British Museum: fig. 8. Courtesy Vladimir Ovcharenko: cat. 3. Philadelphia, © Barnes Foundation: fig. 4. © 2012 Paul Smith / Featureflash: fig. 5. © Juergen Teller, All Rights Reserved: fig. 14. Courtesy Michael Werner Gallery: cat. 84. York Museums Trust (York Art Gallery). Presented by the Contemporary Art Society, 2001: cat. 4. Courtesy the artist and David Zwirner: figs 1, 9, 13, 18; cats 2, 12, 38, 81; figs 10, 16, cats 5–7, 13, 18, 20, 21, 25–7, 30–4, 37, 49, 51, 58, 64, 65, 67, 72, 73, 78–80, 83, 85 (Photo: Jack Hems); cat. 1 (Photo: Elon Schoenholz); cats 16, 19, 22, 23, 28, 29, 35, 36, 40–2, 44–8, 50, 52, 75, 76 (Photo: Anna Arca); cats 24, 39 (Photo: Eva Herzog); cat. 66 (Photo: Jo Moon Price); cat. 77 (Photo: Stephen Arnold).

Additional Copyright

Rose Wylie, © Rose Wylie: all works by the artist. Frank Walter, © The Frank Walter Family: fig. 19. Philip Guston, © The Estate of Philip Guston, courtesy Hauser & Wirth: fig. 2.

Index